M000200758

# Quebec City

## Third Edition

Stéphane Guimont-Marceau
Francois Rémillard

*"Dans la ville où je suis né,
le passé porte le présent
comme un enfant sur les épaules..."*

*"In the town where I was born,
the past carries the present
like a child on it shoulders..."*

Robert Lepage
*Le Confessionnal*

**Travel better,** enjoy more

# ULYSSES

Travel Guides

## Offices

Canada: Ulysses Travel Guides, 4176 St. Denis Street, Montréal, Québec, H2W 2M5, ☎(514) 843-9447, ⇌(514) 843-9448, info@ulysses.ca, www.ulyssesguides.com

Europe: Les Guides de Voyage Ulysse SARL, 127 rue Amelot, 75011 Paris, France, ☎01 43 38 89 50, ⇌01 43 38 89 52, voyage@ulysse.ca, www.ulyssesguides.com

U.S.A.: Ulysses Travel Guides, 305 Madison Avenue, Suite 1166, New York, NY 10165, info@ulysses.ca, www.ulyssesguides.com

## Distributors

U.S.A.: Hunter Publishing, 130 Campus Drive, Edison, NJ 08818, ☎800-255-0343, ⇌(732) 417-1744 or 0482, comments@hunterpublishing.com, www.hunterpublishing.com

Canada: Ulysses Travel Guides, 4176 St. Denis Street, Montréal, Québec, H2W 2M5, ☎(514) 843-9882, ext. 2232, ⇌514-843-9448, info@ulysses.ca, www.ulyssesguides.com

Great Britain and Ireland: Roundhouse Publishing, Millstone, Limers Lane, Northam, North Devon, EX39 2RG, ☎1 202 66 54 32, ⇌1 202 66 62 19, roundhouse.group@ukgateway.net

Other countries: Ulysses Travel Guides, 4176 St. Denis Street, Montréal, Québec, H2W 2M5, ☎(514) 843-9882, ext.2232, ⇌514-843-9448, info@ulysses.ca, www.ulyssesguides.com

Canadian Cataloguing-in-Publication Data (see p 3)
© May 2005, Ulysses Travel Guides.
All rights reserved.
Printed in Canada
ISBN 2-89464-729-8

**Research and Writing**
Stéphane G. Marceau
François Rémillard
Marie-Josée Béliveau

**Publisher**
Claude Morneau

**Production Director**
André Duchesne

**Artistic Director**
Patrick Farei (Atoll)

**Editing Assistants**
Pierre Ledoux
Julie Brodeur
David Sirois

**Copy Editor**
Pierre Ledoux

**Translators**
Janet Logan
Cindy Garayt
Pierre Ledoux

**Cartographers**
Marie-France Denis
André Duchesne
Patrick Thivierge

**Photography**
*Cover*
Patrick Escudero
*Inside pages*
Patrick Escudero
Philippe Renault

**Illustrators**
Myriam Gagné
Lorette Pierson

## Acknowledgements

We acknowledge the financial support of the Government of Canada through the Book Publishing Industry Development Program (BPIDP) for our publishing activities. We would also like to thank the government of Québec for its SODEC income tax program for book publication.

## Library and Archives Canada Cataloguing in Publication

Main entry under title:

Guimont-Marceau, Stéphane, 1969-

Québec City

3rd ed.

(Ulysses travel guide)
Translation of: Ville de Québec.
Includes an index.

ISBN 2-89464-729-8

1. Québec (Québec) - Guidebooks.
I. Rémillard, François. II. Title. III. Series.

FC2946.18.R4513 2005      917.14'471045      C2005-940806-5

# Table of Contents

# Table of Contents *(continued)*

## List of Maps

## Map Symbols

| | | | |
|---|---|---|---|
| ✈ | Airport | H | Hospital |
| ★ | Capital | ? | Tourist information (seasonal service) |
| Funicular | Funicular | ? | Tourist information (permanent service) |
| Train station | Train station | Car ferry | Car ferry |
| Bus station | Bus station | | |

# Symbols

| | |
|---|---|
| ≡ | Air conditioning |
| bkfst incl. | Breakfast included |
| ⇄ | Fax number |
| ℑ | Fireplace |
| ⊘ | Fitness centre |
| ½ b | Half board (lodging + 2 meals) |
| K | Kitchenette |
| ≈ | Pool |
| pb | Private bathroom |
| ℝ | Refrigerator |
| ℜ | Restaurant |
| △ | Sauna |
| sb | Shared bathroom |
| ✹ | Spa |
| ☎ | Telephone number |
| ⚲ | Wheelchair access |
| ⊛ | Whirlpool |
| 🚣 | Ulysses's favourite |

## Attraction Classification

| | |
|---|---|
| ★ | Interesting |
| ★★ | Worth a visit |
| ★★★ | Not to be missed |

## Hotel Classification

| | |
|---|---|
| $ | less than $60 |
| $$ | $60 to $100 |
| $$$ | $101 to $150 |
| $$$$ | $151 to $225 |
| $$$$$ | more than $225 |

Unless otherwise indicated, the prices in the guide are for one standard room, double occupancy in high season.

## Restaurant Classification

| | |
|---|---|
| $ | less than $15 |
| $$ | $15 to $25 |
| $$$ | $26 to $50 |
| $$$$ | more than $50 |

The prices in the guide are for a meal for one person, not including drinks and tip.

All prices in this guide are in Canadian dollars.

# Write to Us

The information contained in this guide was correct at press time. However, mistakes may slip by, omissions are always possible, establishments may move, etc. The authors and publisher hereby disclaim any liability for loss or damage resulting from omissions or errors.

We value your comments, corrections and suggestions, as they allow us to keep each guide up to date. The best contributions will be rewarded with a free book from Ulysses Travel Guides. All you have to do is write us at the following address and indicate which title you would be interested in receiving (see the list at the end of the guide).

## Ulysses Travel Guides

4176 St. Denis Street
Montréal, Québec
Canada H2W 2M5

305 Madison Avenue
Suite 1166, New York
NY 10165

www.ulyssesguides.com
E-mail: text@ulysses.ca

## 🌐 *Where is Québec City?*

**QUÉBEC**
Capital: Québec City
Population: 7,500,000 inhab.
Area: 1,550,000km²
Currency: Canadian dollar

**QUÉBEC CITY**
Population: 508,000 inhab.
Area: 548km²

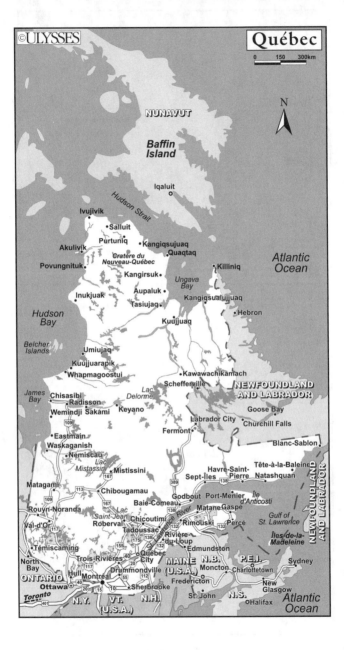

# Portrait

## Rich in history
and architecture, magnificent Québec City is set amidst an exceptional natural landscape.

Compared to other cities in the world, Québec City is not old; however, it is one of the oldest cities in North America and the oldest in Canada. The Haute-Ville (upper town) sits on a promontory, Cap Diamant, which is more than 98m high and juts out over the St. Lawrence River. Jacques Cartier called this rocky out-crop "Cap aux Diamants," believing he had discovered diamonds here. But he quickly learned that these precious stones were nothing more than common iron pyrites. Never-theless, Cap Diamant became the future site of Québec City when Champlain established a fur trading post and fortified buildings, creating the settlement known as "Abitation."

This site played a strategic role in New France's de-fence system. Here the river is only 1 km wide, and it is this narrowing of the St. Lawrence River that gave Québec City its name "Kebec," an Algonquin word meaning "place where the river narrows." Perched on top of Cap Diamant and the site of major fortifications from very early on, the city is now dubbed the "Gibraltar of North America."

This fortification did not succeed, however, in driving back the English troops, who finally captured the city during the Battle of the Plains of Abraham. Yet, the French colony managed to retain its cultural identity after the Conquest. Well protected inside its walls, Québec City's heart continued to beat, making it the centre French Canadian culture in North America.

In 1985, in order to preserve and promote Québec City and its cultural treasures, UNESCO declared the city's historic area—the only walled city in North America—the first World Heritage Site in North America.

This "Vieille Capitale," often simply called "Québec" by the Québécois, is the soul of French speaking America. Thousands of tourists visit it every year and marvel at the city's many charms, its European atmosphere and its inhabitants' *joie de vivre* and hospitality. The architecture and narrow cobblestone streets give the city its character. A romantic place that always fascinates, Québec City has been a source of inspiration to artists for more than three centuries. It is a delight for both the eye and the soul. This little gem is irresistible and whether you visit in the summer, winter, spring or autumn, you cannot help but succumb to its charm.

## History

### The First Europeans

The first Europeans to reach the coast of North America were the Vikings who explored the region in the 10th century. They were followed by whalers and fishers in search of cod.

However, beginning in 1534, **Jacques Cartier** made three journeys that marked a turning point in this segment of North American history and were the first official contacts between France and the New World. Cartier's mission for the king of France, François I, was to

JACQUES CARTIER
1534

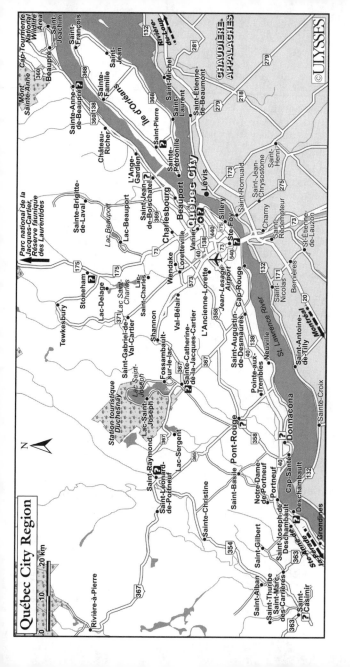

discover a passage to the East and find the gold and other riches that France needed so badly at the time. After Cartier's failure to fulfill his mission, France abandoned these new lands, considering them unimportant.

A few centuries later, the considerable profit that could be made in the fur trade rekindled French interest in New France. In 1608, **Samuel de Champlain** chose the site where Québec City is now located to set up the first permanent trading post. Champlain was surprised not to find the Aboriginal people that Cartier had described following his journeys. During this time, the sedentary Iroquois who farmed and hunted had moved south and were replaced by the nomadic Algonquins who subsisted on hunting and gathering. The Algonquins became France's main allies. Unlike the Iroquois, they did not have a very strong sense of land ownership and did not show any resistance when the French settled on their territory. The Algonquins agreed to take part in the fur trade with the French.

To understand Québec City's place in history is to appreciate all the advantages of its location. Nestled atop Cap Diamant, the city occupies a strategic location overlooking the only waterway leading to the North American interior. When Samuel de Champlain decided to establish the first permanent outpost to trade furs and built a fort around the few existing buildings here, it was primarily because of Cap Diamant's strategic advantages. Here, the river narrows considerably and it is easy to block passing ships. Champlain had a wooden fortress built here, which he named "Abitation." It enclosed the trading post and the homes of various fur traders.

During that first harsh winter in Québec, 20 of the 28 men that were posted there died of scurvy or malnutrition before ships carrying fresh supplies arrived in the spring of 1609. When Samuel de Champlain died on Christmas Day, 1635, there were about 300 pioneers living in New France.

Between 1627 and 1663, the **Compagnie des Cents Associés** held a monopoly on the fur trade and ensured the slow growth of the colony. Meanwhile, French religious orders became more and more interested in New France. The Récollets arrived first, in 1615; they were then replaced by the Jesuits, who began arriving in 1632.

## The 17th Century

Despite the presence of significant tributaries nearby—water being the only efficient means of transport and communication at the time—Québec City was never able to profit as much from the fur trade as Montréal or Trois-Rivières. Throughout the 17th century, merchants, farmers and craftspeople came to settle in Québec City and its surrounding region. The city's economy diversified, namely thanks to its port (which became one of the busiest in the world), its shipbuilding yard and its lumber, which was exported mainly to France. The fur trade, however, remained the leading area of economic activity up until the beginning of the 19th century.

During the 17th century, Québec City became one of the most important centres of commerce in the New World. It was the apex of an economic triangle formed by Acadia, New France and Louisiana, and would become the seat of French power in America. Also, since religious institutions and political powers looked for protection inside the walls of the Haute-Ville, Québec City quickly became the political, administrative and military centre of New France.

Many colonists settled in Québec City. The Basse-Ville (lower town) developed rapidly, expanding to the point where it was necessary to fill in parts of the St. Lawrence River to gain more land. At this time, the risk of fire was great because of the proximity of the buildings and the use of wood as the main construction material. In August 1682, flames devastated Québec's Basse-Ville, and the city was later rebuilt according to new stan-

dards requiring the use of stone instead of wood for building construction. Unfortunately, many inhabitants did not have the money to abide by these new requirements and were forced to build outside the city walls, creating the first suburbs. Most of the stone houses in Vieux-Québec today date from this period.

## The French-British Rivalry

The economic and strategic importance of Québec City made it a choice target very early on and the capital of New France had to defend itself against a covetous England. These conflicts between France and England had repercussions on the North American colony. Declarations of war and peace treaties were, in fact, the result of European politics and did not correspond with the preoccupations of the colony. Consequently, the citadel fell in 1629 when it was attacked by British forces led by the Kirke brothers, but it was quickly returned to France in 1632.

During the 18th century, the French-English rivalry increased as their colonies developed. The ever increasing pressure of British forces in New France finally resulted in the infamous **Battle of the Plains of Abraham**, part of the Seven Years' War. Arriving near Québec City in July 1759, **General Wolfe**'s troops captured the town on September 13 of the same

# A Brief Summary of Québec's History

**More than 12,000 years ago:**
Nomads from Northern Asia cross the Bering Strait and gradually populate the Americas. With the melting of the glaciers, some of them settle on the peninsula now known as Québec: these are the ancestors of the Aboriginal nations of Québec.

**1534:** Jacques Cartier, a navigator from Saint-Malo in Brittany, France, makes the first of three explorations of the Gulf of St. Lawrence and the St. Lawrence River. These were the first official French contacts with this territory.

**1608:** Samuel de Champlain and his men found Québec City, marking the beginning of a permanent French presence in North America.

**1663:** New France officially becomes a French province. Colonization continues.

**1759:** Québec City falls to British forces. Four years later, the king of France officially relinquishes all of New France, which now has a population of about 60,000 colonists of French origin.

**1837-1838:** The British army suppresses the Patriotes' rebellion.

**1840:** Following the Durham Report, the Union Act seeks to create an English majority and eventually assimilate French Canadians.

**1867:** This year marks the birth of Canadian Confederation. Four provinces, including Québec, sign the agreement. Six others eventually follow suit.

**1914-1918:** Canada participates in World War I. Anglophones and francophones disagree about the level of participation of the country. Canada comes out of the conflict very divided.

**1929-1939:** The economic crash hits Québec hard. In 1933, unemployment reaches 27%.

**1939-1945:** Canada participates in World War II. Once again, anglophones and francophones are divided on the issue of conscription.

**1944-1959:** Premier Maurice Duplessis leads Québec with a strong hand. This period is known as the "grande noirceur," or "great darkness."

**1960:** The Liberal Party is elected, marking the beginning of the Révolution Tranquille, or Quiet Revolution.

**October 1970:** A small terrorist group, the Front de Libération du Québec (FLQ), kidnaps a British diplomat and a Québec cabinet minister, igniting a serious political crisis.

**November 1976:** The Parti Québécois, a party favouring independence for Québec, wins the provincial election.

**May 1980:** A majority of the Québec population votes against holding negotiations aimed at Québec independence.

**1982:** The Canadian Constitution is repatriated without Québec's consent.

**June 1990:** The failure of the Meech Lake Accord on the Canadian Constitution is poorly accepted in Québec. Following this, opinion polls show that a majority of Quebecers are in favour of Québec sovereignty.

**October 22, 1992:** The federal government and the provinces organize a referendum on new constitutional offers. Considered unacceptable, these are rejected by a majority of Quebecers and Canadians.

**October 30, 1995:** The Parti Québecois government holds a referendum on the sovereignty of Québec: 49.4% of Quebecers vote "yes" to a sovereignty project and 50.6% vote "no."

**April 2001:** The third Summit of the Americas is held in Québec City, bringing together 34 of the continent's 35 heads of state.

Portrait

year, before reinforcements could arrive from France. During the night, the English climbed Cap Diamant to the west of the fortified walls and in the morning, to the great surprise of the French, they were on the Plains of Abraham. The battle began and ended a short time later with the defeat of the **Marquis de Montcalm**'s troops at the hands of General Wolfe; neither general survived.

## The British Regime

The **Treaty of Paris**, signed on February 10, 1763, sealed the French defeat by officially giving New France to the British, marking the end of the French colony in Canada. Under the British Regime, Québec City was transformed. For French Canadians, the Conquest meant that they were now under British rule and ties between the colony and France were cut off, leaving Québec an orphan. Significant changes occurred as the English replaced the francophones in political and administrative positions. Many of New France's well-to-do inhabitants decided to return to France at the suggestion of the British government. However, most residents and small merchants could not afford the journey and had no other choice but to remain in the British colony. The summit of Cap Diamant was also where the English set up their government, which now had the task of managing a considerable portion of North America.

Like the rest of the colony, Québec City was able to resist British assimilation thanks to the Catholic Church and a very limited anglophone immigration. Sheltered behind its walls, Québec City remained almost completely francophone for a long time.

However, the situation changed rapidly when the American War of Independence came to an end and the Empire Loyalists, faithful to the British Crown, left the United States to settle on British soil. Many of these new arrivals chose Québec City and Montréal, radically changing the look of the capital, which saw its anglophone population grow considerably.

In addition to this immigration of Empire Loyalists, many immigrants arrived from the British Isles to settle in Québec City and work in factories or as stevedores in the port. Among them were a significant number of Irish immigrants who had an important common trait with the local population: the Catholic religion. Anglophones represented approximately 40% of the population in the Québec City region, which at that time was enjoying a significant economic growth. This great anglophone immigration, however, was offset by a large influx of francophones from rural Québec.

## The 19th Century

The beginning of the 19th century was marked by a period of prosperity, primarily as a result of Napoleon's maritime embargo against England, which then suffered from a great lack of raw materials. This demand made Québec City an important trade link between the colony, the West Indies and England. Québec City's port, with its various shipyards set up by the French Regime, continued to develop until the invention of iron hulls and the digging of the channel in the St. Lawrence River, enabling heavy-tonnage ships to reach Montréal and eliminating any advantages for Québec City. From then on, Québec City's importance began to decline in favour of Montréal, which had an excellent railway system that further helped establish it as the centre of industrial and economic power in Québec and Canada.

## The 20th Century

Although Québec City lost its economic importance at the beginning of the 20th century and was now limited to light industry such as footwear, it continued to play a significant role in politics and administration as the capital of the province of Québec.

This state of affairs continued until the *Révolution Tranquille* (Quiet Revolution) in the 1960s. This social and political "revolution" marked the end of a long period spent under the yoke of religion and tradition, and set the province astir. Morals and institutions were modernized; political habits evolved. The province of Québec saw the size of its government increase remarkably and Québec City, at the centre of this wave of change, was transformed as well.

At the same time, the nationalist movement made its appearance in Québec as the province's francophones expressed their desire to end the anglophone minority's control over the development of Québec society. During this period, Québec City's anglophone population began to decline, representing only 1 or 2% of the region's total population.

The reduction of the State and the decentralization of power in favour of Montréal and the regions affected employment stability in the area. Although unemployment in Québec City is fairly low, the city now relies mostly on its great industrial and technological potential. In fact, Québec City has a market of more than 500,000 consumers. Tourism is another important source of revenue, with various tourist attractions such as Vieux-Québec, Mont-Sainte-Anne and Montmorency Falls. But one of the most promising areas of economic development remains the advanced technology sector that includes

Portrait

biotechnology, computers, optics and telecommunications.

On the international scene, the third Summit of the Americas, bringing together 34 of the continent's 35 heads of state (Cuba was not invited), was held in Québec City in April of 2001. The main topic of the summit was the creation of an immense free-trade area that would include the 800 million residents of the Americas, from Ellesmere Island to Tierra del Fuego. But the FTAA (Free Trade Area of the Americas) faced a great deal of opposition. The summit attracted protesters from across the continent, angry that these talks were being held behind closed doors, excluding the population that would be most affected by these discussions. To ensure the privacy of the closed-door meetings, a temporary wall (named "the wall of shame" by locals) was built around a large security perimeter in the heart of Vieux-Québec. This 3m-high, 4km-long fence somehow managed to keep the protesters at bay. In addition, a significant police force was deployed for the event, drowning the city in a cloud of tear gas for the duration of the summit.

## Politics

Political life in Québec City is deeply marked, monopolized even, by the duality between two levels of government: the federal government and the provincial government. To gain a better understanding of the political situation in Québec, one must first comprehend its historical context. Québec City is the cradle of French culture in North America. The Canadian Confederation, created in 1867, had important consequences for all francophones in Québec. One of the most significant impacts was the minority position in which it placed the French Canadian population, whose culture differs from the anglophone majority of Canada. The government set up in 1867 was a copy of the British model, giving legislative power to a Parliament elected by universal vote. The new constitution introduced a two-tiered regime composed of the federal government and the provincial government. In Québec City the parliament is called the National Assembly while in Ottawa this role belongs to the House of Commons. As a result of this new division of power, the minority position of francophones within Canada was confirmed. Within Québec, however, their authority increased thanks to the creation of a provincial government, which would manage the major areas francophones have always tried to preserve, such as education, culture and French civil law.

Québec has always been in favour of provincial autonomy as opposed to a centralized federal government. From the first years of the Constitution, politicians like **Honoré Mercier** pushed for more autonomy for the provinces. Among other things, he claimed that only in Québec were the rights of French Canadians efficiently respected. However, when he became Premier, he praised the French Catholic character of Québec without questioning federalism. From then on, the influence of Québec's political leaders and the ethnic and linguistic tensions between francophones and anglophones gave Québec an increasingly active role in the struggle for provincial autonomy.

Over the last 40 years, the relationship between the federal government and the province has taken a different turn. In fact, federal-provincial exchanges have been intense and rather tumultuous since the Quiet Revolution. The 1960s even saw the creation of an extremist group, the Front de Libération du Québec (FLQ), that demanded Québec independence. The group's political activities resulted in the 1970 **October Crisis**, during which Québec was subjected to the War Measures Act and the Canadian army was brought in to restore order.

The various Québec governments that have since followed have all been considered lobbyists for a distinct language and culture and have all claimed a special status as well as increased power for Québec. The Québec government believes it understands the needs

of the Québécois population better than the federal government, and demands the right to greater autonomy, power and resources.

The event that would radically change the political scene was the election of the Parti Québécois in 1976. This party succeeded very quickly in uniting sovereignist forces, particularly thanks to the personality and charisma of its founder, René Lévesque. This political party whose *raison d'être* was Québec sovereignty, proposed the 1980 referendum on the question of statehood and asked the Québec people for permission to negotiate sovereignty-association with the rest of Canada. The Québécois voted 60% against sovereignty-association. The same party, with Jacques Parizeau as its leader, would again ask the Québécois to express their opinion on the same question on October 31, 1995. This time the results were much closer: 50.6% of the population voted against the Québec government's independence project, while 49.4% declared they were in favour. In the eyes of many, the issue was once again postponed but it remains present today in many political speeches.

The attitude of Québec's political leaders regarding relations between the state and the economy changed radically when **Jean Lesage**'s Liberal Party came to power in the 1960s. This redefinition of the state's role in the economy disrupted the social, political and economic life of the province, particularly in Québec City. The number of employees in the public administration sector grew from 15,000 to 45,000 between the 1960s and the 1980s. This new direction, mapped out by the Quiet Revolution, was generally maintained throughout the 1960s, 1970s and even the 1980s. Québec's political leaders were inspired by their liberal European counterparts, supporting the Keynesian principles of a welfare state, making it a major participant in the economy and a partner in private enterprise. The presence of a large public administration provides the Vieille Capitale region and its inhabitants with steady, well-paid jobs.

The government's new economic role increased the presence and importance of francophones within the Québec economy. This phenomenon was mainly due to the growth of the public and semi-public sectors and the state's contribution to the private sector. The rise of francophones was felt in all sectors of the economy but especially in the areas of finance and public administration. However, this kind of state intervention on the part of Québec City and Ottawa has its drawbacks. Since the beginning of the 1980s, the Canadian and Québec governments, increasingly restricted by tight budgetary constraints, have found it more and more difficult to apply their interventionist politics and have incurred high budget deficits year after year.

To remedy this situation, radical, difficult decisions had to be made. To reduce the deficit, powers were decentralized and the cost of the public service was reduced by cutting jobs and eliminating raises. This created a problem since the Québec City region's economy is strongly oriented towards the public service sector. However, these cuts were eventually compensated for by growth in other sectors, showing that the vigour and ingenuity of the region could allow it to quickly and successfully adjust to an unfavourable situation.

## Economy

The historic and romantic aspects of Québec City are so often emphasized that it is easy to forget that this city is also the province's second most important economic centre. Situated on the banks of the St. Lawrence River, Québec City has more than 500,000 inhabitants. Its economy is strongly oriented towards the service industries and public administration, which employ about 85% of the population. A significant increase in employment has also taken place in areas such as tourism, finance and business, at the expense of the manufacturing industry.

## Municipal Mergers

In 2001, the Québec government passed a law requiring most of Québec's municipalities to merge with their neighbours in order to create larger regional entities. On January 1, 2002, several towns and villages lost their official name and became part of a bigger city. Québec City now includes the 13 municipalities that made up the former Communauté urbaine de Québec, creating a new megacity of more than 500,000 inhabitants divided into eight boroughs. The mergers involved plenty of hiccups, and the process is far from being complete. This is why we have decided, for the time being, not to modify most town names in this guide. In most towns that must be renamed, the choice of a new name is much cause for debate, and we believe that it is still too soon to use place names that will actually take years to be adopted. Nevertheless, you will have no trouble finding your way around the city of Québec.

The colossus that the Québec public administration represents is a result of the Quiet Revolution. Supporters of the principles of a welfare state wanted to make the province of Québec a major player in the economy and a partner in private enterprise. Subsequently, the welfare state aimed to modernize and improve the role of French Canadians in the Québec economy. Between the 1960s and the 1980s, the number of jobs in this sector tripled, and francophone control of the economy grew from 47% to 60%. This increase in the region's public sector also had important repercussions on the region's economy since, on average, one job in the public service results in the creation of another job in the private sector.

During the 1980s, and more particularly in the 1990s, the government attempted to reverse the situation. The welfare state and its numerous expenditures had made Canada one of the most indebted countries of all the industrialized nations. The solution seemed quite simple: cut expenses. This means that the public service has to limit its spending as much as possible by slashing employment and subsidies, followed by the privatization and decentralization of the administration.

Even though Québec City has one of the lowest unemployment rates in the province, the general transformations that the province's economy has gone through have affected Québec City and its region's employment stability. The reduction and decentralization of the Québec government has therefore forced Québec City to refocus its priorities.

To cope with government decentralization in favour of Montréal and the province's other regions and to compensate for job losses, Québec City has had to diversify its economy. Boasting with rich energy resources, a port deep enough to stay open all year and a solid road and railway network, Québec City is an ideal link between the major agricultural and economic centres of North America.

During the past few years, the Québec City region has put a great deal of effort into attracting new industries. Its qualified workforce, quality of life and accessibility have tipped the scale in its favour for several businesses that are now established here, such as manufacturers, telecommunications companies and high-tech businesses. However, despite the number of new jobs they have created, these big businesses haven't been popular with all of Québec City's residents; many are concerned by the pollution problems that come with such large industries, while others fear that a badly planned industrial configuration might one day disfigure their historic city.

**Université Laval** (Laval University) also plays an important role in the region's economic development by providing a qualified work force. It features a research and development department whose primary task is promoting and managing the transfer of technology from the university to various companies in the area. The creation of a technological park, an initiative of Université Laval and the Groupe d'Action Pour l'Avancement Technologique et Industriel de la Région de Québec (a group working for technological and industrial advancement in the Québec City Region) is a good example of the influence this institution has had on the region's economic vitality.

The province's capital has succeeded in revitalizing its economy with its specialized work force and the possibilities for research and development that are offered by the university and leading industries. In addition, Québec City is the seat of the provincial government and despite the reductions that were imposed on the public service, it will continue to be a driving force in the region.

Tourism also occupies an important place in the region's economy, generating approximately the same number of jobs as the manufacturing sector. Tourism is thus an important and ever growing economic sector in the region. Cruise ships from Europe and the United States stop in Québec City more and more often, especially since Pointe-à-Carcy was renovated. With Mont-Sainte-Anne close by, Montmorency Falls just a few minutes from downtown, a carnival in the winter and numerous festivals in the summer, tourism is booming all year long.

## Culture

Québec City has always enjoyed a very impressive and varied cultural life. Numerous artists such as **Cornelius Krieghoff**, **Maurice Cullen**, **James Wilson Morrice**, **Clarence Gagnon**, **Adrien Hébert**, **Jean-Paul Lemieux**, **Jean-Guy Desrosiers** and others have been influenced by this city and at the same time have enriched its image.

Several artists have found inspiration in the region and have chosen to settle in Québec City or its surroundings. For example, **Félix Leclerc** (1914-1988), a composer, poet and performer, was the first Québec singer to achieve success in Europe, opening the way for many other Québec artists.

Leclerc liked to spend his free time on Île d'Orléans, a place that was close to his heart and that is featured prominently in his work.

Today, Québec City continues to be the birthplace of several interesting artistic projects. Performing-arts centres like **Méduse** (see p 121) and **Ex Machina** (see p 92) are only two examples in a city where theatres and other artistic institutions abound. Québec's film industry is also quite rich.

The aforementioned Ex Machina was founded by **Robert Lepage** in 1994. Born in the Haute-Ville section of Québec City on December 12, 1957, this director and producer has enjoyed a remarkable international success. Not unlike Félix Leclerc, it took his huge popularity in Europe to make Québec recognize Lepage's immense talent. This talent is particularly evident in his plays *Les Plaques Tectoniques*, *La Trilogie des Dragons* and *Les Aiguilles et l'Opium* as well as his films *Le Confessionnal*, *Le Polygraphe*, *Nô*, *Possible Worlds* and *La Face Cachée de la Lune*. *Le Confessionnal* takes place in Québec City and draws a parallel with the movie *I Confess*, filmed here by Alfred Hitchcock in the 1950s. Lepage's film presents magnificent images of Québec City. From opera to theatre and cinema to rock concerts… Robert Lepage has done it all.

Portrait

## Québec's Emblems

In 1999, the Québec government adopted the blue flag iris as its floral emblem. Until then, the province's official flower had been the white lily (*fleur-de-lys*) that adorns its flag, commemorating the French origins of the founders of Québec. But because the white lily doesn't actually grow here, the iris was chosen. Indeed, not only is the iris indigenous to the province, but it also symbolizes its people in several ways: it grows in wet environments, which are omnipresent in Québec; it blossoms in late June, during St. Jean Baptiste Day, Québec's national holiday; it is usually blue, the colour of the Québec flag, but can also come in many different varieties, just like the province's various cultural communities. Québec's official tree is the yellow birch, while its aviary emblem is the beautiful snowy owl.

## Literature

During the 19th century, Québec City was the setting of many novels. Although the most popular genre at the time was European-style adventure stories, Québec literature was usually limited to glorifying the past and idealizing country life, and was clearly behind the times when compared to Western literature in general. In the beginning, the use of Québec City as a setting was hardly recognizable but has become increasingly evident over the years. As more novels have been published, from *Les Anciens Canadiens* by **Philippe Aubert de Gaspé** to **Roger Lemelin**'s well known *Au pied de la pente douce* (1944) and *Les Plouffe* (1948), Québec City's image has changed from that of a vague, undefined place to a very lively, bustling French Canadian city. Even though it was once conquered by the British and is not as commercially significant as other cities, Québec remains the intellectual capital of French Canada and a symbol of resistance for French Canadians.

Roger Lemelin (1919-1994), a successful writer who described the colourful poor neighbourhoods of Québec City in his novels *Au pied de la pente douce*, *Les Plouffe* and *Le Crime d'Ovide Plouffe* (1982), was born in Québec City. These last two works became very popular and were adapted for radio and television, then for the movies. In 1974, Lemelin was elected as a foreign member to France's Académie Goncourt.

Famed novelist **Anne Hébert** (1916-2000) was born in Sainte-Catherine-de-la-Jacques-Cartier, in the Québec City region. Her novel *L'Enfant chargé de songes* (1992) brings the city to life as though it were an actual character.

Several contemporary writers also originate from this region, such as **Chrystine Brouillet**, whose forte is detective novels, novelists **Yves Thériault**, **Monique Proulx** and **Marie-Claire Blais**, as well as poet **Pierre Morency**.

## Architecture

Québec City is first and foremost the only walled city on the North American continent. The city was fortified for security reasons and its position on top of Cap Diamant was strategic. Champlain had Fort Saint-Louis built at the beginning of the 17th century. Originally, the walls served to defend against British threats and ward off Aboriginal attacks. Very early on, major fortification work transformed Québec City into a veritable stronghold: the city saw the construction of the Batterie Royale in 1691, the Dauphine Redoubt in 1712, and in 1720, the walls that more or less correspond to the ramparts we see today. The buildings inside the walls and in Vieux-Québec give the city its Old French Regime look.

Québec City has one of the richest architectural heritages in North America. As the cradle of New France, it is especially evocative of Europe in its architecture and atmosphere. But its architecture had to be adapted, particularly because of the harsh winters and lack of specialized workers and materials. The buildings here are simple and efficient without extravagance. A typical house of this period was rectangular in shape with a two-sided sloping roof covered with cedar shingles. To cope with the cold Québec City winters, this type of habitation was fitted with only a few windows and one or two fireplaces. Interiors were quite rustic, since the main preoccupation was to keep warm at all times.

## Let There Be Light!

Following in the footsteps of other cities of the world, Québec City has endeavoured to shine a light on its many beautiful attractions. According to this plan, a tasteful lighting system was set up to highlight the shapes and details of the city's most noteworthy buildings and sites. The **Hôtel du Parlement**, the **Château Frontenac** and the **Pont de Québec** all now light up the sky of this seductive city.

Although this type of dwelling was found mainly in the countryside, the same kind of architecture could also be seen within the city itself. As well as having to deal with the cold, the city's inhabitants had to worry about fires. The proximity of the buildings and the wood used in their construction meant that fires could spread very quickly. Following the great fire of 1682 which almost completely destroyed the Basse-Ville, the intendants of New France issued two edicts in 1721 and in 1727 regulating construction in order to reduce the risk of fire inside the city

walls. From then on, the use of wood and the construction of mansard roofs—their structure was complex and compact, presenting a great danger for fire—were both prohibited. All buildings had to be made of stone and equipped with firewalls. In addition, the floors that separated a house's various storeys had to be covered with terra cotta tiles. All of these changes led to the realignment of Basse-Ville streets and the creation of Place Royale.

In neighbourhoods like Petit-Champlain you will find stone houses dating from this era, such as the Louis-Jolliet House (16 Rue du Petit-Champlain) or the Demers House (28 Boulevard Champlain). The decision to forbid the use of wood also resulted in the creation of the first suburbs outside city walls, since the poorer settlers were unable to meet the costly building requirements and were forced to move out of town,

Following the British victory on the Plains of Abraham, New France became part of the British Empire and the face of Québec City gradually changed as its anglophone population increased. For instance, on Grande Allée, a previously simple tree-lined country road, large domains appeared where the English built Second Empire and, later on, Victorian mansions. Today, these buildings have been transformed into bars or restaurants with terraces overlooking Grande Allée.

# Practical Information

T he information in this chapter will help you better plan your trip, not only well in advance, but also once you've arrived in Québec City.

I mportant details on entrance formalities and other procedures, as well as general information, have been compiled for visitors from other countries. We will also explain how to use this guide. We wish you a great trip to Québec City!

The area code for Québec City and its region is **418**.

## Entrance Formalities

### Passports

A valid passport is usually sufficient for most visitors planning to stay less than three months in Canada. U.S. citizens do not

need a passport, but it is, however, a good form of identification. US citizens and citizens of Western Europe do not need a visa. For a complete list of countries whose citizens require a visa, see the **Canadian Citizenship and Immigration** Web site *(www.cic.gc.ca)* or contact the Canadian embassy or consulate nearest you.

## Extended Visits

Visitors must submit a request to extend their visit **in writing three weeks before** the expiration of their visa (the date is usually written on your passport) to an Immigration Canada office. To make such a request, you must present a valid passport, a return ticket, proof of sufficient funds to cover the stay and a $75 non-refundable filing-fee. In some cases (work, study), however, the request must be made **before** arriving in Canada.

## Customs

If you are bringing gifts into Canada, remember that certain restrictions apply:

**Smokers** (minimum age is 18 in Québec) can bring in a maximum of 200 cigarettes, 50 cigars, 200g of tobacco or 200 tobacco sticks.

For **wine** and **liquor**, the limit is 1.5 litres. The limit for beer is 24 355ml cans or 341ml bottles. The minimum drinking age in Québec is 18.

There are very strict rules regarding the importation of **plants**, **flowers**, and other **vegetation**; it is therefore not advisable to bring any of these types of products into the country.

If you are travelling with your **pet**, you will need a rabies-vaccination certificate. For more information on travelling with animals, plants or food, contact the **Canadian Food Inspection Agency** *(www.cfia-acia.agr.ca)* or the Canadian embassy or consulate nearest you before your departure for Canada.

## Embassies and Consulates

### Abroad

#### Great Britain

**Canada High Commission**
Macdonald House
One Grosvenor Square
London, W1K 4AB
☎ *(207) 258 6600*
⇥ *(207) 258 6333*
*www.dfait-maeci.gc.ca/canada europa/united_kingdom*

#### United States

**Canadian Embassy**
501 Pennsylvania Ave. NW
Washington, DC, 20001
☎ *(202) 682-1740*
⇥ *(202) 682-7701*
*www.canadianembassy.org*

#### Canadian Consulates General:

1175 Peachtree St. NE
100 Colony Square, Suite 1700,
Atlanta, Georgia, 30361-6205
☎ *(404) 532-2000*
⇥ *(404) 532-2050*
*www.dfait-maeci.gc.ca/can-am/ atlanta*

Three Copley Place, Suite 400
Boston, Massachusetts, 02116
☎*(617) 262-3760*
⇌*(617) 262-3415*
*www.dfait-maeci.gc.ca/can-am/*
*boston*

Two Prudential Plaza, 180 N.
Stetson Ave., Suite 2400, Chicago,
Illinois, 60601-6714
☎*(312) 616-1860*
⇌*(312) 616-1877*
*www.dfait-maeci.gc.ca/can-am/*
*chicago*

St. Paul Place, Suite 1700,
750 N. St. Paul St., Dallas, Texas,
75201
☎*(214) 922-9806*
*www.dfait-maeci.gc.ca/can-am/*
*dallas*

600 Renaissance Center, Suite 1100
Detroit, Michigan, 48234-1798
☎*(313) 567-2340*
⇌*(313) 567-2164*
*www.dfait-maeci.gc.ca/can-am/*
*detroit*

550 South Hope St., 9th floor
Los Angeles, California, 90071-2627
☎*(213) 346-2700*
⇌*(213) 346-2767*
*www.dfait-maeci.gc.ca/can-am/*
*los_angeles*

701 Fourth Ave. S., 9th floor
Minneapolis, Minnesota,
55415-1899
☎*(612) 333-4641*
⇌*(612) 332-4061*
*www.dfait-maeci.gc.ca/can-am/*
*minneapolis*

1251 Avenue of the Americas,
Concourse Level, New York, NY 10020-
1175
☎*(212) 596-1628*
⇌*(212) 596-1790*
*www.dfait-maeci.gc.ca/can-am/*
*new_york*

3000 HSBC Center, Buffalo, NY 14203-
2884.
☎*(716) 852-2477 or 858-9591*
*www.dfait-maeci.gc.ca/can-am/*
*buffalo*

412 Plaza 600, Sixth and
Stewart Sts., Seattle,
Washington 98101-1286
☎*(206) 443-1777*
⇌*(206) 443-9662*
*www.dfait-maeci.gc.ca/can-am/*
*seattle*

Practical
Information

## In Montréal

### Great Britain

1000 de la Gauchetière Ouest
Suite 4200, H3B 4W5
☎*(514) 866-5863*
⇌*(514) 866-0202*
*www.britainincanada.org/contact/*
*montreal.htm*

### United States

Place Félix-Martin
1155 Rue Saint-Alexandre, H3B 1Z1
☎*(514) 398-9695*
*Mailing address*:
C.P. 65 Station Desjardins
Montréal, H5B 1G1
*www.usembassycanada.gov*

## In Québec City

### United States

**Consulate General**
2 Place Terrasse Dufferin, G1R 4T9
☎ *(418) 692-2095*
*www.usembassycanada.gov*

## Tourist Information

Tourist information is available from Tourisme Québec, the Délégations Générales du Québec abroad and the various offices of the Office du Tourisme et des Congrès de la région de Québec. A tourist information service is also available from guides on mopeds in Vieux-Québec during the summer. The mopeds are painted green and have a flag with a question mark on it.

**Tourisme Québec**
PO Box 979, Montréal, H3C 2W3
☎ *(514) 873-2015*
*or 877-266-5687*
*www.bonjourquebec.com*

## In Canada and Abroad

### Canada

**Bureau du Québec**
20 Queen St. W., Suite 1504
Toronto, Ontario, M5H 3S3
☎ *(416) 977-6713*
⇥ *(416) 596-1407*
*www.saic.gouv.qc.ca/bureaux_du_quebec/bureau_quebec_toronto.htm*

### Great Britain

**Québec Government House**
59 Pall Mall, London SWIY 5JH
☎ *(44) 207 766-5900*
⇥ *(44) 207 930-7938*
*www.mri.gouv.qc.ca/london/en/index.asp*

### United States

**Québec Government House**
One Rockefeller Plaza, 26th Floor,
New York, NY 10020-2102
☎ *(212) 397-0200 or 843-0950*
⇥ *(212) 757-4753 or 376-8984*
*www.mri.gouv.qc.ca/usa/en*

## In Quebec city and Abroad

### In Québec City

**Centre Infotouriste**
12 Rue Sainte-Anne, Québec G1R 3X2
☎ *877-266-5687*
The centre infotouriste provides detailed information and supplies road maps, travel brochures, and lodging guides for all of Québec's tourist regions.

**Office du tourisme et des congrès de la région de Québec**
835 Avenue Wilfrid-Laurier, G1R 2L3
☎ *641-6290*
*www.quebecregion.com*

### Sainte-Foy

**Bureau d'information touristique**
3300 Avenue des Hôtels, G1W 5A8
☎ *641-6290*
*www.quebecregion.com*

## Beauport

**Bureau touristique du Parc de la Chute-Montmorency**
4300 Boulevard Sainte-Anne,
G1C 7M5 (Route 138)
*mid-Jun to late August*
☎641-6290
*www.quebecregion.com*

### Île d'Orléans

**Bureau d'accueil touristique**
490 Côte du Pont, Saint-Pierre,
G0A 4E0
☎828-9411 or 866-941-9411
*www.iledorleans.com*

### Portneuf

**Tourisme Portneuf**
12 rue des Pins, Deschambault,
G0A 1S0
☎286-3002 or 800-409-2012
*www.portneuf.com*

## On the Internet

Here are some Web sites that will help you find out about Québec City online.

**Tourisme Québec**
*www.bonjourquebec.com*

**Office du tourisme et des congrès de la région de Québec**
*www.quebecregion.com*

**Québec City**
*www.ville.quebec.qc.ca*

**Cultural information**
*www.quebecplus.ca*
*www.telegraphe.com*

## Getting There

If you are leaving from Montréal, take the Jean-Lesage Autoroute (route 20 East) as far as the Pierre-Laporte Bridge, cross the bridge and take Boulevard Laurier which will successively change its name to Chemin Saint-Louis and then to Grande Allée. This road leads you directly to the Haute-Ville. You can also arrive by Félix Leclerc Autoroute (route 40 East), which will take you as far as Sainte-Foy and from there signs for Boulevard Charest will lead you to the centre of Basse-Ville. To get to the Haute-Ville, take Rue Dorchester followed by Côte d'Abraham.

Arriving from Ottawa on Autoroute 417, take Félix Leclere Autoroute (route 40 East) to Sainte-Foy and then follow the signs for Boulevard Charest Est. You will arrive in the Basse-Ville. From Toronto, take the Jean-Lesage Autoroute (route 20 East) until the exit for the Pierre-Laporte Bridge. Cross the bridge and follow the signs for Boulevard Laurier which will eventually become Grande Allée.

From the United States, take Highway 55, then Autoroute 20 East. You will enter Québec City by the Pierre-Laporte Bridge and then take Boulevard Laurier.

When arriving in Québec City by car, the most common

route is via Grande Allée. After passing through a typical North American-style suburb, you will come to a rather British-looking part of town with tree-lined streets. Next come the provincial capital's government buildings and finally the imposing medieval-looking gates that hide the historic streets of the old city, Vieux-Québec.

# Airport

## Jean-Lesage Airport

**Aéroport International Jean-Lesage** *(500 Rue Principale, Sainte-Foy, ☎640-2700, www.aeroportdequebec.com)* is the only airport in the vicinity of Québec City. Despite its small size, it does receive international flights and serves Québec and the other Canadian provinces.

### Location

Situated in L'Ancienne-Lorette, the airport is about 20km northwest of Québec City. To get downtown, head south on Route de l'Aéroport to Autoroute 40 Est and then take Boulevard Charest Est. The trip takes about 20min.

### Taxi

A taxi from the airport to downtown costs about $27.

**Taxi Co-op**
☎525-5191

**Taxi Quebec**
☎525-8123

## Car Rentals

Various car rental agencies, such as Budget, Hertz and National, are located at the airport (see p 37).

## Information

For information about airport services (arrivals, departures, etc.) call ☎640-2600, 24hrs a day for a recorded message. Call the same number and choose option "0" to speak to an agent on Monday to Friday, from 8am to 4:30pm. There is no toll-free line for general information. Here are the telephone numbers of several airline companies that you might want to call:

**Air Canada**
☎888-422-7533
*www.aircanada.com*

**Air Canada Jazz**
☎888-422-7533
*www.flyjazz.ca*

**Air Transat**
☎877-872-6728
*www.transat.com*

**Continental Airlines**
☎800-932-2732 or 800-231-0856
*www.continental.com*

## Foreign Exchange

The **Exchange Corporation Canada** *(☎872-0360)* foreign exchange office is open every day from 9am to 9pm.

# Table of Distances (in kilometres)

## Via the shortest route

| | Baie-Comeau | Boston (Mass.) | Charlottetown (P.E.I.) | Chibougamau | Chicoutimi | Gaspé | Halifax (N.S.) | Gatineau / Ottawa | Montréal | New York (N.Y.) | Niagara Falls (Ont.) | Québec City | Rouyn-Noranda | Sherbrooke | Toronto (Ont.) |
|---|---|---|---|---|---|---|---|---|---|---|---|---|---|---|---|
| Boston (Mass.) | 1040 | | | | | | | | | | | | | | |
| Charlottetown (P.E.I.) | 724 | 1081 | | | | | | | | | | | | | |
| Chibougamau | 679 | 1152 | 1347 | | | | | | | | | | | | |
| Chicoutimi | 316 | 849 | 992 | 363 | | | | | | | | | | | |
| Gaspé | 337 | 1247 | 867 | 1039 | 649 | | | | | | | | | | |
| Halifax (N.S.) | 807 | 1165 | 265 | 1430 | 1076 | 952 | | | | | | | | | |
| Gatineau / Ottawa | 869 | 701 | 1404 | 725 | 662 | 1124 | 1488 | | | | | | | | |
| Montréal | 676 | 512 | 1194 | 700 | 464 | 930 | 1290 | 207 | | | | | | | |
| New York (N.Y.) | 1239 | 352 | 1421 | 1308 | 1045 | 1550 | 1508 | 814 | 608 | | | | | | |
| Niagara Falls (Ont.) | 1334 | 767 | 1836 | 1298 | 1126 | 1590 | 1919 | 543 | 670 | 685 | | | | | |
| Québec City | 422 | 648 | 984 | 515 | 211 | 700 | 1056 | 451 | 253 | 834 | 925 | | | | |
| Rouyn-Noranda | 1304 | 1136 | 1833 | 493 | 831 | 1559 | 1916 | 536 | 638 | 1246 | 858 | 877 | | | |
| Sherbrooke | 662 | 426 | 1187 | 724 | 451 | 915 | 1271 | 347 | 147 | 657 | 827 | 240 | 782 | | |
| Toronto (Ont.) | 1224 | 906 | 1746 | 1124 | 1000 | 1476 | 1828 | 399 | 546 | 823 | 141 | 802 | 606 | 693 | |
| Trois-Rivières | 545 | 566 | 1089 | 574 | 338 | 808 | 1173 | 331 | 142 | 750 | 814 | 130 | 158 | 747 | 688 |

Example: the distance between Québec City and Montréal is 253km.

# Getting Around

## By Car

Québec City has a very good public transportation system and plenty of taxis, so it is not necessary to use your car; it is even preferable to visit the city on foot. Most of the tourist attractions are relatively close to one other and all the tours we suggest are within walking distance. However, for the surrounding areas (Île d'Orléans for example), a car or bicycle is needed to cover the distance.

It is easy to get around by car in Québec City. In Vieux-Québec, parking lots are numerous but expensive. You can park on the street but read the signs limiting parking times carefully and do not forget to feed the parking meters regularly. Inspectors check the streets often and fines are expensive. The signs to leave town are clearly marked.

### Things to Consider

**Driver's License:** As a general rule, foreign driver's licenses are valid for six months from the arrival date in Canada.

**Winter Driving:** Although roads are generally in good condition, the dangers brought on by drastic climatic conditions must be taken into consideration.

**Highway Code:** Turning right on a red light is permitted in the province of Québec, except in Montréal and where otherwise indicated. Priority to the right is the law here; however, it is not always observed, so pay attention. Red signs marked "Arrêt" or "Stop" must always be respected. Come to a complete stop even if there is no apparent danger.

Traffic lights are often located on the opposite side of the intersection, so make sure to stop on the stop line.

When a school bus (usually yellow) has stopped and has its signals flashing, you must come to a complete stop, no matter what direction you are travelling in. Failing to stop at the flashing signals is considered a serious offense and carries a heavy penalty.

Wearing seatbelts in the front and back seats is compulsory at all times.

Pay attention to reserved bus lanes! They are marked by a large white diamond and signs clearly indicating the hours you cannot drive in these lanes, except when making a right turn.

There are no tolls on Québec highways (*autoroutes*), and the speed limit is 100km/h. The speed limit on secondary highways is 90km/h, and 50km/h in urban areas.

**Gas Stations:** Gasoline prices are less expensive than in Europe. Some gas stations (especially in downtown areas) might ask for payment in advance as a security measure, especially after 11pm.

## Accidents and Emergencies

In case of serious accident, fire or any other emergency, dial **911** or **0**.

If you run into trouble on the highway, pull onto the shoulder of the road and turn on the hazard lights. If it is a rental car, contact the rental company as soon as possible. Always file an accident report. If a disagreement arises over who was at fault in an accident, ask for police help.

If you are planning a lengthy car trip, it is a good idea to become a member of the Canadian Automobile Association, or CAA, which can offer help throughout Canada. If you are a member in your home country of an equivalent association (U.S.A.: American Automobile Association; Great Britain: Automobile Association; Australia: Australian Automobile Association), you have the right to some free services. For further information, contact your association or the CAA in Québec City ☎**624-8222**.

## Car Rentals

Generally, a package including airfare, hotel and car or just hotel and car is less expensive than renting a car once you get here. Many travel agencies have agreements with the major car-rental companies (Avis, Budget, Hertz, etc.) and offer good values; contracts often include added bonuses (reduced ticket prices for shows, etc.). Package deals are usually a good bargain. However, if you cannot get a package deal, it is cheaper to rent your car here than it is from abroad. Here are the addresses of the main car rental companies:

**Budget**
7300 Boulevard Wilfrid-Hamel Ouest
☎**872-9885**
*Vieux-Québec*
29 Côte du Palais
☎**692-3660**
*Sainte-Foy*
2481 Chemin Sainte-Foy
☎**651-6518**
*www.budgetmtl.com*

**Discount**
12 Rue Sainte-Anne, Québec
☎**655-2206**
*www.discountcar.com*

**Hertz**
*Jean-Lesage Airport*
☎**871-1571**
*Québec*
580 Grande Allée
☎**647-4949**
*Vieux-Québec*
44 Côte du Palais
☎**694-1224**
2800 Boulevard Laurier,
Hôtel Carillon
☎**658-6795**
*www.hertz.com*

Practical
Information

**National**
*Jean-Lesage Airport*
☎877-9822
*Beauport*
301 Rue Seigneuriale
☎663-8681
*www.nationalcar.com*

**Via Route**
2605 Boulevard Wilfrid-Hamel
☎682-2660
450 de la Gare-du-Palais
☎694-1727
*www.viaroute.com*

**When renting a car, find out if:**
The contract includes unlimited kilometres and if the insurance offered provides full coverage (accident, property damage, hospital costs for you and your passengers, theft).

**Don't forget:**
To rent a car in Québec, you must be at least 21 years of age and have had a driver's license for **at least** one year. If you are between 21 and 25, certain companies will ask for a $500 deposit, and in some cases they will also charge an extra sum for each day you rent the car. These conditions do not apply for those over 25 years of age.

A credit card is extremely useful for the deposit to avoid tying up large sums of money.

Most rental cars have an automatic transmission; however, you can request a car with a manual shift.

Child-safety seats cost extra.

# By Public Transportation

When visiting Québec City, we strongly recommend you use public transportation. Run by the **Réseau de Transport de la Capitale** (RTC), the transit system has a network of bus routes that covers the entire city. There is no subway in Québec City; however, a Métrobus service has recently been established which leaves Beauport or Charlesbourg and goes as far as Sainte-Foy and vice versa. The buses go through Vieux-Québec, along Rue Saint-Jean, Avenue Cartier and across the university campus; they stop opposite the large Sainte-Foy shopping centres and near the Sainte-Foy bus terminal. Métrobuses no. 800 or 801 are fast because they run on reserved lanes (see p 36) and stop less often than other buses. Métrobuses also run often, about every 10min.

You will find the public transportation guide in the telephone book. This map of the bus routes also contains the main landmarks to help you get around.

For unlimited use of public transportation, a monthly bus pass costs $63.40 (on sale at the beginning of each month). You can also buy tickets costing $2.20 each or pay a fare of $2.50 in exact change for each trip. You can also buy a day-pass for $5.65. Students and senior citizens have reduced rates. Children five years of age and under travel free of charge. Tickets can be bought at most pharmacies or corner stores. These outlets also have folders describing the individual bus routes. **Take note, bus drivers do not sell tickets and do not give change**.

When you want to change buses, you must ask the driver for a transfer.

For more information about public transportation:
☎627-2511
www.stcuq.qc.ca

From mid-November to the end of March, there is a shuttle service for people staying in the city who would like to take a day trip to the surrounding countryside. L'**Hiver Express** (*$23 return per person;* ☎525-5191) stops in front of the main hotels in Québec City and Sainte-Foy every morning. These taxis will take you to the region's main tourist recreational sites such as Mont Saint-Anne and pick you up at the end of the afternoon.

## By Bus

The Québec City bus terminal is located in the Gare du Palais. Buses leave for Montréal every hour from 5:30am to 10:30pm (Sun from 6:30am to 10:30pm). There is also a shuttle-bus service that goes directly to Montréal – Pierre

Elliott Trudeau International Airport.

**Gare d'autocars de Québec**
*(terminus)*
320 Rue Abraham-Martin
☎525-3000

The same bus service passes through Sainte-Foy, because buses arriving from Montréal stop in Sainte-Foy before continuing on to the Gare du Palais.

**Gare d'autocars Sainte-Foy**
*(terminus)*
3001 Chemin des Quatre-Bourgeois
☎650-0087

## By Train

Trains from Montréal arrive at the Gare du Palais in the Basse-Ville, and those coming from the east stop at Lévis on the other side of the river, where the ferry crosses.

**ViaRail**
☎888-842-7245
www.viarail.com

**Gare du Palais**
450 Rue de la Gare-du-Palais

**Gare de Charny**
2326 Rue de la Gare Est

**Gare de Sainte-Foy**
3255 Chemin de la Gare

## Hitchhiking

During the summer, hitchhiking is common and is easier outside

Practical Information

large centres. Hitchhiking is prohibited on major highways and expressways.

"Organized" hitchhiking, or ridesharing, with Allo-Stop, works very well in all seasons. This reputed company pairs drivers who want to share their car for a small payment with passengers needing a ride. A membership card is required and costs $6 for a passenger and $7 for a driver per year. The driver receives part (approximately 60%) of the fees paid by the passengers. Destinations include virtually everywhere in the province of Québec. For example, a one-way trip between Québec and Montréal costs $16.

Children under 5 years of age cannot travel with Allo-Stop because of a regulation requiring the use of child-safety seats. Not all drivers accept smokers, and not all passengers want to be exposed to smoke, so check on this ahead of time.

For registration and information:

**Allo-Stop Québec**
665 Rue Saint-Jean
☎*522-0056*

## By Ferry

Even if you have no reason to go to Lévis on the south shore of the St. Lawrence River, you should take the ferry trip just for the view. The ferry dock is across from Place-Royale; you should have no trouble finding it. The return trip from Lévis gives you a magnificent view of Québec City. A one-way trip costs $2 during winter and $2.50 in summer for an adult, and $8.50 for a car in winter and $9.85 during summer (maximum six passengers). The timetable varies from one season to the next so it is better to check directly for the departure times.

**Société des Traversiers du Québec**
10 Rue des Traversiers
☎*643-8420 or 877-787-7483*
*www.traversiers.gouv.qc.ca*

## By Bicycle

One of the best ways to get around in the summer is on a bicycle. Bicycle paths and shared road spaces have been laid out to give cyclists access to certain parts of the city. To help you get around, there is a brochure as well as a map showing the bicycle paths and shared road spaces in the city and its surrounding area. Also, consult the Ulysses Travel Guide *Le Québec cyclable* to obtain maps of those trails.

Cars are not always attentive and cyclists must be careful. Cyclists must follow the rules of the road and although it is not obligatory in Québec, we strongly recommend that you wear a helmet.

**Promo-Vélo** *(PO Box 700, Succ. Haute-Ville, Québec, G1R 4S9, www.promo-velo.org)* can provide you with information on the different types of tours in the region.

### Bicycle Rentals

Some bicycle shops have a rental service. These shops are listed in the chapter on outdoor activities (see p 164) For other addresses consult the yellow pages under "Bicyclettes-Location" or "Bicycle Rental." Insurance is a good idea. Some places include theft insurance in the rental fee, but be sure to confirm this when you rent the bicycle.

## Guided Tours

Several tourist agencies organize tours that give visitors the opportunity to discover the city in various ways. A walking tour provides a more intimate perspective of a neighbourhood than a tour bus. Cruises also provide a unique perspective of the city and its outline from the water. Although there are many options, a few should be mentioned as they are particularly worthwhile.

## On Foot

In the tourist information office on Avenue Wilfrid-Laurier, the company Voxsys offers the **CD Tour** *($15; 835 Avenue Wilfrid-Laurier,* ☎*641-6290 or 654-*

*1115)*. This outfit rents out portable audio-tours for various parts of the city. The tours are recorded on laser disc, enabling visitors to stop where and when they please. In the lively recordings, historic figures are brought back to life to tell visitors about the major events that shaped Québec City.

Another option is to take a "Québec, Fortified City" walking tour, offered by the **Centre d'Initiation aux Fortifications de Québec** *(walking tour $10; 90 min; June and late Aug to early Oct, 1pm; late June to late Aug, 10am, 1:30pm and 3pm; visit of the centre $3.50; early May to early Oct 10am to 5pm;* ☎*648-7016)* (see p 61). Tours start at the kiosk on Terrasse Dufferin.

The **Société Historique de Québec** *($12; 72 Côte de la Montagne,* ☎*692-0556)* offers guided tours of Vieux-Québec. There are a number of themes from which to choose. The visits last a little over 2 hours and allow you to discover the many historical aspects of Québec City.

**Les Tours Voir Québec** *($18; duration: about 2hrs; during winter, 10am and 2pm; during summer, 9:30am, 11am, 1:30pm, 3pm; 12 Rue Ste-Anne,* ☎*694-2001, www.toursvoir quebec.com)* offers tours that relive history through short anecdotes detailing how the city has evolved. They also organize bus tours in the city and its surrounding region.

## By Bus

**Les Tours Voir Québec** (see above).

**Les Tours du Vieux-Québec**
☎664-0460 or 800-267-8687
*www.toursvieuxquebec.com*
Guided tours of the city and its surroundings are given in the comfort of a small air-conditioned bus. Visits to the area around Québec City include Côte-de-Beaupré, Sainte-Anne-de-Beaupré and Île d'Orléans. Tours of Québec's old town last about 2 hours, cost $25 per person and are given all year long.

**Autocars Dupont**
☎649-9226 or 888-558-7668
*www.tourdupont.com*
Autocars Dupont gives classical tours of the city and excursions to the surrounding area in a luxury bus, an air-conditioned minibus or a trolley. The city tour lasts 2 hours and costs $27. These tours are given throughout the year.

## By Calèche (Horse-Drawn Carriage)

**Calèches du Vieux-Québec**
☎683-9222
*$75/45min*
You can visit Vieux-Québec by *calèche* all year long. This original way of discovering the city adds to its charm. *Calèches* can be found almost anywhere in the old town.

## By Boat

The **Croisières AML** (☎692-2634 or 800-563-4643, *www.croisieres aml.com*) and the **Croisières Groupe Dufour** (☎800-463-5250, *www.famille dufour.com*) both offer cruises on the St. Lawrence River that allow you to discover Québec City from another point of view (see p 165).

## Money and Banking

There are several banks and *caisses populaires* (credit unions) in Vieux-Québec that exchange foreign currency. In most cases these institutions charge a commission. The *bureau de change* (exchange bureau) may not charge a fee but their rates are less competitive. You should compare rates and ask about fees. Most banks will exchange U.S. dollars.

**Caisse Populaire Desjardins du Vieux-Québec**
19 Rue Desjardins
☎522-6806

**Échange de Devises Montréal**
12 Rue Sainte-Anne
☎694-1014
46, Rue Petit-Champlain
☎694-0011

**Transchange International**
Promenades du Vieux-Québec
43 Rue de Buade
☎694-6906

## Traveller's Cheques

Traveller's cheques are usually accepted in most department stores and hotels but it is more convenient to change them at the above mentioned places. In Québec City you can buy traveller's cheques in Canadian or U.S. dollars in most banks.

## Credit Cards

Most major credit cards are accepted in stores, restaurants and hotels. While the main advantage of credit cards is that they allow visitors to avoid carrying large sums of money, using a credit card also makes leaving a deposit for a car rental much easier. Also, some cards, gold cards for example, automatically insure you when you rent a car. In addition, the exchange rate on a credit card is generally better than those given by exchange bureaus or banks. The most commonly accepted credit cards are Visa, MasterCard and American Express.

By using a credit card, you can avoid service charges when exchanging money. By over-paying your credit card (to avoid interest charges) you can then withdraw against it. You can thus avoid carrying large amounts of money or traveller's cheques. Withdrawals can be made directly from an automatic teller using the personal

identification number for your card.

## Banks

Most bank services are available to tourists. Those travellers who are planning extended stays should note however that non residents cannot open a bank account. The best way to get money in this case is to carry travellers' cheques. Withdrawing money from your overseas account can be costly, as commission costs are high. However, some automatic teller machines accept foreign bank cards, thus allowing you to make withdrawals. The other choice is a postal money order, for which no commission is charged; however they can be time consuming to process. Those travellers who have gained resident status, permanent or not (such as immigrants or students), can open a bank account. To do so, be sure to bring your passport and proof of residence status with you to the bank.

**Caisse Populaire Desjardins du Vieux-Québec**
19 Rue Desjardins
☎ 522-6806

**Banque Royale**
700 Place d'Youville
☎ 692-6800

**Banque Nationale**
150 Boulevard René-Lévesque Est
☎ 647-6100

Practical Information

## Exchange Rates*

| | | | |
|---|---|---|---|
| $1 CAN = $0.81 US | | $1 US | = $1.24 CAN |
| $1 CAN = £0.43 | | £1 | = $2.34 CAN |
| $1 CAN = €0.63 | | €1 | = $1.59 CAN |

*Samples only—rates may fluctuate

## Currency

The monetary unit in Québec is the Canadian dollar ($), which is divided into cents (¢). One dollar= 100 cents.

Bills come in 5-, 10-, 20-, 50-, 100-, 500- and 1000- dollar denominations, and coins come in 1-, 5-, 10- and 25-cent pieces and in 1- and 2-dollar coins.

## Automated Teller Machines (ATMs)

Most banks have ATMs that allow you to make cash withdrawals. You can use your card as you normally would—you'll be given Canadian dollars with a receipt, and the equivalent amount will be debited from your account. All this will take no more time than it would at your own bank! That said, the network can sometimes experi-ence communication problems that will prevent you from obtaining money. If your transaction is refused by the ATM at one bank, try another bank where you might have better luck. In any case, take precautions so that you do not find yourself empty-handed.

## Insurance

## Cancellation

Your travel agent will usually offer you cancellation insurance when you buy your airline ticket or vacation package. This insurance allows you to be reimbursed for the ticket or package deal if your trip must be cancelled due to serious illness or death.

## Theft

Most residential insurance policies protect some of your goods from theft, even if the theft occurs in a foreign country. To make a claim, you must fill out a police report. It may not be necessary to take out further insurance, depending on the amount covered by your current home policy. As policies vary considerably, you are advised to check with your insurance company.

## Health

This is the most useful kind of insurance for travellers and should be purchased before your departure. Your insurance plan should be as complete as possible because health-care costs add up quickly. When buying insurance, make sure it covers all types of medical costs, such as hospitalization, nursing services and doctor's fees. Make sure your limit is high enough, as these expenses can be costly. A repatriation clause is also vital in case the required care is not available on site. Furthermore, since you may have to pay immediately, check your policy to see what

provisions it includes for such situations. To avoid any problems during your vacation, always keep proof of your insurance policy on you.

## Health

Vaccinations are not necessary for people coming from Europe, the United States and Australia. On the other hand, it is strongly suggested, particularly for medium or long-term stays, that visitors take out health and accident insurance. There are different types, so it is best to shop around. Bring along all medication, especially prescription drugs. Unless otherwise stated, the water is drinkable throughout Québec.

In case of an emergency, dial ☎911.

## Time Difference

Québec is 6hrs behind continental Europe and 3hrs ahead of the North American west coast. The entire province of Québec (save for the Îles de la Madeleine, which are an hour ahead) operates on Eastern Standard Time. Keep in mind that there are several time zones across Canada. Daylight Savings Time (+1hr) starts on the first Sunday in April and finishes the last Sunday in October (-1hr).

Practical Information

# Business Hours and Holidays

## Stores

The law on business hours allows stores to be open the following hours:

- **Monday to Wednesday** from 8am to 9pm; most stores open at 9:30am and close at 5:30pm.

- **Thursday and Friday** from 8am to 9pm; most open at 9:30am.

- **Saturday** from 8am to 5pm; most open at 9:30am.

- **Sunday** from 8am to 5pm; most open at noon. Not all stores open on Sundays.

*Dépanneurs* (convenience stores that sell food) are found throughout Québec and are open later, sometimes 24hrs a day.

## Holidays

**January 1st and 2nd**

**Easter Monday**

**3rd Monday in May**
*Fête de Dollard and Victoria Day*

**June 24**
*Saint-Jean-Baptiste Day, Québec's national holiday*

**July 1st**
*Canada Day*

**1st Monday in September**
*Labour Day*

**2nd Monday in October**
*Thanksgiving*

**November 11**
*Remembrance Day; only banks and federal government services are closed*

**December 25 and 26**
*Christmas*

# Climate and Clothing

Québec's seasonal extremes set the province apart from much of the world. Temperatures can rise above 30°C in summer and drop to -25°C in winter. Visiting Québec during the two "main" seasons (summer and winter) is like experiencing two totally different countries, with the seasons influencing not only the scenery, but the lifestyles and behaviour of the province's residents. Because of the extremes in Québec City's weather, you should choose clothing appropriate to the season of your visit.

## Winter

*"Mon pays ce n'est pas un pays, c'est l'hiver..."*

("My country is not a country, it is winter")

– Gilles Vigneault

Mid-November to the end of March is the best time for skiing, snowmobiling, skating, snowshoeing and other winter sports. In general, there are five or six large snowstorms every winter. Howling winds often make the temperatures bitterly cold, causing "drifting snow" (very fine snow that is blown by the wind). One bright spot is that though the weather may be freezing cold, Quebec still gets more hours of sunshine than most of Europe.

With sweaters, gloves, a scarf and a hat (called "a tuque"), you will be ready to confront winter. Well... almost! Remember, don't think you can ignore the cold. Here are a few tips:

Wear a coat, preferably a long one with a hood. Otherwise be sure to buy yourself a hat or a good pair of earmuffs.

If you are fond of your shoes, buy a pair of galoshes. They are a kind of rubber overshoe that is very practical for protecting against the corrosive salts used to melt the ice. They are easy to find and are inexpensive.

Visitors usually find that stores and other public places are overheated. The trick is to remove your scarf and open your coat the moment you step indoors.

If you feel a sudden chill while window-shopping, do not hesitate to enter a store to get warm. This way you will avoid catching a cold.

If you are going skiing, do not forget your sunglasses.

## Spring

Spring is short, lasting roughly from the end of March to the end of May, and is heralded by the arrival of "slush," a mixture of melted snow and mud, and the break up of the ice on the St. Lawrence River. As the snow disappears, long-buried plants and grass, yellowed by frost and mud, come to life again. Nature's welcomed reawakening is spectacular. One of the other signs that announce spring is the return of the snow geese flying in long *V* formations. Their calls mingle with those of the Québécois shouting, "It's spring!"

Heavy sweaters, woolen clothes and scarves are recommended for the in-between seasons of spring and autumn. Do not forget your umbrella and a raincoat.

Practical Information

## Summer

Summer in Québec blossoms from the end of May to the end of August and may surprise some who think of Québec as a land of snow and igloos. The heat can be quite extreme and often seems much hotter because of the accompanying humidity. The vegetation becomes lush, and don't be surprised to see some rather exotic-looking red and green peppers growing in window boxes. City streets are decorated with flowers, and restaurant terraces are always full.

Bring T-shirts, light shirts and trousers, shorts and sunglasses; a sweater will also be useful in the evening.

## Autumn

The autumn colours can last from September to November. Maple trees offer one of the most beautiful living pictures on the North American continent. Leaves are transformed into a kaleidoscope of colours from bright green to scarlet red, to golden yellow. Temperatures will stay warm for a while, but eventually the days and especially the nights will become quite cold.

Like in spring, heavy sweaters, wool clothing and scarves are recommended for autumn, as are a raincoat and an umbrella.

## Indian Summer

This relatively short period (only a few days) during the late fall feels like summer's triumphant return! Referred to as "Indian Summer", it is in fact the result of warm air currents from the Gulf of Mexico. It is called Indian Summer because it heralded the last hunt before winter. Aboriginals took advantage of the warm weather to stock up on provisions before the cold weather arrived.

## Security

Québec City is not a violent place. The quality of life here is quite outstanding and you should feel perfectly safe.

If you take normal precautions, you should not be overly worried about personal security. However, in case of an emergency, dial ☎911.

## Telecommunications

You do not need to dial the area code for the Québec City region (418) if you make a local call. For long-distance calls, dial 1 followed by the area code you are calling, then the telephone number. Telephone numbers preceded by 800, 866, 877 or 888 mean you can call without incurring long-distance charges if you are dialing from Canada and often even from the United States.

To reach the telephone operator, dial **0**.

Considerably less expensive than in Europe, public phones are scattered throughout the city and are easy to use; some even accept credit cards. Local calls cost $0.25 for unlimited time. For long distance calls, equip yourself with quarters ($0.25 coins), or purchase a $10, $15 or $20 telephone card, on sale at newsstands and in convenience stores. Paying by credit card or with the prepaid "HELLO!" card is also possible, but be advised that they are considerably more expensive.

When calling abroad you can use a local operator and pay local phone rates. First dial **011** then the international country code followed by the phone number.

To call Great Britian, dial **011** + **44** + the area code (London's is **171** or **181**) + the number you are trying to reach. The same goes for Australia, New Zealand and most European countries.

Another way to call abroad is by using the direct access numbers listed below to contact an operator in your home country.

**United States**
**AT&T**
☎*800-225-5288*
**MCI**
☎*800-888-8000*

**Great Britain**
**British Telecom Direct**
☎*800-408-6420*

**Australia**
**Australia Telstra Direct**
☎*800-663-0683*

**New Zealand**
**New Zealand Telecom Direct**
☎*800-663-0684*

## Post Offices

Major post offices are open from 8am to 5:45pm. However, smaller outlets can be found all over the city, either in shopping centres, in *"dépan-neurs"*, and some pharmacies that are open much later than regular post offices.

**Bureau de Poste Principal**
300 Rue Saint-Paul
☎*800-267-1177*

**Station B**
59 Rue Dalhousie
☎*800-267-1177*

**Succursale Haute-Ville**
5 Rue du Fort
☎*800-267-1177*

## Taxes and Tipping

### Taxes

The ticket price on items usually **does not include tax**. There are two taxes, the 7% GST (federal Goods and Services Tax, or TPS in French) and the

Practical Information

vincial sales tax,
ich) on goods
. They are
apply to most
goods, services, restaurants and
hotels.

There are some exceptions to
this taxation system, such as
books, which are only taxed
7% and food (except for ready-
made meals), which is not
taxed at all.

### Tax Refunds
### for Non-Residents

Non-residents can be refunded
for GST, or federal tax, paid on
purchases made while in Québec. To obtain a refund, it is
important to keep your re-
ceipts. For further information,
call ☎ *800-668-4748*.

## Tipping

Tipping applies to all table service, in restaurants or other
places where customers are
served at their tables (fast-food
service is therefore not included
in this category). Tipping is also
compulsory in bars, nightclubs
and taxis.

Depending on the quality of the
service, patrons must leave
approximately **15%** of the bill
before tax. Unlike in Europe,
the tip is not included in the bill,
and clients must calculate the
amount themselves and give it
to the server. "Service charges"
and "tip" have the same mean-

ing in North America; do not
forget to leave it.

## Québec Cuisine

Although many restaurant
dishes are similar to those
served in the rest of Canada or
the United States, some of
them are prepared in a typically
Québécois way. These unique
dishes should definitely be
tasted:

*La soupe aux pois*
pea soup

*La tourtière*
meat pie

*Le pâté chinois*
(also known as shepherd's pie)
a layered pie consisting of
ground beef, potatoes, and
corn

*Les cretons*
a type of pâté of ground pork
cooked with onions in fat

*Le jambon au sirop d'érable*
ham with maple syrup

*Les fèves au lard*
baked beans

*Le ragoût de pattes de cochon*
pigs'-feet stew

*Le cipaille*
layered pie with different types
of meat

*La tarte aux pacanes*
pecan pie

*La tarte au sucre*
sugar pie

*La tarte aux bleuets*
blueberry pie

*Le sucre à la crème*
rich maple-syrup fudge

In the country, you may also have the opportunity to enjoy some exceptional regional specialties like venison, hare, beaver, Atlantic salmon, Arctic char and Abitibi caviar.

## Wine, Beer and Alcohol

In Québec, the provincial government is responsible for regulating alcohol which is sold in liquor stores known as Société des Alcool du Québec (SAQ). If you wish to purchase wine, imported beer or hard liquor, you must go to a branch of the SAQ *(www.saq.com)*. Some outlets, known as "Sélection," offer a more varied and specialized selection of wines and spirits. SAQ outlets can be found throughout the city, but their opening hours are fairly limited, with the exception of so-called "Express" branches which are open later but offer a more limited choice. As a general rule, their opening hours are the same as those of stores. Convenience and grocery stores are authorized to sell Canadian beer and a few wines, but the choice is slim and the quality of the wines is mediocre.

You must be at least 18 years old to purchase alcohol, the sale of which is not permitted after 11pm.

**A few SAQ addresses:**

1059 Avenue Cartier
☎*643-4334*

853 Rue Saint-Jean
☎*643-4337*

**SAQ Sélection**
400 Boulevard Jean-Lesage, near the Gare du Palais
☎*643-4339*

**SAQ Signature**
1 Rue des Carrières
☎*692-1182*

### Beer

Two huge breweries share the largest part of the beer market in Québec: Labatt and Molson-O'Keefe. They each produce different types of beer, mostly light ales, with varying levels of alcohol. In bars, restaurants, and nightclubs, draft beer is cheaper than bottled beer.

Practical Information

Besides these large breweries, some interesting independent micro-breweries have sprung up in the past few years. The variety and taste of these beers make them quite popular in Québec. However, because they are microbrews, they are not available everywhere. Here are a few of the micro-brewery beers: McAuslan (Griffon, St-Ambroise), Le Cheval Blanc (Coup de Grisou, Loch Ness), Les Brasseurs du Nord (Boréale) and GMT (Belle Gueule).

## Advice for Smokers

Smoking is considered a problem that must be eliminated. It is prohibited to smoke in most public places.

Smoking sections in public places (restaurants, cafés) must be closed off. Cigarettes are still sold in many places though (bars, grocery and convenience stores, and newspaper and magazine shops). You must be 18 years old to buy cigarettes.

## Senior Citizens

Older people who would like to meet people their age can do so through the organization listed below. It provides information about activities and local clubs throughout Québec:

**Fédération de l'Âge d'Or du Québec**
4545 Avenue Pierre-de-Coubertin, C.P. 1000, Succursale M, Montréal, H1V 3R2
*☎(514) 252-3017 or 800-828-3344*

Reduced transportation fares and entertainment tickets are often made available to seniors. Do not hesitate to ask.

## Gay and Lesbian Life

Québec City provides some services for the gay community, which is mainly concentrated in the Faubourg Saint-Jean-Baptiste area.

There is a telephone service called **Gai Écoute** (*☎888-505-1010*), and several support groups have been set up to meet the community's various needs. For information about these groups, call Gris-Québec (*☎523-4808*).

The free magazines *Fugues* and *Être Québec* are published monthly and are available in bars. They include information on the gay community's favourite meeting places.

## Travellers with Disabilities

Kéroul, an association that specializes in tourism for people with disabilities, publishes a guide, *Accessible Québec*, which lists the places that are accessible to people with disabilities throughout the province. These places are classified according to tourist regions. In most of Quebec's regions, there are associations that organize leisure and sports activities as well. For the addresses of these associations, contact the Association Québécoise de Loisir pour Personnes Handicapées.

**Kéroul**
4545 Avenue Pierre-de-Coubertin,
C.P. 1000 Succursale M
Montreal H1V 3R2
☎ *(514) 252-3104*
*www.keroul.qc.ca*

**Association Régionale de Loisir pour Personnes Handicapées/ Québec–Chaudière-Appalaches**
4545 Avenue Pierre-de-Coubertin,
C.P. 1000 Succursale M
Montreal H1V 3R2
☎ *(514) 252-3144*

# Children

Children in Québec are treated like royalty. Facilities are available almost everywhere you go, whether it be in transportation or during leisure activities. Generally, children under five years of age travel for free, and those under 12 are eligible for fare reductions. The same rules apply for various leisure activities and shows. Find out before you purchase tickets. High chairs and children's menus are available in most restaurants,

while a few of the larger stores provide a babysitting service while parents shop.

# Pets

As a rule, animals are not allowed in most public places. If you decide to travel with your dog, you will not be able to take it on a bus. It is also impossible to go shopping with a dog in most places (even shopping centres) and certain covered markets. However, some hotels accept pets; make sure to check before leaving home. Animals are not permitted in food stores or restaurants.

# Miscellaneous

**Barbers and Hairstylists:** As in restaurants, it is customary to tip 10% to 15% of the bill before taxes.

**Drugs:** Recreational drugs are against the law and are not tolerated (even "soft" drugs). Anyone caught with drugs in their possession risks severe consequences.

**Économusées:** Economuseums are educational, working museums found almost everywhere in Québec. They are intended to present Québec's traditional arts and crafts and are located in forges, flour mills, sculpture studios and other places where you can watch people at work on their craft.

Practical Information

**Electricity:** Voltage is 110 volts throughout Canada, the same as in the United States. Electric plugs have two parallel, flat pins. Adaptors are available here.

**Laundromats:** Laundromats and dry cleaners can be found almost everywhere in urban areas. In most cases, detergent is sold on site. Although change machines are sometimes provided, it is best to bring plenty of quarters (25-cent coins) with you.

**Museums:** Most museums charge admission; however, permanent exhibits at some museums can be free, while reductions are offered for temporary exhibits. Reduced prices are available for seniors, children, and students. Call the museum for further details.

**Newspapers:** International newspapers are readily available here. Québec City's major newspapers are *Le Soleil* and *Le Journal de Québec*.

**Pharmacies:** In addition to traditional pharmacies, there are huge chain stores (medical- and beauty- product supermarkets). Do not be surprised to find chocolates and detergent next to cough drops and headache medication.

**Public Washrooms:** Most shopping centres have public toilets. But if you cannot find one, you may be able to use the facilities in a bar or a restaurant.

**Religion:** Almost all religions are represented. Unlike English Canada, the majority of the Québec population is Catholic, although most Quebecers are not practising.

**Weather:** For road conditions, call ☎ *800-355-0511*; for weather forecasts, call ☎ *648-7766*.

*Musée national des beaux-arts du Québec*

# Weights and Measures

Although the metric system has been in use in Canada for more than 20 years, some people continue to use the Imperial system in casual conversation. Here are some equivalents:

**Weights**
1 pound (lb) = 454 grams (g)
1 kilogram (kg) = 2.2 pounds (lbs)

**Linear Measure**
1 inch (in) = 2.54 centimetres (cm)
1 foot (ft) = 30 centimetres (cm)
1 mile (mi) = 1.6 kilometres (km)
1 kilometre (km) = 0.63 miles (mi)
1 metre (m) = 39.37 inches (in)

**Land Measure**
1 acre = 0.4 hectare (ha)
1 hectare (ha) = 2.471 acres

**Volume Measure**
1 U.S. gallon (gal) = 3.79 litres

# Temperature

To convert °F into °C:
subtract 32, divide by 9, multiply by 5.

To convert °C into °F:
multiply by 9, divide by 5, add 32.

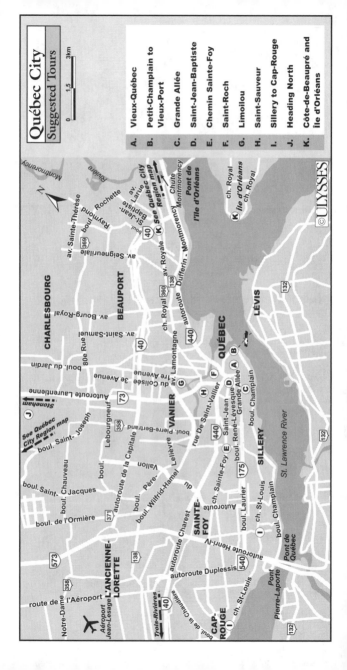

Québec City
Suggested Tours

0   1,5   3km

A. Vieux-Québec
B. Petit-Champlain to Vieux-Port
C. Grande Allée
D. Saint-Jean-Baptiste
E. Chemin Sainte-Foy
F. Saint-Roch
G. Limoilou
H. Saint-Sauveur
I. Sillery to Cap-Rouge
J. Heading North
K. Côte-de-Beaupré and Île d'Orléans

© ULYSSES

# Exploring

# Québec City comprises
eight districts totalling about half a million
people, the majority of whom speak French.

It is difficult to pinpoint a specific downtown area in this
city, since some of the nearby
suburbs are attracting more and
more people. In fact, two or
three areas, such as Vieux-
Québec or Grande Allée, could
claim this title. On the other
hand, it is easier to locate
Haute-Ville (uppertown) and
Basse-Ville (lowertown), as they
are often called by the Québécois. It is not difficult to distin-
guish them because the former,
more bourgeois, is perched
high on the promontory, while
the latter is spread out at the
foot of its north side.

In the first nine tours of this
chapter, you will discover
Québec City and its nearby
suburbs. The last two excursions will take you outside the
city to the Basilica of Sainte-
Anne-de-Beaupré and beautiful
Île d'Orléans, among other
places. The city tours are designed to maximize walking and
the use of public transportation,

since visiting the city this way
will allow you to better experience the life that flows through
its arteries. If you prefer, you
can visit the city by car, but a
car will be necessary to follow
the last three tours.

Each tour includes information about the main tourist attractions and provides a historical and cultural overview. The attractions are classified according to a star rating so that you can set your priorities according to your schedule.

| | |
|---|---|
| ★ | Interesting |
| ★★ | Worth a visit |
| ★★★ | Not to be missed |

The address, opening hours and cost of admission are featured in brackets with each attraction. The admission price given is for one adult. Keep in mind that some places offer discounts to children, students and seniors, as well as family rates. Many of these attractions are only open during the tourist season; this will be indicated in the above- mentioned brackets. However, during the off season, some will welcome you if you make an appointment, especially if you are with a group.

Follow this guide and let yourself be enticed by one of the most beautiful cities in the world!

# Tour A: Vieux-Québec

*(two to three days)*

Vieux-Québec is divided into two parts by Cap Diamant. The part that spreads out between the river and the cliff is featured in the next tour (see p 81). The section covering the plateau atop Cap Diamant is informally called Vieux-Québec. As the administrative and institutional centre of the city, it is adorned with convents, chapels and public buildings whose construction dates back, in some cases, to the 17th century. The walls of Haute-Ville, dominated by the Citadelle, surround this section of Vieux-Québec and give it the characteristic look of a fortress. These same walls long contained the development of the town, resulting in a densely built-up bourgeois and aristocratic milieu. With time, the picturesque urban planning of the 19th century contributed to the present-day image of Québec City through the construction of such magnificent buildings as the Château Frontenac and the creation of such public spaces as Terrasse Dufferin, in the *belle époque* spirit.

*The Vieux-Québec walking tour begins at Porte Saint-Louis, near the parliament buildings.*

# A Vieux-Québec

## ATTRACTIONS

1. Club de la Garnison
2. Fortifications of Québec National Historic Site
3. Chalmers-Wesley United Church
4. Sanctuaire Notre-Dame-du-Sacré-Coeur
5. Maison Cirice-Têtu
6. Cavalier-du-Moulin Rue Mont-Carmel
7. Jardin des Gouverneurs
8. Terrasse Dufferin
9. Château Frontenac
10. Place d'Armes
11. Centre Infotouriste
12. Musée du Fort
13. Musée de Cire de Québec
14. Ancien Palais de Justice (former courthouse)
15. Maison Maillou
16. Maison Kent
17. Musée d' Art Inuit Brousseau
18. Maison Jacquet
19. Monastère des Ursulines
20. Musée des Ursulines
21. Holy Trinity Anglican Cathedral
22. Hôtel Clarendon
23. Édifice Price
24. Maison Antoine-Anfelson
25. Place de l'Hôtel-de-Ville
26. Hôtel de Ville
27. Centre d'interprétation de la vie urbaine de la Ville de Québec
28. Basilique-Cathédrale Notre-Dame-de-Québec
29. Séminaire de Québec
30. Musée de l'Amérique Française
31. Holt Renfrew and Promenades du Vieux-Québec
32. Rue du Trésor
33. Québec Expérience
34. Bureau de Poste (Édifice Louis-S.-Saint-Laurent) and Parks Canada Information Service
35. Monument to Monseigneur François de Montmorency Laval
36. Palais Archiépiscopal
37. Parc Montmorency
38. Old Université Laval
39. Rue des Remparts
40. Maison Montcalm
41. Maison François-Xavier-Garneau
42. Musée Bon-Pasteur
43. Chapelle and Musée de l'Hôtel-Dieu and Musée des Augustines du Monastère de l'Hôtel-Dieu
44. Methodist Church (Institut Canadien)
45. Ancienne Prison de Québec (the old jail)
46. St. Andrew's Presbyterian Church
47. Artillery Park National Historic Site
48. Old Anglican orphanage
49. Église des Jésuites
50. Maison McGreevy
51. Citadelle and Musée du Royal 22ᵉ Régiment

*Porte Saint-Louis*

**Porte Saint-Louis** *(at the beginning of the street of the same name)*, a gateway, is the result of Québec City merchants' pressuring the government between 1870 and 1875 to tear down the wall surrounding the city. The Governor General of Canada at the time, Lord Dufferin, was opposed to the idea and instead put forward a plan drafted by Irishman William H. Lynn to showcase the walls while improving traffic circulation. The design he submitted exhibits a Victorian romanticism in its use of grand gateways that bring to mind images of medieval castles and horsemen. The pepper-box tower of Porte Saint-Louis, built in 1878, makes for a striking first impression upon arriving in downtown Québec City.

Past Porte Saint-Louis, to the left and facing Parc de l'Esplanade, are the **busts** of British Prime Minister Winston Churchill and U.S. President Franklin D. Roosevelt. The two statues commemorate the Québec Conferences that were held by the Allies in 1943 and 1944.

On the right, on the opposite side of the street, is the **Club de la Garnison** *(97 Rue Saint-Louis)*, reserved for army officers, as well as the road leading to the Citadelle. As a visit to the citadel may require 2 to 3hrs, it is best to set aside extra time to take a tour of the premises (see p 80).

The **Fortifications of Québec National Historic Site ★** *($3.50; early May to mid-Oct every day 9am to 5pm, rest of the year 10am to 5pm; mid-Oct to mid-May reservation required; ☎648-7016)* displays models and maps outlining the development of Québec City's defense system and you can visit the **Poudrière de l'Esplanade**. Booklets are available with a complete tour of the city's fortifications, and the **Centre d'Initiation aux Fortifications** offers two guided tours *($10)*. Information plaques have been placed along the wall, providing another means of discovering the city's history. The walkway on top of the wall can be reached by using the stairs next to the city gates.

Québec City's first wall was made of earth and wooden posts. It was erected on the west side of the city in 1693, according to the plans of engineer Dubois Berthelot de Beaucours, to protect Québec City from the Iroquois. Work on much stronger stone fortifications began in 1745, designed by engineer Chaussegros de Léry, when England and France entered a new era of conflict. However, the wall remained unfinished when the city was seized by the British in 1759. The British saw to the completion of the project at the end of the 18th century. Some work on the Citadelle began in 1693; however, the structure as we now know it was essentially built between 1820 and 1832. Nevertheless, the Citadelle is largely designed along the principles advanced by Vauban in the 17th century—principles that suit the location admirably.

*Continue along Rue Saint-Louis and turn right on Rue Sainte-Ursule.*

Until the end of the 19th century, Québec City had a small but influential community of Scottish Presbyterians, most of whom were involved in shipping and the lumber trade. The **Chalmers-Wesley United Church** *(78 Rue Sainte-Ursule, ☎692-2640)*, an attractive Gothic Revival structure, is presently used by a variety of groups, testifying to the decline in the Scottish Presbyterian community. The church was built in 1852 and designed by John Wells, an architect known for a number of famous buildings, including the Bank of Montreal headquarters. The elegant Gothic Revival spire of the church contributes to the picturesque aspect of the city. The church's organ was restored in 1985. Concerts are presented at the church every Sunday night from the beginning of July until the middle of August. Donations are appreciated.

The **Sanctuaire Notre-Dame-du-Sacré-Coeur** *(free admission; Oct to Apr every day 7:30am to 6pm; Apr to Oct every day 7am to 8pm; 71 Rue Sainte-Ursule, ☎692-3787)* faces Chalmers-Wesley United Church. The sanctuary was originally built for the Sacré Cœur missionaries. This place of worship, erected in 1910 and designed by François-Xavier Berlinguet, is now open to everyone. The sanctuary has a Gothic Revival facade. Its two rather narrow steeples seem dwarfed by the size of the building. The interior of the structure, with its stained

**Exploring**

glass windows and murals, is more attractive.

*Return to Avenue Sainte-Geneviève and then turn left.*

In addition to the city's major historical landmarks, Québec's appeal lies in its smaller, less imposing buildings, each of which has its own separate history. It is enjoyable to simply wander the narrow streets of the old city, taking in the subtleties of an architecture so atypical of North America. The **Maison Cirice-Têtu** ★ *(25 Avenue Sainte-Geneviève)* house was built in 1852. It was designed by Charles Baillargé, a member of a celebrated family of architects who, beginning in the 18th century, left an important mark on the architecture of Québec City and its surroundings. The Greek Revival facade of the house, a masterpiece of the genre, is tastefully decorated with palmettes and the discreet use of laurel. The main floor has huge bay windows that open onto a single expansive living room in the London style. From the time of its construction, the house incorporated all the modern amenities: central heating, hot running water and multiple bathrooms.

A short detour down Rue Mont-Carmel (to the left) brings you to one of the remnants of Québec City's earliest fortifications, located in an out-of-the-way spot behind a row of houses. The **Cavalier-du-Moulin** was built in 1693 by engi-

## Baillargé or Baillairgé

Recent historical studies have prompted us to use the name Baillargé to designate this famous family of Québec architects. However, documents signed by members of the family reveal that they themselves used both Baillargé and Baillairgé. Don't be surprised, therefore, if you come across both; the reference is always to the same family.

neer Dubois Berthelot de Beaucours. It is a redoubt set within the city walls that was meant to be destroyed in the event of a successful enemy invasion. The fortification is named for the windmill, or *moulin*, that used to sit on top of it.

The charming square known as **Jardin des Gouverneurs** ★ was originally the private garden of the governor of New France. The square was laid out in 1647 for Charles Huault de Montmagny to the west of Château Saint-Louis, the residence of the governor, which is no longer standing. A monument to opposing military leaders Wolfe and Montcalm, both of whom died on the battlefields of the Plains of Abraham, was erected during the restoration of the garden in 1827.

A walk on the wooden planks of the **Terrasse Dufferin** ★ ★ ★, overlooking the St. Lawrence River, provides a different sensation than the pavement we are used to. It was built in 1879 at the request of the governor general of the time, Lord Dufferin. The boardwalk's open-air pavilions and ornate streetlamps were designed by Charles Baillargé and were inspired by the style of French urban architecture that was common under Napoleon III. Terrasse Dufferin is one of Québec City's most popular sights and is the preferred meeting place for young people. The view of the river, the south shore and Île d'Orléans is magnificent. During the winter months, a huge ice slide is set up at the western end of the boardwalk.

Terrasse Dufferin is located where the Château Saint-Louis, the long-destroyed elaborate residence of the governor of New France, used to stand. Built at the very edge of the escarpment, this three-storey building had a long, private stone terrace on the river side, while the main entrance, consisting of a fortified facade, opened onto Place d'Armes and featured pavilions with imperial-type roofs. The château was built in the 17th century by architect François de la Joüe and was enlarged in 1719 by engineer Chaussegros de Léry. Its rooms, linked one to the other, were the scene of elegant receptions given for the French nobility. Plans for the future of the entire continent were drawn up in this building. Château Saint-Louis was badly damaged in the British invasion of the city at the time of the Conquest and was later remodelled according to British tastes, before being destroyed by a fire in 1834.

Exploring

*Terrasse Dufferin*

There are two **monuments** at the far end of Terrasse Dufferin. One is dedicated to the memory of Samuel de Champlain, the founder of Québec City and father of New France. It was designed by Parisian sculptor Paul Chevré and erected in 1898. The second monument informs visitors that Vieux-Québec was recognized as a World Heritage Site by UNESCO in 1985. Québec City is the first city in North America to be included on this list. A staircase just to the left of the Champlain monument leads to the Place-Royale quarter in Basse-Ville (Tour B). At the other end of the Terrasse, you'll find another staircase leading to the **Promenade des Gouverneurs** (see p 108).

The first half of the 19th century saw the emergence of Québec City's tourism industry when the romantic European nature of the city began to attract growing numbers of American visitors. In 1890, the Canadian Pacific Railway company, under Cornelius Van Horne, decided to create a chain of distinguished hotels across Canada. The first of these hotels (see p 179) was the **Château Frontenac ★ ★ ★** *(1 Rue des Carrières)*, named in honour of one of the best-known governors of New France, Louis de Buade, comte de Frontenac (1622-1698).

The magnificent Château Frontenac, symbol of the province's capital city, is probably the most famous sight in Québec. Ironically, the hotel was designed by an American architect, Bruce Price (1845-1903) who was known for his New York skyscrapers. The look of the hotel, which combines certain elements of the Scottish manors and the châteaux of the Loire Valley in France, has come to be considered a national archetype style called "Château Style." Bruce Price, who also designed Montréal's Windsor train station and the famous Tuxedo Park development near New York, was inspired by the picturesque location that was chosen for the hotel and by the mix of French and English cultures in Canada.

The Château Frontenac was built in phases. Price's initial wing overlooked Terrasse Dufferin and was completed in 1893. Three sections were later added, the most important of these being the central tower (1923), the work of architects Edward and William Sutherland Maxwell. To fully appreciate the château, one must go inside to explore the main hall, decorated in a style popular in

*Château Frontenac*

A few of Vieux-Québec's picturesque old houses. - *Patrick Escudero*

The magnificent Château Frontenac, symbol of the province's capital city.
- *Patrick Escudero*

18th-century Parisian *hôtels particuliers*, and visit the Bar Maritime in the large main tower overlooking the river.

The Château Frontenac has been the site of a number of important events in history. In 1944, the Québec Conference was held here. At this historic meeting, U.S. President Franklin D. Roosevelt, British Prime Minister Winston Churchill and Canadian Prime Minister Mackenzie King met to discuss the future of post-war Europe. On the way out of the courtyard is a stone with the inscription of the Order of Malta, dated 1647, the only remaining piece of Château Saint-Louis. **Tours** *($8; May to mid-Oct every day 10am to 6pm; mid-Oct to end of Apr Sat and Sun 1pm to 5pm;* ☎*691-2166)* of Château Frontenac are given by guides dressed in period costumes.

Until the construction of the Citadelle, **Place d'Armes ★** was a military parade ground. It became a public square in 1832. In 1916, the *Monument de la Foi* (Monument of Faith) was erected in Place d'Armes to mark the tricentennial of the arrival of the Récollet religious order in Québec. Abbot Adolphe Garneau's statue rests on a base designed by David Ouellet.

*At the other end of the square are the Centre Infotouriste (the tourist information centre) and two museums. The back of the* **Holy Trinity Anglican Cathedral** *(see p 68) is also visible from here.*

The **Centre Infotouriste** *(12 Rue Sainte-Anne)* is located in the former Union Hotel, a white building with a copper roof. A group of wealthy Quebecers saw the need for a luxury hotel in Québec City and commissioned British architect Edward Cannon to head the project which was completed in 1803.

On either side of the Centre Infotouriste are two popular tourist attractions. Using an elaborate model of the city along with a sound and light show, the **Musée du Fort** *($7.50; mid-Jan to Feb closed; Feb and March Thu-Sun 10pm to 4pm; Apr to Nov every day 10am to 5pm; 10 Rue Sainte-Anne,* ☎*692-2175)* recreates the six sieges of Québec City, starting with the capture of the town by the Kirke brothers in 1629 and ending with the American invasion of 1775.

The **Musée de Cire de Québec** *($3; May to Oct every day 8:30am to 9pm, rest of the year every day 9am to 4pm; 22 Rue Sainte-Anne,* ☎*692-2289)* displays wax likenesses of some 60 individuals grouped in 16 settings that depict Québec City's history and recent events. You will see Lara Fabian and Roch Voisine (contemporary pop-music stars) alongside Churchill, Champlain and Wolfe.

*Return to Rue St-Louis.*

Exploring

The **Ancien Palais de Justice (Former Courthouse)** ★ (*12 Rue Saint-Louis*) is the city's original courthouse, built in 1883 by Eugène-Étienne Taché, the architect of the parliament buildings. The courthouse resembles the parliament in a number of ways. Its French Renaissance Revival design preceded the Château style as the "official" style of the city's major building projects. The interior of the building was renovated between 1922 and 1930; it has several large rooms with attractive woodwork. Since 1987, the Ancien Palais de Justice building has been home to Québec's Ministry of Finance.

**Maison Maillou** (*17 Rue Saint-Louis*) is the location of the seat of Québec's chamber of commerce. This attractive French Regime house was built in 1736 by architect Jean Maillou. It was saved from destruction after the stock market crash of 1929 led to the abandonment of plans to expand the Château Frontenac.

The history of **Maison Kent** (*24 Rue Saint-Louis*), once a residence of Queen Victoria's father, the Duke of Kent, is somewhat cloudy. There is some disagreement as to whether the house was built in the 17th or 18th century. It is clear, however, from its English sash windows and low-pitched roof, that the house underwent major renovations during the 19th century. The agreement that handed Québec over to the British in 1759 was signed in this house. Ironically, it is now occupied by the Consulate General of France.

*Continue on Rue Saint-Louis.*

The Galerie d'Art Inuit Brousseau is well known for the quality of its works of art and now includes a small museum to house the owner's private collection: the **Musée d'Art Inuit Brousseau** ★ (*$6; every day 9:30am to 5pm; 39 Rue St-Louis,* ☎*694-1828, www.inuitart.ca*). Each of the five exhibition rooms has its own theme such as history, the materials that were used, etc. The works are well placed and it is a pleasure to visit the bright, airy and modern display rooms. The historical and cultural notes are interesting and quite thorough. At the end of the tour you can watch a documentary video on the artists whose works are presented or return to the adjoining shop to purchase some for yourself.

**Maison Jacquet** ★ (*34 Rue Saint-Louis*), a small, red-roofed building covered in white roughcast dating from 1677, is the oldest house in Haute-Ville; it is the only house in Vieux-Québec that still looks just as it did in the 17th century. The house is distinguished from those built during the following century by its high, steep roof covering a living area with a very low ceiling. The house is named for François Jacquet, who once owned the land on which it stands. It was built by architect François de la Joüe in

*Maison Jacquet*

1690, for his own use. In 1815, the house was acquired by Philippe Aubert de Gaspé, author of the famous novel *Les Anciens Canadiens* (The Canadians of Old). The restaurant that now occupies the house takes its name from this book.

*Turn right on Rue du Parloir.*

At the corner of rue Donnacona, you will find the **Monastère des Ursulines** ★ ★ ★ *(18 Rue Donnacona)*. In 1535, Sainte Angèle Merici founded the first Ursuline community in Brescia, Italy. After the community had established itself in France, it became a cloistered order dedicated to teaching (1620). With the help of a benefactor, Madame de la Peltrie, the Ursulines arrived in Québec City in 1639 and, in 1641, founded a monastery and convent where generations of young girls have received a good education. The Ursulines'

convent is the longest running girls' school in North America.

Only the museum and chapel, a small part of the huge Ursulines complex where several dozen nuns still live, are open to the public.

The Sainte-Ursuline chapel was rebuilt in 1901 on the site of the original 1722 chapel. Part of the magnificent interior decoration of the first chapel, created by Pierre-Nöel Levasseur between 1726 and 1736, survived and is present in the newer structure. The work includes a pulpit surmounted by a trumpeting angel and a beautiful altarpiece in the Louis XIV style. The tabernacle of the high altar is embellished with fine gilding applied by the Ursulines. The Sacred Heart tabernacle, a masterpiece of the genre, is attributed to Jaques Leblond, also known as Latour, and dates from around 1770. Some of

Exploring

the paintings decorating the church come from the collection of Father Jean-Louis Desjardins, a former chaplain of the Ursulines. In 1820, Desjardins bought several dozen paintings from an art dealer in Paris. The paintings had previously hung in Paris churches but were removed during the French Revolution. Works from this collection can still be seen in churches all over Québec. At the entrance hangs *Jésus chez Simon le Pharisien* (Jesus with Simon the Pharisee) by Philippe de Champaigne, and to the right of the nave hangs *La Parabole des Dix Vierges* (The Parable of the Ten Virgins), by Pierre de Cortone.

The chapel was the burial site of the Marquis de Montcalm until 2001, when his remains were transferred to the **Hôpital Général military cemetery** (see p 133). General of the French troops during the decisive Battle of the Plains of Abraham, he was fatally wounded during the conflict, as was his rival General Wolfe. The tomb of blessed Mère Marie de l'Incarnation, the founder of the Ursulines monastery in Québec is still there. An opening provides a view of the nuns' chancel, rebuilt in 1902 by David Ouellet who outfitted it with a cupola-shaped skylight. An interesting painting by an unknown artist, *La France Apportant la Foi aux Indiens de la Nouvelle-France* (France Bringing the Faith to the Indians of New France), also hangs in this section of the chapel.

The entrance to the **Musée des Ursulines** (*$6; May to Sep, Tue-Sat 10am to noon and 1pm to 5pm, Sun 1pm to 5pm; Oct to Dec and Feb to Apr Tue-Sun 1pm to 4:30pm; 12 Rue Donna-cona, ☎694-0694*) is located across from the chapel. The museum outlines nearly four centuries of Ursuline history. On view are various works of art, Louis XIII furniture, impressive embroideries made of gold thread, and 18th-century altar cloths and church robes.

*Continue on Rue Donnacona, and turn left on Rue des Jardins. Note the tiny little house on your left!*

After the British Conquest of Québec, a small group of British administrators and military officers established themselves in Québec City. These men wanted to mark their presence through the construction of prestigious buildings with typically British designs. However, their small numbers resulted in the slow progress of this project until the beginning of the 19th century, when work began on the **Holy Trinity Anglican Cathedral ★★** (*31 Rue des Jardins*) by Majors Robe and Hall, two military engineers inspired by St. Martin's Church in London Fields. The Palladian-style church was completed in 1804. This significant example of non-French architecture changed the look of the city. The church was the first Anglican cathedral built outside Britain and, in its elegant simplicity, is a good example of

British colonial architecture. The roof was made steeper in 1815 so that it would not be weighed down by snow.

The cathedral's interior, soberer than that of most Catholic churches, is adorned with various generous gifts from King George III, including several pieces of silverware and pews made of English oak from the forests of Windsor. The bishop's chair is said to have been carved from an elm tree under which Samuel de Champlain liked to sit. There are stained-glass windows and commemorative plaques which were added over the years. There is also a Casavant organ dating from 1909 that was restored in 1959. Its set of eight bells is one of the oldest in Canada.

*Continue along Rue des Jardins. To the right is a cobblestone section of Rue Sainte-Anne and on the left is the Hôtel Clarendon and the Price building.*

The **Hôtel Clarendon** *(57 Rue Sainte-Anne)* (see p 178) began receiving guests in 1870 in the former Desbarats print shop (1858). It is the oldest hotel still operating in Québec. The Charles Baillargé-designed restaurant on the main floor is also the oldest restaurant (see p 203) in Canada. The Victorian charm of the somber woodwork evokes the *belle époque*. The Hôtel Clarendon was expanded in 1929 by the addition of a brick tower featuring

an Art Deco entrance hall designed by Raoul Chênevert.

The design of **Édifice Price ★** *(65 Rue Sainte-Anne)* manages to adhere to that of traditional North American skyscraper architecture and yet does not look out of place among the historic buildings of Haute-Ville. Architects Ross and MacDonald of Montréal gave the building a tall yet discreet silhouette when they designed it in 1929. It features a copper roof typical of Château-style architecture. The main hall of the building, a fine example of Art Deco design, is covered in polished travertine and bronze bas-reliefs depicting the various activities of the Price company, which specialized in the production of paper.

*Walk back up to Rue des Jardins, and turn left.*

The next stop is quaint **Maison Antoine-Anfelson** at 17 Rue des Jardins, built in 1780. A talented silversmith by the name of Laurent Amiot had a workshop here in the 19th century. The rooms on the second floor of this building feature wonderful Louis XV woodwork.

**Place de l'Hôtel-de-Ville ★**, a small square, was the location of the Notre-Dame market in the 18th century. A monument in honour of Cardinal Taschereau, created by André Vermare, was erected here in 1923.

Exploring

The American Romanesque Revival influence seen in the **Hôtel de Ville** *(2 Rue des Jardins)* stands out in a city where French and British traditions have always dominated the construction of public buildings. The building was completed in 1895 following disagreements among the mayor and the city councillors as to a building plan. Sadly, a Jesuit college dating from 1666 was demolished to make room for the city hall.

Under the pleasant **jardins de l'Hôtel de Ville** gardens, where popular events are held in the summer, is an underground parking lot, a much needed addition in this city of narrow streets.

The **Centre d'interprétation de la vie urbaine de la Ville de Québec** *($3; late Jun to early Sep every day 10am to 5pm; rest of the year Tue-Sun 10am to 5pm; 43 Côte de la Fabrique, ☎641-6172)*, an information centre on urban life in Québec City, is located in the basement of city hall. It addresses questions of urban development and planning. An interesting model of the city provides an understanding of the layout of the area.

The history of Québec City's cathedral underscores the problems faced by builders in New France and the determination of the Québécois in the face of the worst circumstances.

The **Basilique-Cathédrale Notre-Dame-de-Québec** ★★★ *(at the other end of Place de l'Hôtel-de-Ville)* as it stands today is the result of numerous phases of construction and a number of tragedies that left the church in ruins on two occasions. The first church on this site was built in 1632 under the orders of Samuel de Champlain, who was buried nearby four years later. This wooden church was replaced in 1647 by the Église Notre-Dame-de-la-Paix, a stone church in the shape of a Roman cross that would later serve as the model for many rural parish churches. In 1674, New France was assigned its first bishop in residence. Monseigneur François-Xavier de Montmorency-Laval (1623-1708) decided that this small church, after renovations befitting its status as the heart of such an enormous ministry, would become the seat of the Catholic Church in Québec. A grandiose plan was commissioned from architect Claude Baillif, which, despite personal financial contributions from Louis XIV, eventually had to be scaled down. Only the base of the west tower survives from this period. In 1742, the bishop had the church remodelled by engineer Gaspard Chaussegros de Léry, who is responsible for its present layout, featuring an extended nave illuminated from above. The cathedral resembles many urban churches built in France during the same period.

*Basilique-Cathédrale Notre-Dame-de-Québec*

During the siege of Québec in 1759, the cathedral was bombarded and reduced to ruins. It was not rebuilt until the status of Catholics in Québec was settled by the British crown. The oldest Catholic parish north of Mexico was finally allowed to begin the reconstruction of its church in 1770, using the 1742 plans. The work was directed by Jean Baillargé (1726-1805), a member of the well-known family of architects and craftsmen. This marked the beginning of the Baillargé family's extended, fervent involve-ment with the reconstruction and renovation of the church. In 1789, the decoration of the church's interior was entrusted to Jean Baillargé's son François (1759-1830), who had recently returned from three years of studying architecture in Paris at the Académie Royale. He de-signed the chancel's beautiful gilt canopy with winged caryat-ids four years later. The high altar, the first in Québec to be designed to look like the facade of a Basilica, was put into place in 1797. The addition of ba-roque pews and a plaster vault created an interesting contrast. Thus completed, the spectacular interior emphasized the use of gilding, wood and white plasterwork according to typical Québécois traditions.

In 1843, Thomas Baillargé (1791-1859), the son of François, created the present neoclassical facade and attempted to erect a steeple on the east side of the church. Work on the steeple was halted at the halfway point when it was discovered that the 17th century foundations were not strong enough. Charles Baillargé (1826-1906), Thomas Baillargé's cousin, designed the wrought-iron gate around the front square in 1858. Between 1920 and 1922, the church was carefully restored, but just a few weeks after the work was completed a fire seriously damaged the building. Raoul Chênevert and Maxime Roisin, who had already come to Québec from Paris to take on the reconstruction of the Basilica in Sainte-Anne-de-Beaupré, were put in charge of yet another restoration of the cathedral. In 1959, a mausoleum was added in the basement of the church. It holds the remains of Québec bishops and various governors (Frontenac, Vaudreuil, de Callière). In recent years, several masterpieces that have been hanging in the church have been stolen, leaving bare walls and increasing the need to safeguard the remaining paintings, including the beautiful *Saint-Jérôme*, by Jacques-Louis David (1780).

During the 17th century, the **Séminaire de Québec ★ ★ ★** *(late Jun to late Aug; 1 Côte de la Fabrique,* ☎*692-3981)* religious complex was an oasis of European civilization in a rugged and hostile territory. To get an idea of how it must have appeared to students of the day, go through the old gate (decorated with the seminary's coat of arms) and into the courtyard before proceeding through the opposite entryway to the reception desk.

The seminary was founded in 1663 by Monseigneur Francois de Laval, on orders from the Séminaire des Missions Étrangères de Paris (seminary of foreign missions), with which it remained affiliated until 1763. As headquarters of the clergy throughout the colony, it was at the seminary that future priests studied, that parochial funds were administered, and that ministerial appointments were made. Louis XIV's Minister, Colbert, further required the seminary to establish a smaller school devoted to the conversion and education of native people. Following the British Conquest and the subsequent banishing of the Jesuits, the seminary became a college devoted to classical education. It also served as housing for the bishop of Québec after his palace was destroyed during the invasion. In 1852, the seminary founded the Université Laval, the first French-language university in North America. The Séminaire's vast ensemble of buildings now includes the priests' residence, a private school for boys and girls, the faculty of architecture of Université Laval, and the Musée de l'Amérique Française (see below), which manages these historic buildings.

Today's seminary is the result of rebuilding efforts following numerous fires and bombardments. Across from the old gate the wing devoted to the offices of the Procurator can be seen, complete with sundial. During the 1690 attack of Admiral Phipps, it was in the vaulted cellars of this wing that the citizens of Québec City took refuge.

It also contains the private chapel of Monseigneur Briand (1785), decorated with sculpted olive branches by Pierre Emond. Forming a right angle with the chapel is the beautiful parlor wing, constructed in 1696. The use of segmented arch windows in this attractive building betrays the direct influence of French models, which were used prior to making adaptations to Québec's climate. Guided tours leave from the Musée de l'Amérique Française.

The exterior chapel was built in 1890 to replace the original, which dated from 1752 and burned down in 1888. In order to avoid any such recurrence, the interior, which is similar to that of Église de la Trinité in Paris, was covered over in tin and zinc and painted in *trompe l'oeil*, following the design of

Paul Alexandre de Cardonnel and Joseph-Ferdinand Peachy. The chapel contains the most significant collection of relics in North America, including those of Saint-Augustine and Saint-Anselm, the martyrs of Tonkin, Saint Charles Borromé and Ignatius of Loyola. Some religious relics are both large and authentic while others are rather small and dubious. On the left is a funeral chapel housing a tomb containing the remains of Monseigneur de Laval, the first bishop of North America.

The **Musée de l'Amérique Française** ★★ *($5, $13 package with Musée de la Civilisation and Centre d'Interprétation de la Place-Royale; late Jun to early Sep every day 9:30am to 5pm; early Sep to late Jun Tue-Sun 10am to 5pm; 2 Côte de la Fabrique, ☎692-2843 or 866-710-8031, www.mcq.org)* is dedicated to the seven North American communities that were formed by French immigration. Other than the Québécois, they include the Acadians, the Franco-Ontarians, the francophones from the West, the Metis and the francophones from Louisiana and New England. It contains over 450,000 artifacts including silverware, paintings, oriental art and numismatics, as well as scientific instruments collected for educational purposes over the course of the last three centuries by the priests of the seminary. The museum occupies five floors of what used to be the residences of the

Exploring

Université Laval. The first Egyptian mummy brought to America is on view, as are several items that belonged to Monseigneur de Laval. Temporary exhibitions are also held presenting various figures from history.

*On returning to Place de l'Hôtel-de-Ville, turn left on Rue De Buade.*

The old **Holt Renfrew** store *(43 Rue De Buade)*, which opened in 1837, faces the cathedral. The store originally sold furs, which it supplied by appointment to Her Majesty the Queen, and for many years Holt's held the exclusive rights for the Canadian distribution of Dior and Saint-Laurent creations. Holt's is now closed, having given way to the boutiques of the **Promenades du Vieux-Québec**.

A little further on is the entrance to **Rue du Trésor**, which also leads to Place d'Armes and Rue Sainte-Anne. Artists come here to sell paintings, drawings and silkscreens, many of which depict views of Québec City.

**Québec Expérience** *($7.50; mid-May to mid-Oct every day 10am to 10pm; mid-Oct to mid-May every day 10am to 4:45pm; 8 Rue du Trésor, 3rd floor, ☎694-4000)*, is an elaborate show depicting the history of Québec City. This lively three-dimensional multimedia presentation takes viewers back in time to relive the great moments in the city's history

## Rue du Trésor

This pretty little street where artists work during the summer has been called "Rue du Trésor" since the time of the French regime. In fact, colonists would pass through this street on their way to pay their taxes to the treasury, which was located where Maison Maillou now stands. Strangely enough, this building now houses the Chambre de Commerce de Québec. One could say that true callings are not always lost with time!

through its important historical figures. A wonderful way to learn about Québec City's past, these half-hour shows are a big hit with the kids. Presented in both French and English.

The **Bureau de Poste** ★ *(3 passage du Chien-d'Or)*, Canada's first post office, opened in Québec City in 1837. For a long time it was housed in the old Hôtel du Chien d'Or, a solid dwelling built around 1753 for a wealthy Bordeaux merchant, who ordered a bas-relief depicting a dog gnawing a bone installed above the doorway. The following inscription appeared underneath the bas-relief, which was relocated to the pediment of the present post office in 1872: *"Je suis un chien qui ronge l'os, en le rongeant je prends mon repos. Un temps viendra qui n'est pas venu où je mordrai qui m'aura mordu."* (I am a dog gnawing a bone, as I gnaw, I rest at home. Though it's not yet here there'll come a time when those who bit me will be paid in kind.) It is said that the message was destined for Intendant Bigot, a man known for being a swindler, who was so outraged he had the Bordeaux merchant killed.

The dome of the post office and the facade overlooking the river were added at the beginning of the 20th century. The building was renamed **Édifice Louis-S.-Saint-Laurent**, in honour of the former prime minister of Canada. Besides the traditional post and philatelic services, a **Parks Canada Information Service** *(free admission; Mon-Fri 8am to 4:30pm, Sat and Sun 10am to 5pm; 3 passage du Chien-d'Or, ☎648-4177)* office was added to illustrate Canada's natural and historical heritage.

Facing the post office stands a **monument to Monseigneur François de Montmorency Laval** (1623-1708), the first bishop of Québec whose diocese covered two thirds of the North American continent. Designed by Philippe Hébert and erected in 1908, the monument features an attractive staircase leading to Côte de la

Montagne and from there to Basse-Ville.

The Laval Bishop's monument is located directly in front of the **Palais Archiépiscopal** *(2 Rue Port-Dauphin)* or archbishopric, which was rebuilt by Thomas Baillargé in 1844. The first archbishopric stood on what is now Parc Montmorency. Designed by Claude Baillif and built between 1692 and 1700, the original palace was, by all accounts, one of the most gorgeous of its kind in New France. Drawings show an impressive building, complete with a recessed chapel whose interior was reminiscent of Paris's Val-de-Grâce. Though the chapel was destroyed in 1759, the rest of the building was restored and then occupied by the Legislative Assembly of Lower Canada from 1792 to 1840. It was demolished in 1848 to make room for the new parliamentary buildings, which went up in flames only four years later.

**Parc Montmorency** ★ was laid out in 1875 after the city walls were lowered along Rue des Remparts and the governor general of Canada, Lord Dufferin, discovered the magnificent view from the promontory. George-Étienne Cartier, prime minister of the Dominion of Canada and one of the Fathers of Confederation, is honoured with a statue here, as are Louis Hébert, Guillaume Couillard and Marie Rollet, some of the original farmers of New France. These last three disembarked in

1617 and were granted the fiefdom of Sault-au-Matelot, on the future site of the seminary, in 1623. These attractive bronzes are the work of Montréal sculptor Alfred Laliberté.

*Continue along rue des Remparts.*

The halls of the **old Université Laval** ★ can be seen through a gap in the wall of the ramparts. Built in 1856 in the gardens of the seminary, they were completed in 1875 with the addition of an impressive mansard roof surmounted by three silver lanterns. When the spotlights shine on them at night, it creates the atmosphere of a royal gala. Note that Université Laval is now located on a large campus in **Sainte-Foy** (see p 116).

Following **Rue des Remparts**, Basse-Ville (lower town) comes into view and you'll see a lot of old cannons. The patrician manors on the street along the ramparts provide a picturesque backdrop for the old Latin quarter which extends behind them. The narrow streets and 18th-century houses in this neighbourhood are worth the detour.

**Maison Montcalm** *(45 to 51 Rue des Remparts)* originally was a single very large residence constructed in 1727; it is now divided into three houses. Home to the Marquis de Montcalm at the time of the Battle of the Plains of Abraham, the building subsequently housed the officers of the British army before being subdivided and returned to private use. In the first half of the 19th century, many houses in Québec were covered in the sort of imitation stone boards that still protect the masonry of the Montcalm house. It was believed that this type of covering lent a more refined look to the houses.

*Take Rue Saint-Flavien.*

At the corner of Rue Couillard is **Maison François-Xavier-Garneau** *($5; May to Feb Sun 1pm to 4pm, tours on the hour; 14 Rue Saint-Flavien, ☎692-2240)*. Québec City businessman Louis Garneau recently bought this neoclassical house (1862) where historian and poet François-Xavier-Garneau lived during the last years of his life. Throughout the summer, an actor dressed in period costume is on site to make the past come alive as you visit the rooms and admire the objects on display.

Nearby, on Rue Couillard, is the **Musée Bon-Pasteur** ★ *($2; year-round 1pm to 5pm, closed Mon; 14 Rue Couillard, ☎694-0243)*. Founded in 1993, it tells the story of the Bon Pasteur (Good Shepherd) community of nuns, which has been serving the poor of Québec City since 1850. The museum is located in the Béthanie house, an eclectic brick structure built around 1887 to shelter unwed mothers and their children. The museum occupies three floors of an 1878 addition and houses furniture as well as sacred objects manufactured or collected by the nuns, as well as a video documentary that recounts an adoption.

*Walk back on Rue Couillard. Go down Rue Hamel until Rue Charlevoix, where you turn left.*

The Augustinian nurses founded their first convent in Québec in Sillery. Uneasy about the Iroquois, they relocated to Québec City in 1642 and began construction of the present complex, the **Chapelle** and **Musée de l'Hôtel-Dieu ★ ★** *(32 Rue Charlevoix)*, which includes a convent, a hospital and a chapel. Rebuilt several times, today's buildings mostly date from the 20th century. The oldest remaining part is the 1756 convent, built on the vaulted foundations from 1695, hidden behind the 1800 chapel. This chapel was erected using material from various French buildings destroyed during the Seven Years' War. The stone was taken from the palace of the intendant, while its first ornaments came from the 17th-century Jesuit church. Today, only the iron balustrade of the bell tower bears witness to the original chapel. The present neoclassical facade was designed by Thomas Baillargé in 1839 after he completed the new interior in 1835. The nun's chancel can be seen to the right. Abbot Louis-Joseph Desjardins used the chapel as an auction house in 1817 and again in 1821, after he pur-

chased the collection of a bankrupt Parisian banker who had amassed works confiscated from Paris churches during the French Revolution. *La Vision de Sainte-Thérèse d'Avila* (Saint Theresa of Avila's Vision), a work by François-Guillaume Ménageot which originally hung in the Carmel de Saint-Denis near Paris, can be seen in one of the side altars.

The **Musée des Augustines du Monastère de l'Hôtel-Dieu** *(free admission, $3 guided tours; Tue-Sat, 9:30am to noon and 1:30pm to 5pm; Sun 1:30pm to 5pm; 32 Rue Charlevoix, ☎692-2492)* is a museum which traces the history of the Augustinian community in New France through pieces of furniture, paintings, and medical instruments. On display is the chest that contained the meagre belongings of the founders (pre-1639), as well as pieces from the Château Saint-Louis, the residence of the first governors under the French Regime, including portraits of Louis XIV and Cardinal Richelieu. Upon request, visitors can see the chapel and the vaulted cellars. The remains of Blessed Marie-Catherine de Saint-Augustin, the founder of the community in New France, are kept in an adjoining chapel, as is a beautiful gilded reliquary in the Louis XIV style, sculpted in 1717 by Noël Levasseur.

*Follow the small street opposite the chapel (Rue Collins). At the corner of Rue Saint-Jean is a pleasant view of Côte de la*

Exploring

*Fabrique, with the Hôtel de Ville on the right and Cathédrale Notre-Dame in the background on the left. Turn right on Rue Saint-Jean, a lovely commercial street in the heart of Vieux-Québec.*

A short detour to the left down Rue Saint-Stanislas provides a view of the old **Methodist Church**, a beautiful Gothic Revival building dating from 1850. Today it houses the **Institut Canadien** *(42 Rue Saint-Stanislas)*, a centre for literature and the arts. Before the Quiet Revolution of the 1960s, this centre was the focus of many a contentious dispute with the clergy over its "audacious" choice of books. The institute is home to a theatre and a branch of the municipal library.

The neighbouring building, number 44, is the **Ancienne Prison de Québec** (the old jail) built in 1808 by François Baillargé. In 1868 it was renovated to accommodate Morrin College, affiliated with Montréal's McGill University. This venerable institution of English-speaking Québec also houses the library of the **Québec Literary and Historical Society**, a learned society founded in 1824. The building on the corner of Rue Cook and Rue Dauphine surmounted by a Palladian steeple is **St. Andrew's Presbyterian Church**, completed in 1811.

*Return to Rue Saint-Jean, which you'll cross. Turn left on Rue McMahon, and continue on to*

*the reception and information centre at the Artillery Park.*

**Artillery Park National Historic Site ★ ★** *($4; early Apr to mid-Oct every day 10am to 5pm, rest of the year hours vary; 2 Rue d'Auteuil, ☎648-4205)*, also called Lieu Historique National du Parc-de-l'Artillerie, takes up part of an enormous military installation running alongside the walls of the city. The reception and information centre is located in the old foundry where munitions were manufactured until 1964. On display is a fascinating model of Québec City, which was built between 1795 and 1810 by military engineer Jean-Baptiste Duberger for strategic planning. The model has only recently been returned to Québec City, after having been sent to England in 1813. It is an unparalleled source of information on the layout of the city in the years following the British Conquest.

The walk continues with a visit to the Dauphine Redoubt, a beautiful white roughcast building near Rue McMahon. In 1712, military engineer Dubois Berthelot de Beaucours drafted plans for the redoubt which was completed by Chaussegros de Léry in 1747. A redoubt is an independent fortified structure that serves as a retreat in case the troops are obliged to fall back. The redoubt was never really used for this purpose but rather as a military barracks. Behind it are several barracks and an old cartridge factory constructed by the British in the 19th century. The officers' barracks (1820), which has been converted into a children's centre for heritage interpretation, makes a nice end to the visit. You can take part in a 1hr guided tour led by characters in period costumes or visit on your own with an audioguide. There are also two other exhibits on the site: the first is a collection of antique toys and the second features dolls in an economuseum named **Les Dames de Soie** ("the silk ladies").

*Walk back up Rue d'Auteuil.*

The newest of Québec City's gates, **Porte Saint-Jean** actually has rather ancient origins. As of 1693 it was one of only three entrances to the city. It was reinforced by Chaussegros de Léry in 1757, and then rebuilt by the British. To satisfy merchants who were clamouring for the total destruction of the walls, a "modern" gate equipped with tandem carriage tunnels and corresponding pedestrian passageways was erected in 1867. However, this structure did not fit in with Lord Dufferin's romantic vision of the city and was eliminated in 1898. The present gate did not replace it until 1936.

Number 29, on the left, is an **old Anglican orphanage** built for the Society for Promoting Christian Knowledge in 1824, and was the first Gothic Revival style building in Québec City.

Its architecture was portentous, as it inaugurated the romantic current that would eventually permeate the city.

The last of Québec's Jesuits died in 1800, his community having been banished by the British and then, in 1774, by the Pope himself. The community was resuscitated in 1814, however, and returned to Québec City in 1840. Since its college and church on Place de l'Hôtel-de-Ville were no longer available, they were welcomed by the Congregationists, a brotherhood founded by the Jesuit Ponert in 1657 with a view to propagating the cult of the Virgin. These latter parishioners built the **Église des Jésuites ★** *(20 rue Dauphine, ☎694-9616)*. François Baillargé designed the plans for the church, which was completed in 1818. The facade was redone in 1930. The decoration of the interior began with the construction of the counterfeit vaulting. Its centrepiece is Pierre-Noël Levasseur's altar (1770). Since 1925, the Jesuit church has been Québec's sanctuary for the worship of Canada's martyred saints.

**Porte Kent**, like Porte Saint-Louis, is the result of Lord Dufferin's romantic vision of the city. The plans for this gate, Vieux-Québec's prettiest, were drawn up in 1878 by Charles Baillargé, following the suggestions of Irishman William H. Lynn.

Exploring

*Climb the stairway to the top of Porte Kent and walk along the wall towards Porte Saint-Louis.*

On the other side of the walls stands the Hôtel du Parlement and inside, several patrician homes along the Rue d'Auteuil. Number 69, **Maison McGreevy** *(no visiting)* stands out by its sheer size. The house is the work of Thomas Fuller, the architect of the Parliament Buildings in Ottawa, as well as New York's State Capitol. It was built in 1868 by McGreevy, a construction entrepreneur who also built Canada's first parliament buildings. Behind the rather commercial-looking facade of yellow Nepean sandstone is a perfectly preserved Victorian interior.

*Climb down the stairway from the wall at Porte Saint-Louis. Côte de la Citadelle is on the other side of Rue Saint-Louis.*

Québec City's **Citadelle ★ ★ ★** *(at the far end of the Côte de la Citadelle; ☎694-2815)* (citadel) represents three centuries of North American military history and is still in use. Since 1920, it has housed the Royal 22nd Regiment of the Canadian Army, a regiment distinguished for its bravery during World War II. Within the circumference of the enclosure are some 25 buildings, including the officers' mess, the hospital, the prison, and the official residence of the governor general of Canada, as well as the first observatory in Canada. The Citadelle's history began in

1693, when engineer Dubois Berthelot de Beaucours had the Cap Diamant redoubt built at the highest point of Québec City's defensive system, some 100m above the river. Today, this solid construction is included inside the King's bastion.

Throughout the 18th century, French and then British engineers developed projects for a citadel that remained unfulfilled. Chaussegros de Léry's powderhouse of 1750, which now houses the Museum of the Royal 22nd Regiment, and the temporary excavation works to the west (1783) are the only works of any scope accomplished during this period. The citadel that appears today was built between 1820 and 1832 by Colonel Elias Walker Durnford. Dubbed the "Gibraltar of America," and built according to principles expounded by Vauban in the 17th century, the citadel has never borne the brunt of a single cannonball, though it has acted as an important element of dissuasion.

The **Musée du Royal 22$^e$ Régiment** *($8; Nov to March with reservations only, Apr every day 10am to 4pm, May and Jun every day 9am to 5pm, Jul every day 9am to 6pm, Sep every day 9am to 4pm, Oct every day 10am to 3pm; ☎694-2815)* is a museum that offers an interesting collection of weapons, uniforms, insignia and military documents spanning almost 400 years. It is possible to take a guided tour of the whole

## Small Panes of Glass

Why do the windows of the old houses in Québec City and the rest of the province have several small panes of glass instead of one large one? You might think it is because of the cold and the snow. But the answer is even more down-to-earth. During colonial times, glass had to be imported from France. Needless to say, much of it was broken en route. As a result, the merchants decided to import smaller pieces of glass so there would be less risk of breakage. Furthermore, it was sometimes transported in large barrels of molasses for added protection!

installation where you'll witness the changing of the guard, the retreat, and the firing of the cannon. The changing of the guard lasts 30min and takes place every day from the end of June until the beginning of September at 6pm, weather permitting. The retreat lasts 30min and occurs according to a variable schedule during the summer.

## Tour B: Petit-Champlain to Vieux-Port

*(two days)*

Québec's port and commercial area is a narrow *U*-shaped piece of land wedged near the waters of the St. Lawrence River. This area is sometimes called the Basse-Ville of Vieux-Québec because of its location at the foot of the Cap Diamant escarpment. The cradle of New France, Place-Royale is where Samuel de Champlain (1567-1635) founded the settlement he called "Abitation" in 1608, which would eventually become Québec City. In the summer of 1759, three quarters of the city were badly damaged by British bombardment. It took 20 years to repair and rebuild the houses. In the 19th century, the construction of multiple embankments allowed the expansion of the town and enabled the area around Place-Royale to be linked by road with the area around the intendant's palace. The port's decline at the beginning of the 20th century led to the gradual abandonment of

Exploring

Place-Royale; restoration work began in 1959. The Petit-Champlain district has been reclaimed by artisans who have set up shop here, especially on the Rue du Petit-Champlain. This area now caters mostly to tourists, who visit the numerous studios to watch the craftspeople at work and to buy their wares.

*This walking tour begins at Porte Prescott, which straddles Côte de la Montagne. Those who do not enjoy walking would be well advised to take the funicular from Terrasse Dufferin and to begin the tour at the start of Rue Petit-Champlain.*

The **Funiculaire** (Funicular) *($1.50; ☎692-1132)* began operating in November 1879. It was installed by entrepreneur W. A. Griffith in order to link the lower and upper towns. When the funicular was first built, water was transferred from one reservoir to another to make it function. It was converted to electricity in 1906, at the same time that Terrasse Dufferin was illuminated. The funicular is an outdoor elevator that eliminates the need to take the *Escalier Casse-Cou*, or "break-neck stairway," or to go around Côte de la Montagne. The funicular was completely overhauled in 1998. It operates from 7:30am until at least 11pm.

**Porte Prescott** *(Côte de la Montagne)* can be reached from Côte de la Montagne or from Terrasse Dufferin by means of a stairway and a charming footbridge on the left of the funicular's entryway. This discreetly postmodern structure was built in 1983 by the architectural firm of Gauthier, Guité, Roy, which sought to evoke the 1797 gate by Gother Mann. It allows pedestrians to cross directly from Terrasse Dufferin to Parc Montmorency.

*Descend Côte de la Montagne and take the Escalier Casse-Cou on the right.*

The **Escalier Casse-Cou** *(Côte de la Montagne)*, which literally means "the break-neck stairway," has been here since 1682. Until the beginning of the 20th century, it had been made of planks that were in constant need of repair or replacement. It connects the various businesses situated on different levels. At the foot of the stair-

*Escalier Casse-Cou*

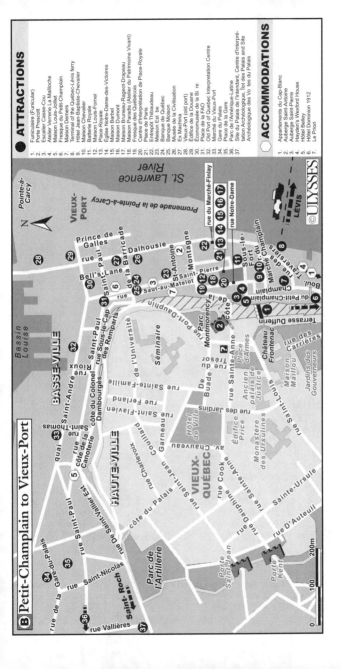

# B Petit-Champlain to Vieux-Port

**HAUTE-VILLE**

**BASSE-VILLE**

**VIEUX-PORT**

**VIEUX-QUÉBEC**

Pointe-à-Carcy

St. Lawrence River

Promenade de la Pointe-à-Carcy

LÉVIS

Bassin Louise

© ULYSSES

N

0   100   200m

● **ATTRACTIONS**

1. Funiculaire (Funicular)
2. Porte Prescott
3. Escalier Casse-Cou
4. Atelier Verrerie La Mailloche
5. Maison Louis-Jolliet
6. Fresque du Petit-Champlain
7. Maison Demers
8. Terminal of the Québec-Lévis ferry
9. Hôtel Jean-Baptiste-Chevalier
10. Maison Chevalier
11. Batterie Royale
12. Maison Louis-Fornel
13. Place-Royale
14. Église Notre-Dame-des-Victoires
15. Maison Barbel
16. Maison Dumont
17. Maison Bruneau-Rageot-Drapeau
18. Maison Paradis (Atelier du Patrimoine Vivant)
19. Fresque des Québécois
20. Centre d'interprétation de Place-Royale
21. Place de Paris
22. Entrepôt Thibaudeau
23. Maison Est be
24. Banque de Québec
25. Banque Molson
26. Musée de la Civilisation
27. Ex Machina
28. Vieux-Port (old port)
29. Économusée de la Bi re
30. Place de la FAO
31. Old Port-of-Québec Interpretation Centre
32. Édifice de la Douane
33. Marché du Vieux-Port
34. Place de la Gare
35. Gare de la Gare
36. Parc de l'Amérique-Latine
37. Site du Palais de l'Intendant, Centre d'interpré-
    tation Archéologique, îlot des Palais and Site
    Archéologique des Vo tes du Palais

◇ **ACCOMMODATIONS**

1. Appartements du Cap-Blanc
2. Auberge Saint-Antoine
3. Auberge Saint-Pierre
4. Hayden's Wexford House
5. Hôtel Belley
6. Hôtel Dominion 1912
7. Le Priori

rue du Marché-Finlay
rue Notre-Dame

way is **Rue du Petit-Champlain**, a narrow pedestrian street flanked by charming craft shops and pleasant cafés located in 17th and 18th century houses. Some of the houses at the foot of the cape were destroyed by rockslides prior to the cliff's reinforcement during the 19th century.

At the foot of the Escalier Casse-Cou, a small *économusée* (economuseum) unveils the secrets of glass-blowing. At **Atelier Verrerie La Mailloche** *(free admission; late Jun to early Nov Wed-Sun 10am to noon and 1:30pm to 4:30pm, rest of the year Mon-Fri 10am to noon and 1:30pm to 4:30pm; 58 Rue Sous-le-Fort, ☎694-0445)*, visitors can observe the fascinating spectacle of artisans shaping molten glass according to traditional techniques. The finished products are sold in a shop on the second floor.

**Maison Louis-Jolliet ★**
*(16 Rue du Petit-Champlain)* is one of the earliest houses of Vieux-Québec (1683) and one of the few works of Claude Baillif still standing. The house was built after the great fire of 1682 which destroyed Basse-Ville. It was this tragedy that prompted the authorities to require that stone be used in all buildings. The fire also paved the way for some improvements in urban planning: roads were straightened and Place-Royale was created. Louis Jolliet (1645-1700) was the man who, along with Father Marquette, discovered the

## S-Shaped Linchpins

You have perhaps noticed the *S*-shaped pieces of iron that decorate the walls of some of this neighbourhood's old houses. These objects are linchpins that hold the stones in the walls on which the weight of the roof rests.

Mississippi and explored Hudson Bay. During the last years of his life, he taught hydrography at the Séminaire de Québec. The interior of the house was completely gutted and now contains the lower platform of the funicular (see above).

*Follow Rue du Petit-Champlain until the end, where it meets Boulevard Champlain. You will see a colourful fresco on the facade of the last house.*

You will probably need a few minutes to admire the many details that make up the beautiful **Fresque du Petit-Champlain** *(102 Rue du Petit-Champlain)*. Some 35 characters, both famous and unknown, who shaped the history of the province of Québec, and most particularly of Québec City and the Petit-Champlain district, come to life in six rooms. From the first floor to the attic, they are presented in various settings, such as artisan workshops and an inn. You'll feel as though the walls suddenly open up on different chapters in history!

*Retrace your steps and take the stairway that leads to Boulevard Champlain. At the foot of the stairway, make sure to turn around and admire the exceptional view from below of the Château Frontenac.*

**Maison Demers ★** *(28 Boulevard Champlain)* was built in 1689 by mason Jean Lerouge. This impressive residence is an example of the bourgeois style of Québec's Basse-Ville. A two-storey residential facade looks on to Rue du Petit-Champlain while the rear, which was used as a warehouse, extends down another two storeys to open directly onto l'Anse du Cul-de-Sac.

The cove called l'**Anse du Cul-de-Sac**, also known as the Anse aux Barques, was Québec City's first port. In 1745, Intendant Gilles Hocquart ordered the construction of a major shipyard in the western part of the cove. Several French battleships were built there using Canadian lumber. In 1854, the terminus of the Grand Trunk railway was built on the embankments, and in 1858 the Marché Champlain went up, only to be destroyed by fire in 1899. The location is presently occupied by administrative buildings and by the

**terminal of the Québec-Lévis ferry**. A short return trip on the ferry provides a spectacular view of Vieux-Québec as a whole. Taking the ferry (see p 40) in the winter affords a rare chance to come face to face with the ice floes on the St. Lawrence River.

*Follow Boulevard Champlain east as far as Rue du Marché-Champlain. The ferry boards from the south end of this road.*

**Hôtel Jean-Baptiste-Chevalier ★★** *(60 Rue du Marché-Champlain)*, a former hotel, was the first building in the Place-Royale area to be restored. The hôtel is really three separate houses from three different periods: **Maison de l'Armateur Chevalier** (home of Chevalier the shipowner), built in a square in 1752; **Maison Frérot**, with a mansard roof (1683); and **Maison Dolbec**, dating from 1713. These houses were all repaired or partially rebuilt after the British Conquest. As a group, they were rescued from deterioration in 1955 by Gérard Morisset, the director of the Inventaire des Oeuvres d'Art, who suggested that they be purchased and restored by the government of Québec. This decision had a domino effect that prevented the demolition of Place-Royale.

**Maison Chevalier** *(free admission; March to late Jun, Tue-Sun 10am to 5pm; late Jun to early Sep, every day 9:30am to 5pm; early Sep to late Oct, Wed-Sun*

Exploring

*10am to 5pm; late Oct to March, Sat and Sun 10am to 5pm; 50 Rue du Marché-Champlain, ☎643-2158)* harbours an annex of the Musée de la Civilisation, where an interesting exhibit, *Habiter au Passé* (Living in the Past) portrays the daily lives of the merchants of New France. The exhibit features furniture as well as everyday items. The original, stately Louis XV wood-work (circa 1764) can also be seen.

*Take Rue Notre-Dame and turn right onto Rue Sous-le-Fort.*

With no walls to protect Basse-Ville, other means of defending it from the cannon-fire of ships in the river had to be found. Following the attack by Admiral Phipps in 1690, it was decided to set up the **Batterie Royale ★** *(at the far end of Rue Sous-le-Fort)*, according to a plan drawn up by Claude Baillif. The strategic position of the battery allowed for the bombardment of any enemy ships foolhardy enough to venture into the narrows in front of the city. The ruins of the battery, long hidden under storehouses, were dis-covered in 1974. The crenellations, removed in the 19th century, were recon-structed, as was the wooden portal, discernible in a sketch from 1699.

The two rough stone houses on Rue Saint-Pierre, next to the battery, were built for Charles Guillemin in the early 18th cen-tury. The narrowness of the

## Vaults

The houses in Vieux-Québec often had vaulted cellars to support the building; because of their cool temperature, food and drink were often stored there. Some of these cellars have survived and can be visited. Maison Fornel, on Place-Royale, which houses the Association Québec-France, opens its vaults to visitors *(9am to 4pm)* and even presents small exhibi-tions. The entrances are at 25 Rue Saint-Pierre and 9 Place-Royale.

house on the left shows just how precious land was in Basse-Ville during the French Regime. Each lot, irregular or not, had to be used. A little further along, at number 25 Rue Saint-Pierre, is the **maison Louis-Fornel**, where a number of artifacts are on display in vaults. This vaulted basement was built in the 17th century from the ruins of Champlain's stronghold, and extends right under the square.

*Continue along Rue Saint-Pierre, and turn left on Rue de la Place to go up to Place-Royale.*

**Place-Royale ★★★** is the most European quarter of any city in North America. It resembles a village in northwestern France. Place-Royale is laden with symbolism, as it was on this very spot that New France was founded in 1608. After many unsuccessful attempts, this became the official departure point of French exploits in America. Under the French Regime, Place-Royale was the only densely populated area in a vast, untamed colony. Today, it contains the most significant concentration of 17th- and 18th-century buildings in the Americas north of Mexico.

The square itself was laid out in 1673 by Governor Frontenac as a market. It replaced the garden of Champlain's Abitation, a stronghold that went up in flames in 1682, along with the rest of Basse-Ville. In 1686, Intendant Jean Bochart de Champigny erected a **bronze bust of Louis XIV** in

the middle of the square, hence the name of the square, Place-Royale. In 1928, François Bokanowski, then the French Minister of Commerce and Communications, presented Québécois Athanase David with a bronze replica of the marble bust of Louis XIV in the Gallerie de Diane at Versailles to replace the missing statue. The bronze, by Alexis Rudier, was not set up until 1931, for fear of offending England.

Small, unpretentious **Église Notre-Dame-des-Victoires ★★** *(free admission; early May to mid-Oct every day 9am to 4:30pm, rest of the year 10am to 4:30pm; closed during weddings, baptisms and funeral ceremonies; 32 rue Sous-le-Fort; ☎692-1650)* is the oldest church in Canada. Designed by Claude Baillif, it dates from 1688. It was built on the foundations of Champlain's *Abitation* and incorporates some of its walls. Beside the church, black granite

Exploring

*Place-Royale*

marks the remains of the foundations of the second Abitation de Champlain. These vestiges were discovered in 1976.

Initially dedicated to the Infant Jesus, it was rechristened Notre-Dame-de-la-Victoire after Admiral Phipp's attack of 1690 failed. It was later renamed Notre-Dame-des-Victoires (the plural) in memory of the misfortune of British Admiral Walker, whose fleet ran aground on Île-aux-Oeufs during a storm in 1711. The bombardments of the Conquest left nothing standing but the walls of the church, spoiling the Levasseur's lovely interior. The church was restored in 1766, but was not fully rebuilt until the current steeple was added in 1861.

Raphaël Giroux is responsible for most of the present interior, which was undertaken between 1854 and 1857, but the strange "fortress" tabernacle of the main altar is a later work by David Ouellet (1878). Lastly, in 1888, Jean Tardivel painted the historical scenes on the vault and on the wall of the chancel. Most striking, though, are the various pieces in the church: the *ex-voto* (an offering) that hangs from the centre of the vault depicting the *Brézé*, a ship that came to Canada in 1664 carrying soldiers of the Carignan Regiment; and the beautiful tabernacle in the Sainte-Geneviève chapel, attributed to Pierre-Noël Levasseur (circa 1730). Among the paintings are works by Boyermans and Van

## Rue des Pains-Bénits

If you visit the city during the holidays, consider visiting Place-Royale, especially on January 3. This is the feast day of Sainte Geneviève, patron saint of the chapel adjoining Église Notre-Dame-des-Victoires. Every year since the colony was established, blessed bread rolls are distributed to the people to celebrate this event. The little street that runs along the east side of the church is called "Rue des Pains-Bénits" (blessed-bread street). While eating your bread, you can admire the nativity scene inside the church.

Loo, originally from the collection of Abbot Desjardins.

Under the French Regime, the square attracted many merchants and ship owners who commissioned the building of attractive residences. The tall house on the southwest corner of the square and on Rue de la Place, **Maison Barbel**, was built in 1754 for the formidable businesswoman Anne-Marie Barbel, widow of Louis Fornel. At the time, she owned a pottery factory on Rivière Saint-

Charles and held the lease on the lucrative trading post at Tadoussac.

**Maison Dumont** *(1 Place-Royale)* was designed in 1689 by the tireless Claude Baillif for vintner Eustache Lambert Dumont. The house incorporated elements of the old store of the Compagnie des Habitants (1647). Visitors can see its huge vaulted basement now used, as it was in the past, to store casks and bottles of wine. Turned into an inn in the 19th century, the house was a favourite stopover for U.S. President Howard Taft (1857-1930) on his way to his annual summer vacation in La Malbaie.

**Maison Bruneau-Rageot-Drapeau**, at number 3A, is a house built in 1763 using the walls of the old Nicolas Jérémie house. Jérémie was a Montagnais interpreter and a clerk at the fur-trading posts of Hudson Bay.

**Maison Paradis**, on Rue Notre-Dame, houses the **Atelier du Patrimoine Vivant** *(free admission; late Jun to mid-Oct every day 10am to 5pm; 42 Rue Notre-Dame, ☎647-1598).* In these studios, various artisans hone their skills using traditional methods.

If you continue on Rue Notre-Dame towards Côte de la Montagne and then turn around, you will be surprised by the colourful sight. On the blind wall of Maison Soumande, in front of Parc de La Cetière,

are displayed the colours of the **Fresque des Québécois ★★**. In fact, if they're not careful, passersby may actually miss the fresco: it is a *trompe l'œil!* A team of French and Québec artists created this fresco with the guidance of specialists (historians, geographers, etc.) who made sure the painting was realistic and educational. On a surface area of 420m², they brought together Québec City's architecture and famous sites such as Cap Diamant, the ramparts, a bookshop, houses of Vieux-Québec—in short, the different places that the town's inhabitants encounter every day. Just like the crowd of admiring onlookers that gathers rain or shine, you can amuse yourself for quite a while trying to identify the historical figures and the role they played. From top to bottom and from left to right, you will see Marie Guyart, Catherine de Longpré, François-Xavier Garneau, Louis-Joseph Papineau, Jean Talon, the Comte de Frontenac, Marie Fitzbach, Marcelle Mallet, Louis Jolliet, Alphonse Desjardins, Lord Dufferin, Félix Leclerc and, finally, Samuel de Champlain, who started it all.

Return to Place-Royale and visit the **Centre d'Interprétation de Place-Royale ★★** *($4, free admission on Tue from early Nov to late May and on Sat from 10am to noon during Jan and Feb; $13 package with Musée de la Civilisation and Musée de l'Amérique Française; early Sep to late Jun Tue-Sun 10am to*

Exploring

*5pm; late Jun to early Sep every day 9:30am to 5pm; 27 Rue Notre-Dame, ☎646-3167, www.mcq.org)*, which was inaugurated in the fall of 1999. To accommodate the centre, both the Hazeur and Smith houses, which had burned down, were rebuilt in a modern style while using a large portion of the original materials. The omnipresent glass lets you admire the exposed rooms as well as the buildings' architecture from all angles. Along the glass walls between the two houses, a stairway goes down Côte de la Montagne to Place-Royale. From the staircase, you can see some of the centre's treasures. On each of the three levels, an exhibition presents chapters of Place-Royale's history. There are also artifacts that were discovered during archaeological digs under the square. Whether they are whole objects or tiny pieces that are difficult to identify, they are all instructive. You can also watch a multimedia show and admire various scale models, such as the one representing the second Abitation de Champlain in 1635.

You will learn, among other things, that the first hotel to be established in Québec City was opened in 1648 by a Mr. Boidon. Coincidentally, his name in French (*bois donc*) means "have a drink!". The hotel tradition continued on Place-Royale until the middle of the 20th century, when the last hotel was destroyed by fire. Visitors had been welcomed, lodged and nourished there for 300 years. In the basement, the vaults of the house are transformed into a playroom where young and old can dress up as one of the former occupants. A great (and original) idea!

*Continue along Rue de la Place until it opens onto Place de Paris.*

**Place de Paris** ★ *(along Rue du Marché-Finlay)* is an elegant and sophisticated combination of contemporary art and traditional surroundings conceived by Québécois architect Jean Jobin in 1987. A large sculpture by French artist Jean-Pierre Raynault dominates the centre of the square. The work was presented to the city by Jacques Chirac, who was then mayor of Paris, on behalf of his city. Entitled *Dialogue avec l'Histoire* (Dialogue with History), the black granite and white marble work is said to evoke the first human presence in the area and forms a pair with the bust of Louis XIV visible in the background. The Québécois have dubbed it the Colossus of Québec because of its imposing dimensions. From the square, which was once a market, there is a splendid view of the Batterie Royale, the Château Frontenac and the St. Lawrence River.

**Entrepôt Thibaudeau** *(215 Rue du Marché-Finlay)* is a huge building whose stone facade faces Rue Dalhousie. It represents the last prosperous days of the area before its decline at the end of the 19th century. The Second Empire building is distinguished by its mansard roof and by its segmental arch openings. It was built in 1880, following the plans of Joseph-Ferdinand Peachy, for Isidore Thibaudeau, president and founder of the Banque Nationale and importer of European novelties.

*Head back up the street towards Rue Saint-Pierre and turn right.*

Further along at number 92 is yet another imposing merchant's house, **Maison Estèbe** (1752). It is now part of the Musée de la Civilisation, whose smooth stone walls can be seen along Rue Saint-Pierre. Guillaume Estèbe was a businessman and the director of the Saint-Maurice ironworks in Trois-Rivières. Having participated in a number of unsavoury schemes with Intendant Bigot during the Seven Years' War, he was locked-up in the Bastille for a few months on embezzlement charges. The house where he lived for five years with his wife and 14 children is built on an embankment that used to front onto a large private wharf which is now the courtyard of the museum. The courtyard is accessible through the gateway on the left. The 21-room interior escaped the bombardments of 1759. Some of the rooms feature handsome Louis XV woodwork. Near Rue de la Barricade is the old **Banque de Québec** building (Edward Staveley, architect, 1861). Across the street, the old **Banque Molson** occupies an 18th-century house.

*Turn right onto Rue Saint-Jacques. The entrance to the Musée de la Civilisation is on Rue Dalhousie, on the right.*

The **Musée de la Civilisation** ★ ★ *($8, Tue free admission, except in summer; $13 package with Musée de l'Amérique Française and Centre d'Interprétation de la Place-Royale; early Sep to late Jun Tue-Sun 10am to 5pm; late Jun to early Sep every day 9:30am to 6:30pm; 85 Rue Dalhousie, ☎643-2158, www.mcq.org)* is housed in a building that was completed in 1988 in the traditional architectural style of Québec City, with its stylized roof, dormer windows and a belltower like those common to the area. Architect Moshe Safdie, who also designed the revolutionary Habitat '67 in Montréal, Ottawa's National Gallery and Vancouver's Public Library, designed a sculptural building with a monumental exterior staircase at its centre.

*Musée de la Civilisation*

Exploring

The lobby provides a charming view of Maison Estèbe and its wharf while preserving a contemporary look that is underlined by Astri Reuch's sculpture, **La Débâcle**.

The Musée de la Civilisation presents a great variety of temporary exhibitions. Themes such as humour, circus and song, for example, have been the object of very lively displays. Travelling exhibitions also recount the world's great civilisations, while permanent exhibitions provide a portrait of the local culture. *Mémoires* recounts the history of the Québec people; *Nous les Premières Nations*, developed in collaboration with First Nations peoples, is a large exhibition tracing the history of the 11 Aboriginal nations that originally inhabited Québec. You can view many objects as well as audiovisual materials like the work of filmmaker Arthur Lamothe. Some of the more remarkable items are the Aboriginal artifacts, the large French Regime fishing craft unearthed during excavations for the museum itself, some highly ornate 19th-century horse-drawn hearses, and some Chinese *objets d'art* and pieces of furniture, including an imperial bed, from the collection of the Jesuits. You can also visit the museum's vaulted cellar, which dates from the 18th century.

*Head northeast, towards the Vieux-Port, through Rue Dalhousie.*

Beside the Musée de la Civilisation is a lavish *beaux-arts* fire station dating from 1912 that now houses **Ex Machina** *(103 rue Dalhousie)*, a multi-disciplinary artistic production centre founded by Robert Lepage. Note the high tower with a copper dome rising on the southeast corner like a church spire, which was inspired by the tower of the Hôtel du Parlement. Firefighters used to hang their hoses in the tower to dry and to prevent damage, since in those days hoses were made of fabric. The building has been expanded and in order to keep its character, a false wall similar to the original stone wall—but made of plastic—has been erected in front of the new part.

The **Vieux-Port** ★ *(160 Rue Dalhousie)* (old port) is often criticized for being overly American in a city with such a pronounced European sensibility. It was refurbished by the Canadian government on the occasion of the maritime celebration, *Québec 1534-1984*. Various metallic structures were designed to enliven the promenade, at the end of which is the handsome **Édifice de la Douane** *(2 Quai St-André)* (customs house). With its dome and columns, it features a lovely neoclassical architecture. At the time the structure was built (1856-1857), the river actually flowed right next to it.

The entire port area between
, Place-Royale and the entrance

of **Bassin Louise** is known as **Pointe-à-Carcy**. A pleasure boat harbour was added here in 2002.

An **Économusée de la Bière** *(free admission; every day noon to 3pm; 37 Quai Saint-André, ☎692-2877)* (beer economuseum) has been set up in an established Vieux-Port bar, L'Inox. By reading the information panels on the walls, you will learn more about the long and glorious history of beer. You can also discover the secrets of beer-brewing by taking a guided tour. Since L'Inox itself is a micro-brewery, it is possible to have the master brewer take you behind the scenes which are visible from the bar through a glass wall (reservations are necessary). Not only will he explain how he makes the beer, he will also offer you a taste of his work.

*Take Rue Saint-Pierre on your left.*

**Place de la FAO** is located at the intersection of Rue Saint-Pierre, Rue Saint-Paul and Rue Sault-au-Matelot. This square honours the United Nations Food and Agriculture Organisation whose first meeting was held at the Château Frontenac in 1945. The sculpture at the centre of the square represents the prow of a boat as it emerges from the waves, its female figurehead, *La Vivrière*, firmly grasping all kinds of fruit, vegetables and grains.

In the square at the corner of Rue Saint-Pierre stands an imposing building with a large round portico which formerly housed the **Canadian Imperial Bank of Commerce**.

*Take Rue Sault-au-Matelot to Rue de la Barricade. This street is named in honour of the barricade that was set up against invading revolutionaries coming from what was to become the United States. They attempted to take Québec City on December 31, 1775.*

On the right, Rue de la Barricade leads to **Rue Sous-le-Cap**. This narrow passage was once wedged between the St. Lawrence River and the Cap Diamant escarpment. At the end of the 19th century, the street housed working-class families of Irish origin. Today's inhabitants, finding the houses too small, have renovated the little cottages on the side of the cliff and connected them to their houses by walkways crossing the street at clothesline height. One almost enters Rue Sous-le-Cap on tiptoe because of the feeling that you're walking into another world. At the end of the street is Côte du Colonel-Dambourgès and then Rue Saint-Paul.

**Rue Saint-Paul** is a most pleasant street, lined with antique shops that overflow with beautiful Québec heritage furniture.

*To get to the Centre d'Interprétation du Vieux-Port-de-Québec, take Rue Rioux or Rue des Navigateurs, which both meet up with Quai Saint-André.*

Exploring

In the days of sailboats, Québec City was one of the most important gateways to America, since many vessels could not make their way any farther against the current. Its bustling port was surrounded by shipyards that made great use of the plentiful and high-quality Canadian lumber. The first royal shipyards appeared under the French Regime in the cove known as l'Anse du Cul-de-Sac. The Napoleonic blockade of 1806 forced the British to turn to their Canadian colony for wood and for the construction of battleships. This was a great boost for a number of shipyards and made fortunes for many of their owners. The **Old Port of Québec Interpretation Centre** *($3.50; early May to early Sep every day 10am to 5pm, early Sep to mid-Oct noon to 4pm; 100 Rue Saint-André, ☎648-3300)* is a national historic site that concentrates on those flourishing days of navigation in Québec. You can also take part in guided tours *($8)* of the Vieux-Port accompanied by characters in period costumes.

*Take the promenade that runs along the basin to the Vieux-Port market.*

Most of Québec City's public markets were shut down in the 1960s because they had become obsolete in an age of air-conditioned supermarkets and frozen food. However, people continued to yearn for fruit and vegetables fresh from the farm as well as the contact with the farmers. Moreover, the market was one of the only non-aseptic places people could congregate. Thus, the markets gradually began to reappear at the beginning of the 1980s. **Marché du Vieux-Port ★** *(corner of Rue Saint-Thomas and Rue Saint-André)* was built in 1987 by architectural partners Belzile, Brassard, Galienne and Lavoie. It is the successor to two other markets, Finlay and Champlain, that no longer exist. In the summer, the market is a pleasant place to stroll and take in the view of the Marina Bassin Louise at the edge of the market.

*Continue along Rue Saint-Paul. Turn right on Rue Abraham-Martin and then left on Rue de la Gare-du-Palais until you reach the train station.*

For over 50 years, the citizens of Québec City clamoured for a train station worthy of their city. Canadian Pacific finally fulfilled their wish in 1915. Designed by New York architect Harry Edward Prindle in the same style as the Château Frontenac, the **Gare du Palais ★** *(Rue de la Gare-du-Palais)* gives visitors a taste of the romance and charm that await them in Québec City. The 18m-high arrival hall that extends behind the giant window of the facade is bathed in sunlight from the leaded glass skylight on the roof. The faïence tiles and multicoloured bricks in the walls lend a striking aspect to the

*Gare du Palais*

entire ambiance. The station was closed for almost 10 years (from 1976 to 1985) at the time when railway companies were imitating airlines and moving their stations to the suburbs. Fortunately, it was reopened with great pomp, and now houses the bus and train stations. Across from it, **Place de la Gare** offers a lovely spot where you can relax and admire an impressive fountain designed by Charles Daudelin.

The building on the right is Raoul Chênevert's 1938 **post office**. It illustrates the persistence of the Château style of architecture that is so emblematic of the city.

A little further on Boulevard Jean-Lesage is **Parc de l'Amérique-Latine**. There, two monuments honour the memory of two of the most important figures in Latin American history. The monuments to great liberators Simón Bolívar and José Martí were offered by the governments of Venezuela and Cuba respectively.

*Return to Rue Saint-Paul by Boulevard Jean-Lesage, which becomes Rue Vallière. At the corner of Rue Saint-Nicolas and Rue Saint-Paul, you are in the heart of the Quartier du Palais, so named because it surrounds the Palais de l'Intendant. To reach it, head west on Rue De Saint-Vallier.*

The block bordered by Ruelle de l'Ancien-Chantier, Rue Saint-Vallier Est, Rue Saint-Paul and Rue Saint-Nicolas is known as **L'Îlot Saint-Nicolas**. It was restored with verve by architects De Blois, Côté, Leahy.

The handsome stone building on the corner and the two others behind it on Rue Saint-Nicolas housed the famous **Cabaret Chez Gérard** from 1938 to 1978. It was here that Charles Trenet, Rina Ketty and many other famous French singers performed. Charles

Exploring

Aznavour actually got his start here. In the bohemian days of the 1950s, he sang here every night for many months for a mere pittance.

The big Scottish-brick building with the pinnacle inscribed "**Les Maisons Lecourt**" was erected across from l'Îlot Saint-Nicolas using the remnants of Intendant Bigot's "royal store." Nick-named *La Fripone* (The Rogue's) because of the extortionary prices Bigot and his accomplices exacted from the miserable populace, the location was one of only two in the city during the French Regime where one could moor a boat (the other being l'Anse du Cul-de-Sac). In the 17th century, warehouses and wharfs were built along the estuary of the Saint-Charles, as was a shipyard with a dry dock that bequeathed the street its name, Rue de l'Ancien-Chantier, meaning "old shipyard."

The **Site du Palais de l'Intendant** ★ and the **Centre d'Interprétation Archéologique** are part of **l'Îlot des Palais** *($3; late Jun to early Sep every day 10am to 5pm, rest of the year with reservations only; 8 Rue Vallière, ☎641-6173)* and the **Site Archéologique des Voûtes du Palais**, (the palace vaults archaeological site). The intendant oversaw the day-to-day affairs of the colony. The royal stores, the few state enterprises and the prison were all located near his residence. With so

many opportunities to enrich himself, it was only natural that his should be the most splendid mansion in New France. The remains of one wing of the palace can still be seen in the shape of the segment of brown brick foundation wall that is now aboveground. The location was originally the site of the brewery that was set up by the first intendant, Jean Talon (1625-1694). Talon took great effort to populate and develop the colony. For his trouble, he was made secretary of the king's cabinet upon his return to France. His brewery was replaced by a palace designed by engineer La Guer Morville in 1716. This elegant building had a classical cut-stone entrance that led to a horseshoe-shaped staircase. Twenty or so ceremonial rooms were used for receptions and the meetings of the Conseil Supérieur.

The palace was spared British cannon-fire only to be burned to the ground during the American invasion of 1775-76. The arches of its cellars were used as the foundation of the Boswell brewery in 1872, bringing the site full circle. Visitors are free to inspect the cellars where the archeological information centre is located. The centre displays artifacts and ruins from the site itself.

*To return to Haute-Ville, climb Côte du Palais at the end of Rue Saint-Nicolas.*

★ ★

# Tour C:
# Grande Allée

*(one day)*

Grande Allée appears on 17th-century maps, but it was not completed until the first half of the 19th century, when the city grew beyond its walls. Grande Allée originally was a country road linking the town to Chemin du Roi, and then to Montréal. At that time, it was bordered by the large agricultural properties of the nobility and clergy of the French Regime. After the British Conquest, many of the domains were turned into country estates by English merchants who set their manors well back from the road. The neoclassical town then spilled over into the area before the Victorian city had a chance to stamp the landscape with its distinctive style. Today's Grande Allée is the most pleas-

ant route into the old city and the focus of extramural Haute-Ville. Although it links the capital's various ministries, a portion of it is a cheerful street, as many of its bourgeois houses have been converted into restaurants and bars.

*This walking tour starts at Porte Saint-Louis and gradually works its way away from the walled city.*

On the right is Paul Chevré's monument to historian François-Xavier Garneau. On the left is the *Croix du Sacrifice*, where Remembrance Day services are held every year on November 11.

The **Hôtel du Parlement** ★ ★ ★ *(free admission; guided tours late Jun to early Sep Mon-Fri 9am to 4:30pm, Sat and Sun 10am to 4:30pm, early Sep to Jun Mon-Fri 9am to 4:30pm; at the corner of Honoré-Mercier and Grande Allée Est, ☎643-7239, www.assnat.qc.ca)* is known to the Québécois as

**Exploring**

*Hôtel du Parlement*

l'Assemblée Nationale, or the National Assembly. The seat of the government of Québec, this imposing building was erected between 1877 and 1886. It has a lavish French Renaissance Revival exterior intended to reflect the unique cultural status of Québec in the North American context. Eugène-Étienne Taché (1836-1912) looked to the Louvre for inspiration in both the plan of the quadrangular building and its decor. Originally destined to incorporate the two houses of parliament characteristic of the British system of government, as well as all of the ministries, it is today part of a group of buildings on either side of Grande Allée.

The numerous statues of the parliament's main facade constitute a sort of pantheon of Québec. The 22 bronzes of important figures in the history of Québec were cast by such well-known artists as Louis-Philippe Hébert and Alfred Laliberté. A raised inscription on the wall near the central passage identifies the statues. In front of the main entrance a bronze by Hébert entitled *La Halte dans la Forêt* (The Pause in the Forest) depicts an Aboriginal family. The work, which is meant to honour the original inhabitants of Québec, was displayed at Paris's World's Fair in 1889. *Le Pêcheur à la Nigog* (Fisherman at the Nigog), by the same artist, hangs in the niche by the fountain.

The building's interior is a veritable compendium of the icons of Québec's history. The handsome woodwork is done in the tradition of religious architecture.

The members of parliament, called *députés*, sit in the National Assembly, or Salon Bleu (Blue Chamber), where

*La Halte dans la Forêt* by Louis-Philippe Hébert

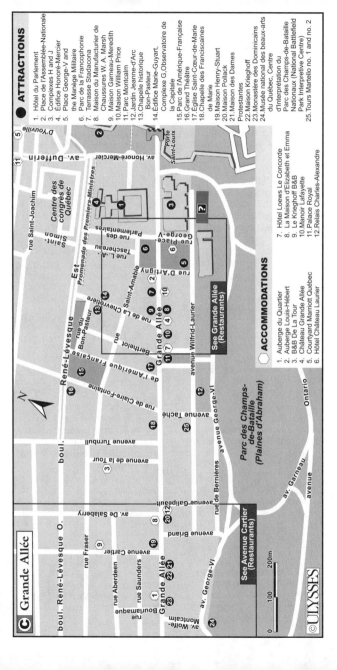

## C Grande Allée

**● ATTRACTIONS**

1. Hôtel du Parlement
2. Place de l'Assemblée-Nationale
3. Complexes H and J
4. Édifice Honoré-Mercier
5. Place George-V and the Manège Militaire
6. Parc de la Francophonie
7. Terrasse Stadacona
8. Maison du Manufacturier de Chaussures W. A. Marsh
9. Maison Garneau-Meredith
10. Maison William Price
11. Parc Montcalm
12. Jardin Jeanne-d'Arc
13. Chapelle historique Bon-Pasteur
14. Édifice Marie-Guyart, Complexe G, Observatoire de la Capitale
15. Parc de l'Amérique-Française
16. Grand Théâtre
17. Église Saint-Cœur-de-Marie
18. Chapelle des Franciscaines de Marie
19. Maison Henry-Stuart
20. Maison Pollack
21. Maison des Dames Protestantes
22. Maison Krieghoff
23. Monastère des Dominicains
24. Musée national des beaux-arts du Québec, Centre d'Interprétation du Parc des Champs-de-Bataille Nationaux (National Battlefield Park Interpretive Centre)
25. Tours Martello no. 1 and no. 2

**◆ ACCOMMODATIONS**

1. Auberge du Quartier
2. Auberge Louis-Hébert
3. B&B De La Tour
4. Château Grande Allée
5. Courtyard Marriott Québec
6. Hôtel Château Laurier
7. Hôtel Loews Le Concorde
8. La Maison d'Elizabeth et Emma
9. Le Krieghoff B&B
10. Manoir Lafayette
11. Palace Royal
12. Relais Charles-Alexandre

© ULYSSES

Charles Huot's painting, *La Première Séance de l'Assemblée Législative du Bas-Canada en 1792* (The First Session of the Legislative Assembly of Lower Canada in 1792), hangs over the chair of the president of the Assembly. A large work by the same artist covers the ceiling and evokes the motto of Québec, *Je me souviens* (I remember). The Salon Rouge (Red Chamber), intended for the Conseil Législatif, an unelected body that was eliminated in 1968, is now used for parliamentary commissions. A painting entitled *Le Conseil Souverain* (The Sovereign Council), a reminder of the style of government in the days of New France, graces this chamber.

Several of the windows of the parliament building boast gorgeous Art Nouveau stained glass by master glazier Henri Perdriau, a native of Saint-Pierre de Montélimar in Vendée, France. Undeniably, the most spectacular is the one that adorns the entrance to the elegant **Le Parlementaire** (see p 212) restaurant. This feature was designed by architect Omer Marchand in 1917. National Assembly debates are open to the public, but a pass is required.

In the Parc de l'Hôtel du Parlement, there are three important monuments: one in honour of Honoré Mercier, Premier of Québec from 1887 to 1891; another in honour of Maurice Duplessis, Premier during the *grande noirceur*, or

"great darkness," (1936-1939 and 1944-1959), as well as the one representing René Lévesque, who holds a special place in the hearts of the Québécois and was the Premier from 1976 to 1985. Also, the **Promenade des Premiers-Ministres** presents panels listing the Premiers that have led Québec since 1867.

In front of the Assemblée Nationale you'll notice the beautiful **Place de l'Assemblée-Nationale**, divided in two by handsome Avenue Honoré-Mercier. On the wall's side, many events are hosted throughout the year. In July, a stage is erected for the Summer Festival and in February, the Ice Palace, the focus of carnival festivities, is located here.

The dizzying growth of the civil service during the Quiet Revolution of the 1960s compelled the government to construct several modern buildings to house its various ministries. A row of beautiful Second Empire houses was demolished to make way for **Complexes H and J** *(on Grande Allée opposite the Hôtel du Parlement)*. Dubbed "the bunker" by the Québécois, Pierre Saint-Gelais's 1970 building used to house the Premier's office.

Since the spring of 2002, the offices of the Conseil Exécutif and the Premier's cabinet have been located in the beautiful **Édifice Honoré-Mercier** *(835 Boulevard René-Lévesque Est)*, on the north side of the Hôtel du Parlement. In fact, this is actually a homecoming since the building housed the Premier's offices up until 1972. Before the move, the building was entirely renovated but the beauty of its architecture was preserved including its marble features, plaster mouldings and woodwork. It was built between 1922 and 1925 according to the designs of architect Chênevert.

*Take Grande Allée westward, leaving Vieux-Québec. On the left you will come to Rue Place-George-V, which runs along the square of the same name. Take this street to Avenue Wilfrid-Laurier.*

**Place George-V** and the **Manège Militaire ★** *(Avenue Wilfrid-Laurier)*, an expanse of lawn, is used as the training area and parade ground of the military's equestrians. There are cannons and a statue in memory of the two soldiers who perished attempting to douse the flames of the 1889 fire in the suburb of Saint-Sauveur. Otherwise, the grounds serve mainly to highlight the amusing Château-style facade of the Manège Militaire, (military riding academy) built in 1888 and designed by Eugène-Étienne Taché, who also designed the Hôtel du Parlement.

The Centre d'Interprétation du Parc des Champs-de-Bataille is on Avenue Wilfrid-Laurier behind the H and J Buildings, which border the Plains of Abraham. Housed in one of the Citadelle buildings, the **Maison de la Découverte ★** *(free admission; late Jun to mid-Oct 8:30am to 5:30pm; mid-Oct to late Jun 8:30 to 5pm; 835 Avenue Wilfrid-Laurier, ☎648-4071)* should please Québec City natives as much as visitors. Upstairs, at the Office du Tourisme de la région de Québec, travellers can get help finding their way around. And on the ground floor, questions are answered about the Parc des Champs-de-Bataille, its history and the many activities that go on here. There are also a few services and an entrance to the Plains of Abraham. Various guided tours leave from here. One of them takes place on board the "Bus d'Abraham," guided by Abraham Martin himself!

*Go back towards Grande Allée.*

**Parc de la Francophonie** *(between Rue Saint-Augustin and Rue d'Artigny)* and **Complexe G**, which appears in the background, both occupy the site of the old Saint-Louis quarter, today almost entirely vanished. Parc de la Francophonie was laid out for open-air shows. It also takes the name Le Pigeonnier (dovecote), from the interesting concrete structure at its centre, based on an idea by landscape architects Schreiber and Williams, in 1973.

*Continue west on Grande Allée, along its liveliest section.*

A little further to the west, the fabric of the old city is again in

Exploring

evidence. **Terrasse Stadacona** *(numbers 640 to 664)*, on the right, is a neoclassical row of English-style townhouses: the multiple houses share a common facade. These houses date from 1847 and have been converted into bars and restaurants with terraces sheltered by multitudes of parasols. Opposite *(numbers 661 to 695)* is a group of Second Empire houses that dates from 1882, a period when Grande Allée was the most fashionable street in Québec City. These houses show the influence of the parliamentary buildings on the residential architecture of the area. Three other houses on Grande Allée are worth mentioning for the eclecticism of their facades: **Maison du Manufacturier de Chaussures W. A. Marsh** *(number 625)*, the house of a prominent shoe manufacturer, was designed in 1899 by Toronto architect Charles John Gibson; **Maison Garneau-Meredith** *(numbers 600 to 614)* from the same year; and **Maison William Price** *(number 575)*, a little Romeo-and-Juliet-style house which is, unfortunately, dwarfed by the **Hôtel Loews Le Concorde** (see p 183). The revolving restaurant (see p 217) of this hotel affords a magnificent view of Haute-Ville and the Plains of Abraham.

In little **Parc Montcalm**, next to the hotel, is a statue commemorating the general's death on September 13, 1759, at the Battle of the Plains of Abraham. The **statue of French General Charles de Gaulle** (1890-1970), which faces away from Montcalm, created quite a controversy when it was erected in the spring of 1997. Farther along, at the entrance to the Plains of Abraham, **Jardin Jeanne-d'Arc ★★** boasts magnificent flowerbeds and a statue of Joan of Arc astride a spirited charger. Note that you are now standing on a huge drinking-water reservoir located under this part of the Plains of Abraham!

*Return to Grande Allée and go east, then turn left on Rue de La Chevrotière.*

Behind the austere facade of the mother house of the Soeurs du Bon-Pasteur, a community devoted to the education of abandoned and delinquent girls, is the charming, Baroque Revival-style **Chapelle historique Bon-Pasteur ★★** *(free admission; Mon-Fri 1pm to 5pm; 1080 Rue de La Chevrotière, ☎522-6221).* Designed by Charles Baillargé in 1866, this tall, narrow chapel houses an authentic baroque tabernacle dating from 1730. Pierre-Noël Levasseur's masterpiece of New France carving is surrounded by devotional miniatures hung on pilasters by the nuns.

Atop the 31 storeys of **Édifice Marie-Guyart** in Complexe G, the **Observatoire de la Capitale** *($5; late Jun to mid-Oct every day 10am to 7pm, mid-Oct to late Jun Tue-Sun 10am to 5pm; 1037 Rue de La Chevrotière,*

☎*644-9841)*, provides a splendid view of Québec City and its surrounding area. At 221m in altitude, it is the highest observation point in the city. For an even better view, use the telescopes.

*Go back and turn right on Rue Saint-Amable. Walk as far as the Parc de l'Amérique Française.*

The **Parc de l'Amérique-Française** is centered around a collection of flags of the various francophone communities of America.

The **Grand Théâtre** *(269 Boulevard René-Lévesque Est,* ☎*643-8131)* is located at the far end of the park. Inaugurated in 1971, this theatre designed by Polish architect Victor Prus was to be a meeting place for the members of Québec City's high society. There was quite a scandal, therefore, when Jordi Bonet's mural was unveiled and the assembled crowd read the lines from a poem by Claude Péloquin: *"Vous êtes pas tannés de mourir, bande de caves"* (Aren't you idiots tired of dying?). The theatre has two halls (Louis-Fréchette and Octave-Crémazie) and presents symphony orchestra concerts as well as theatre, dance and variety shows.

*Go back as far as Rue Scott where you turn right to return to Grande Allée.*

**Église Saint-Cœur-de-Marie** *(530 Grande Allée Est)* was built for the Eudists in 1919 and de-

signed by Ludger Robitaille. It looks more martial than devotional with its bartizans, machicolations and towers. Its large archways are reminiscent of a Mediterranean fortress. Across the road is the most outlandish row of Second Empire houses still standing in Québec City *(455-555 Grande Allée Est)*, the **Terrasse Frontenac**. The product of Joseph-Ferdinand Peachy's imagination (1895), its slender, fantastical peaks look like something from a fairy tale.

The **Chapelle des Franciscaines de Marie** ★ is the chapel of a community of nuns. They commissioned the Sanctuaire de l'Adoration Perpétuelle (Sanctuary of Perpetual Adoration) in 1901. This exuberant Baroque Revival chapel invites the faithful to prayer and celebrates the everlasting presence of God. It features a small columned cupola supported by angels and a sumptuous marble canopy.

Several handsome bourgeois houses dating from the early 20th century face the chapel. Among them, at numbers 433-435, is the residence of John Holt, the proprietor of the Holt Renfrew stores. Both this and the neighbouring house at number 425 are designed like Scottish manors. Undeniably the most elegant, in its mild Flemish and Oriental eclecticism, is the house of Judge P. A. Choquette, designed by architect Georges-Émile Tanguay.

*Continue in the same direction.*

Exploring

*Maison Henry-Stuart*

**Maison Henry-Stuart** *($5; late Jun to early Sep every day 11am to 5pm; 82 Grande Allée Ouest, ☎647-4347 or 800-494-4347)*, on the corner of Cartier and Grande Allée, is one of the few remaining Regency-style Anglo-Norman cottages in Québec City. This type of colonial British architecture is distinguished by a large pavilion roof overhanging a low veranda surrounding the building. The house was built in 1849 and used to mark the border between the city and the country; its original garden still surrounds it. The interior features several pieces of furniture from the Saint-Jean-Port-Joli manor and has been practically untouched since 1911. More or less closed to the public for a number of years, Maison Henry-Stuart and its garden, which belongs to the organisation "Jardins du Québec," now welcome visitors. The house is home to the Conseil des Monuments et Sites de Québec. Tea is served here on summer afternoons.

**Avenue Cartier** is one of the most attractive shopping streets in town. The main artery in the Montcalm residential neighbourhood, it is lined with restaurants (see p 211), shops and specialty food stores that attract the yuppie clientele strolling around here.

In the area of the American-style **Maison Pollack** *(1 Grande Allée Ouest)* is the Renaissance Revival **Maison des Dames Protestantes** *(111 Grande Allée Ouest)*, built in 1862 by architect Michel Lecourt. Also nearby is **Maison Krieghoff** *(115 Grande-Allée Ouest)*, which was occupied in 1859 by the Dutch painter Cornelius Krieghoff.

The **Monastère des Dominicains** ★ *(175 Grande Allée Ouest, closed to the public)* and its church are relatively recent testimonials to the persistence and historical exactitude of 20th century Gothic Revival architecture. This sober British-style building promotes reverence and meditation.

*Turn left on Avenue Wolfe-Montcalm to the entrance to both Parc des Champs-de-Bataille and the Musée national des beaux-arts du Québec.*

Located at the roundabout is the **Monument to General Wolfe**, victor of the decisive Battle of the Plains of Abraham. It is said to stand on the exact spot where he fell. The 1832 monument has been the object of countless demonstrations and acts of vandalism. Toppled again in 1963, it was rebuilt, this time with an inscription in French.

The **Musée national des beaux-arts du Québec ★ ★ ★** *($10, free admission to the permanent collection; early Jun to early Sep every day 10am to 6pm, Wed to 9pm; early Sep to late May Tue-Sun 11am to 5pm, Wed to 9pm; Parc des Champs de Bataille, ☎644-6460 or 866-220-2150, www.mnba.qc.ca)* was renovated and expanded in 1992. The older, west-facing 1933 Classical Revival building is on the right. The entrance, parallel to Avenue Wolfe-Montcalm, is dominated by a glass tower similar to that of the Musée de la Civilisation. The first building is subterraneously linked with the old prison on the left. The latter has been cleverly restored to house exhibits and has been rebaptized "Édifice Ballargé" in honour of its architect. Some of the cells have been preserved.

*Musée national des beaux-arts du Québec*

# Jean-Paul Riopelle

Jean-Paul Riopelle was one of Québec's most renowned painters, and its best-known internationally. Many of the impressive number of paintings he created are exhibited throughout the world. This legendary character, an abstract painter famous for his huge mosaics, left his mark on the world of contemporary art. He was born in Montréal in 1932, and his career took off with the Automatism movement in the 1940s. He was also a co-signatory of the Refus Global artistic manifesto. He lived in Paris for several years but returned to the province of Québec during the last years of his life. He died on March 12, 2002, in his manor on Île aux Grues, on the St. Lawrence River, on the migration path of the snow geese he held so dear to his heart.

A visit to this important museum allows one to become acquainted with the painting, sculpture and silverwork of Québec from the time of New France to today. In 2000, the museum inaugurated a gallery (Salle 3) in honour of painter Jean-Paul Riopelle, who died in 2002, in which his huge mural (42m) *Hommage à Rosa Luxembourg* is displayed. The collections of religious art gathered from Québec's rural parishes are particularly interesting. Also on display are official documents, including the original surrender of Québec (1759). The museum frequently hosts temporary exhibits from the United States and Europe. Many cultural activities are held here, such as conferences, films and concerts.

On the first floor of the museum's Édifice Baillargé is the **Centre d'Interprétation du Parc des Champs-de-Bataille Nationaux (National Battlefield Park Interpretive Centre)** *($5; mid-May to mid-Oct every day 10am to 5:30pm, mid-Oct to mid-May Tue-Sun 10am to 5pm; Édifice Baillargé, level 1, ☎648-5641, www.ccbn-nbc.gc.ca)*, which exhibits a reconstruction of the Battle of the Plains of Abraham and a model of the subsequent development of the area through a multi-media show.

*Turn left on Avenue Georges-VI and right on Avenue Garneau.*

The **Parc des Champs-de-Bataille** ★★★ *(free admission; ☎648-4071)* takes visitors back to July 1759: commanded by General Wolfe, the British fleet arrives in front of Québec City. An attack is launched almost immediately. Almost 40,000 cannonballs crash down on the besieged city. As the summer draws to a close, the British must make a decision before they are surprised by French reinforcements or trapped in the December freeze. On the 13th of September, under cover of night, British troops scale the Cap Diamant escarpment west of the fortifications. The ravines which here and there cut into the otherwise uniform mass of the escarpment allow them to climb while remaining concealed. By morning, the troops have taken position in the fields of Abraham Martin, hence the name given to the park: **Plains of Abraham**. The French are surprised, as they had anticipated a direct attack on the citadel. Their troops, with the aid of a few hundred Aboriginal and (French-) Canadian warriors, throw themselves against the British. The generals of both sides are slain, and the battle draws to a close in bloody chaos. New France is lost!

Parc des Champs-de-Bataille, where the battle took place, was created in 1908 to commemorate the event. With its 101ha, the park is a superb recreational space. Previously occupied by a military training ground, the Ursulines and a few farms, the park was laid out between 1929 and 1939 by landscape architect Frederick Todd. This project provided work for thousands of Québécois during the Depression. Today, the plains are a large green space crisscrossed with paths that were used for all kinds of winter and summer activities. You will find beautiful landscaping here as well as historical and cultural sites such as the **Kiosque Edwin-Bélanger**, which presents outdoor entertainment. At the park's eastern entrance, the **Maison de la Découverte** (see p 101) presents a fine introduction to the Plains, as various exhibitions and activities interpret its history and natural environment.

The **Tours Martello no. 1 and no. 2** ★ (martello towers) are characteristic of British defenses at the beginning of the 19th century. Tower number 1 (1808) is visible from the edge of Avenue Ontario; number 2 (1815) blends into the surrounding buildings on the corner of Avenue Laurier and Avenue Taché. Inside the first tower, an exhibition recounts some of the military strategies used in the 19th century (*$4; late Jun to late Sep every day 10am to 5:30pm*). At Tour

Exploring

Martello no. 2, you can enjoy "Conseil de guerre" (war council) evenings, which consist of murder-mystery dinners. Reservations are required. Further north, on Rue de la Tourelle in the Saint-Jean-Baptiste district, a third tower is used as a site for various meetings and cultural events.

*This marks the end of the Grande Allée walking tour. To return to the walled city, follow Avenue Ontario east to Avenue Georges-VI or take Avenue du Cap-Diamant (in the hilly part of the park) to* **Promenade des Gouverneurs**. *The promenade follows the Citadelle and overlooks the Cap Diamant escarpment, winding up at Terrasse Dufferin. This route affords stunning views of the city, the St. Lawrence River and the south shore.*

# Tour D:
# Saint-Jean-Baptiste

*(two hours)*

A hangout for young people, complete with bars, cafés and boutiques, the Saint-Jean-Baptiste quarter is perched on a hillside between Haute-Ville and Basse-Ville. The abundance of pitched and mansard roofs is reminiscent of parts of the old city, but the orthogonal layout of the streets is quintessentially North American. Despite a terrible fire in 1845, this old

Québec City suburb retains several examples of wooden constructions, which were forbidden inside the city's walls.

*The Saint-Jean-Baptiste tour begins at Porte Saint-Jean, on Place d'Youville. It threads along Rue Saint-Jean, the neighbourhood's main artery.*

**Place d'Youville**, also called "carré d'Youville" (square), is the public space at the entrance of the old section of town. Formerly an important market square, today it is a bustling crossroads and cultural forum. Redevelopment has given the square a large promenade area with some trees and benches. The counterscarp wall, part of the fortifications that were removed in the 19th century, has been highlighted by the use of black granite blocks. In winter, part of the square is covered in ice, much to the delight of skaters who twirl around to the sound of cheerful tunes.

At the beginning of the 20th century, Québec City was in dire need of a new auditorium, its Académie de Musique having burnt to the ground in March 1900. With the help of private enterprise, the mayor undertook the search for a new location. The Canadian government, owner of the fortifications, offered to provide a strip of land along the walls of the city. Although narrow, the lot grew wider toward the back, permitting the construction of a

# D | Saint-Jean-Baptiste

## ATTRACTIONS
1. Place D'Youville
2. Capitole de Québec
3. Palais Montcalm
4. Centre des Congrès de Québec
5. Church and Cemetery of Saint Matthew
6. Épicerie J.-A.-Moisan
7. Choco-Musée Érico
8. Église Saint-Jean-Baptiste

## ACCOMMODATIONS
1. Chez Pierre
2. Delta Québec
3. Hilton Québec
4. Hôtel du Capitole

## RESTAURANTS
1. Carthage
2. Chez Victor
3. Ciccio Café
4. Il Teatro
5. La Campagne
6. La Grolla
7. La Piazzetta
8. La Pointe des Amériques
9. Le Beffroi
10. Le Bonnet d'Âne
11. Le Commensal
12. Le Hobbit
13. Les Épices du Széchouan
14. Que Sera Sera
15. Thang Long

© ULYSSES

suitable hall, the **Capitole de Québec** ★ *(972 Rue Saint-Jean, www.lecapitole.com)*. W. S. Painter, the ingenious Detroit architect who was already at work on the expansion of the Château Frontenac, devised a plan for a curved facade, giving the building a monumental air despite the limited size of the lot. Inaugurated in 1903 as the Auditorium de Québec, the building is one of the most impressive *beaux-arts* realizations in the country.

In 1927, the famous American cinema architect Thomas W. Lamb converted the auditorium into a sumptuous 1,700-seat cinema. Renamed the Théâtre Capitole, the auditorium nevertheless served as a venue for shows until the construction of the Grand Théâtre in 1971. Abandoned for a few years, the Capitole was entirely refurbished in 1992 by architect Denis Saint-Louis. The building now houses a dinner-theatre in its hall, a luxury hotel (see p 184) and a restaurant (see p 220) in the curved facade. The Capitole has recently acquired the adjoining cinema, on front of which is an imposing round sign. The cinema has been converted into a nightclub.

The Montcalm Market was levelled in 1932 to build the

*Capitole de Québec*

multifunctional space called the **Palais Montcalm** *(995 Place d'Youville)*. Also known as the Monument National, this is the venue of choice for political rallies and demonstrations of all kinds. The auditorium has a sparse architecture which draws on both the neoclassical and Art Deco schools. Today, visitors come here to see concerts or exhibitions.

The **Chapelle du Couvent des Soeurs de la Charité** (1856) is visible on leaving Place d'Youville. Its delicate Gothic Revival facade is dwarfed by two huge towers.

*Cross Avenue Dufferin, which was recently restored. Higher up, at the corner of Rue Saint-Joachim, is a large network of buildings that includes the Centre des Congrès, the Place Québec shopping centre and the Hilton and Radisson Gouverneur hotels.*

The **Centre des Congrès de Québec** *(1000 Boulevard René-Lévesque Est, ☎644-4000 or 888-679-4000, www.convention. qc.ca)* was inaugurated in 1996 and is situated north of the Hôtel du Parlement. This large modern building features glass walls   zthat let the daylight stream in. It includes an exhibition hall, several conference rooms and even a ballroom, and is connected to the Place Québec shopping centre and the **Hilton** and **Delta Québec** hotels (see p 184). Its creation has revived this previously dreary part of Boulevard René-Lévesque.

Between the Hilton Québec hotel and the Centre des Congrès is the **Promenade Desjardins**, which recalls the life and work of Alphonse Desjardins, the founder of the Caisses Populaires Desjardins credit union. At the end of the promenade is a great view of the city and the faraway mountains. At the entrance to the Centre des Congrès is the lively sculpture *Le Quatuor d'Airain*, the work of Lucienne Payan-Cornet.

*From Rue Saint-Joachim, take Rue Saint-Augustin, which will lead you to Rue Saint-Jean, where you will turn left.*

There has been a cemetery on the site of the **Church and Cemetery of Saint Matthew ★** *(755 Rue Saint-Jean)* since 1771, when Protestants, whether French Huguenot, English Anglican or Scottish Presbyterian, banded together to found a Protestant graveyard. Several 19th-century tombstones are still standing. The gravestones were carefully restored recently, and the cemetery is now a public garden.

Located in the cemetery along Rue Saint-Jean is a lovely Anglican church. Its Gothic Revival architecture was influenced by the Ecclesiologists, an influential school of Anglican thought that sought to re-establish ties with the traditions of the Middle Ages. In its design, and even in its materials, it looks more like an ancient

**Exploring**

village church than a Victorian church with a Gothic decor. The nave was first erected in 1848; then, in 1870, William Tutin Thomas, the Montréal architect who designed the Canadian Centre for Architecture's Shaughnessy House, drafted an enlargement, giving the church its present bell tower and interior. Québec's Anglican community dwindled in the 20th century, leading to the abandonment of the church. In 1980, it was cleverly converted into a branch of the municipal library. Several of the adornments crafted by British artists have been retained: Percy Bacon's handsome oak choir enclosure, Felix Morgan's alabaster pulpit, and Clutterbuck's beautiful stained glass. The sober vault with its exposed beams is also noteworthy.

*Continue along Rue Saint-Jean.*

At number 699, **Épicerie J.-A.-Moisan** *(699 Rue St-Jean)* was founded in 1871 and claims to be the "oldest grocery store in North America." It does in fact look like a general store from yesteryear, with its wooden floor and shelves, old advertisements and many tin cans.

The owner of the Érico chocolate shop, a favourite among "chocoholics," had the great idea of adding a small chocolate museum to his shop. If this interests you, stop by the **Choco-Musée Érico** *(free admission; 634 Rue Saint-Jean, ☎524-2122, www.chocomusee.com)* to learn how the Mayans used cocoa, find out how this fruit grows, discover different recipes and more. Thanks to a window on the kitchen, you can even observe chocolate "artists" at work. Don't forget to sample!

The **Église Saint-Jean-Baptiste ★** *(410 Rue Saint-Jean)* stands out as Joseph Ferdinand Peachy's masterpiece. A disciple of French eclecticism, Peachy was a wholehearted admirer of the Église de la Trinité in Paris. The resemblance here is striking, as much in the portico as in the interior. Completed in 1885, the building caused the bankruptcy of its architect, who was, unfortunately for him, held responsible for cracks that appeared in the facade during construction. In front of the church is an attractive little square.

For a beautiful view of the city, take the Rue Claire-Fontaine stairs up to the corner of Rue Lockwell, on the right. The climb is steep but the view is worth the effort, especially in the evening when the Basse-Ville lights dance at your feet behind the imposing church. When strolling through this neighbourhood's attractive streets, you will have many opportunities to catch a glimpse of this great view. For example, you can go down Rue Sainte-Claire to the stairs leading to the Saint-Roch neighbourhood, which you will be able to see with the Laurentian mountains in the background.

## Tour E: Chemin Sainte-Foy

*(half a day)*

At the end of the 18th century, the Haute-Ville walls could no longer contain the expanding city. Suburbs were created around Saint-Jean-Baptiste church and Grande Allée. There was, however, an area that retained its pastoral charm up until the beginning of the 20th century: the farmland along an old country road, Chemin Sainte-Foy, leading to the village of the same name. Since 1950, **Sainte-Foy** has become Québec City's largest suburb. Sainte-Foy, like the other suburbs of Québec City, merged on January 1, 2002 to form the new mega-city of Québec. Because of its large shopping centres and exclusively low-rise housing, Sainte-Foy was mainly known as a dormitory suburb. But over the past few years, it has attempted to shed that reputation by creating civic and cultural facilities that would be the envy of more than one Québec town. Long described as a "progressive" city, it has conserved little of its past. This tour travels first through the Montcalm and Saint-Sacrement neighbourhoods, where a relatively well-to-do population lives on shaded streets that at times recall the outskirts of London.

The tour then takes you to the modern campus of Université Laval.

*The tour starts on Chemin Sainte-Foy at the corner of Avenue Cartier and heads west. Turn right on Avenue de l'Alverne.*

The **Former Franciscan Monastery** *(on the northeast corner of Avenue de l'Alverne and Rue des Franciscains)*, today converted into a housing complex, was built in 1901 and was designed around a cloister inspired by the French Regime's monastery style. It is a remnant of one of several religious communities that settled along Chemin Sainte-Foy at the beginning of the 20th century. At that time, great stretches of land, far from the noise of the city, could be bought for a song.

*Turn left on Rue des Franciscains, then left again on Avenue Désy. Turn right on Chemin Sainte-Foy, heading west.*

The land along Chemin Sainte-Foy was granted to notable people and Québec religious communities in the early part of the 17th century, but, shortly after the Conquest, a number of these huge properties were handed over to British dignitaries. Following the example of the domains in **Sillery** (see p 134), several of them would be turned into country gardens with villas. These domains were divided up in the 20th century and residential developments

Exploring

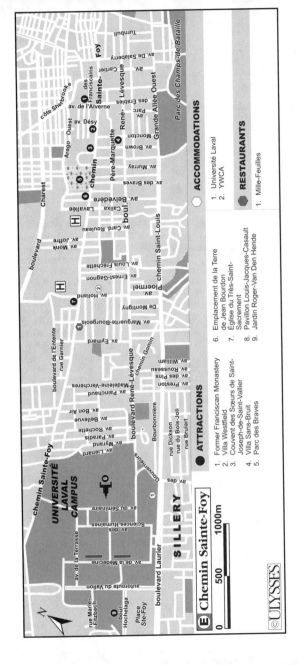

# E Chemin Sainte-Foy

0    500    1000m

N

© ULYSSES

**ATTRACTIONS**

1. Former Franciscan Monastery
2. Villa Westfield
3. Couvent des Sœurs de Saint-Joseph-de-Saint-Vallier
4. Villa Sans-Bruit
5. Parc des Braves

6. Emplacement de la Terre de Jean Bourdon
7. Église du Très-Saint-Sacrement
8. Pavillon Louis-Jacques-Casault
9. Jardin Roger-Van Den Hende

**ACCOMMODATIONS**

1. Université Laval
2. YWCA

**RESTAURANTS**

1. Mille-Feuilles

and institutional buildings replaced most of the villas. However, a few of these residences have survived. Such is the case of the **Villa Westfield** *(private, no visiting; 430 Chemin Sainte-Foy)*, built around 1825 for Charles Grey Stewart, a Lower Canada customs inspector. Its monumental-English-style architecture features neoclassical ornamentation. It was once surrounded by a magnificent English garden.

A little further west is the **Couvent des Sœurs de Saint-Joseph-de-Saint-Vallier** *(560 Chemin Sainte-Foy)*, which was formerly the residence of Andrew Thompson, at which time it was called "Bijou." The house, which forms the central part of the convent, was build in 1874 in the Second Empire style and can be recognized by its mansard roof and curved segmental openings. The wings added by the religious order fit admirably well with the architecture of the house. In 1927, a neo-Romanesque chapel was built in the eastern part of the convent.

*Turn left on Avenue Brown.*

Here you can see the **Villa Sans-Bruit** *(874 Avenue Brown)*, constructed around 1850. The mansard roof was added in 1880 at the time when the house belonged to the Laurie family. Until recently, this area of the Haute-Ville was considered the bastion of Québec City's small anglophone community.

*Head south on Avenue Brown. Turn right on Rue du Père-Marquette where you will find the **Église des Saints-Martyrs-Canadiens** (1929), then turn right again on Avenue des Braves.*

**Avenue des Braves** ★ is in line with the monument of the same name (see below). When the avenue was planned in 1912, it was to be Québec City's most prestigious residential street. Today, you can still see a few opulent stone and brick houses from the 1920s and 1930s. They were built for Québec City's bourgeoisie who at the time were leaving their staid homes in the old city for the more open spaces of the suburbs.

The beautiful residence at number 1080 belonged to Roger Lemelin, author of *Les Plouffe*, from 1953 to 1972. And briefly, between 1994 and 1996, it was the official residence of Québec's Premier at the time, Jacques Parizeau.

*Go back up Avenue des Braves to the monument at the corner of Chemin Sainte-Foy.*

On April 27, 1760, the Chevalier de Lévis arrived from Montréal leading 3,800 men and tried to capture Québec City, which had fallen to the British Army the previous autumn. Although they failed to enter the city, they succeeded in defeating General Murray's troops in Sainte-Foy, making this battle one of the only

Exploring

French victories of the Seven Years' War in New France. **Parc des Braves** ★ was created on the exact site of the battle. Weapons have been found here as well as skeletons of soldiers killed in action. Its name pays tribute to the courage of these valiant young men who made this rash move while waiting for help from a fleet of French reinforcements that would never arrive. In 1855, a **monument** designed by Charles Baillairgé was erected in their memory in the park. The statue of Bellone, a roman war goddess standing atop a cast-iron column, was a gift from Prince Jérôme-Napoléon Bonaparte.

In 1930, landscape architect Frederick Todd redesigned Parc des Braves attracting, wealthy families from the old city to the park's surrounding area. The park has lovely views of Basse-Ville and the Laurentian mountains.

*Continue west on Chemin Sainte-Foy.*

At the corner of Chemin Sainte-Foy and Avenue Belvédère is the **Emplacement de la Terre de Jean Bourdon**. Bourdon was an engineer in New France during the first half of the 17th century and also owned the Pointe-aux-Trembles (Neuville) Seigneury. Around 1645, Bourdon had a farm built on this land, which he fortified with stone. The farm had a small and a large dwelling, a chapel, two barns and three storehouses. Unfortunately,

these buildings disappeared during the upheaval that followed the Conquest.

Large institutions such as the imposing Saint-Sacrement Hospital (number 1050) can also be found along Chemin Sainte-Foy.

**Église du Très-Saint-Sacrement** *(1330 Chemin Sainte-Foy)* is a late neo-Romanesque work from the 1920s by architects Charles Bernier of Montréal and Oscar Beaulé of Québec City. Influenced by late medieval architecture, they gave the church a slender, rather austere nave. However, the stained-glass windows by Marius Plamondon, installed in 1954, add a bit of colour. The noviciate of the Très-Saint-Sacrement is in the back.

*From here, take bus number 7 along Chemin Sainte-Foy to reach the university campus 2km further west. Get off at the corner of Avenue du Séminaire to reach the centre of campus.*

**Université Laval Campus** *(south of Chemin Sainte-Foy and west of Avenue Myrand)*. Université Laval was founded in 1852, making it the oldest French-speaking university in America. It was first established in the heart of the old city, near the seminary and Catholic cathedral before being moved to its current site 100 years later. The university was named in honour of Monseigneur de Laval, the first bishop of New France. Each year this vast campus welcomes some 40,000 students. It features good examples of modern and postmodern Québec architecture: one of the more interesting buildings is the **PEPS** (sports and physical education building), built in 1971, on the right, at the corner of Chemin Sainte-Foy and Avenue du Séminaire.

A little further to the left, **Pavillon Louis-Jacques-Casault** closes off the symmetrical perspective of the campus *(1210 Avenue du Séminaire).* This building was constructed from 1954-1958 according to the designs of Ernest Cormier, who also created the Université de Montréal's main building. In the beginning, Pavillon Louis-Jacques-Casault was to be the "Great Seminary" for priests in training, which explains the presence of a central chapel adorned with medieval-inspired towers. However, with the approach of the *Révolution Tranquille* (Quiet Revolution), such a building was considered a dinosaur, reflecting the architecture of the past despite its recent construction. Since 1980, it has housed the **Direction Générale des Archives Nationales du Québec** *(☎643-8904)* as well as the interesting **Centre Muséographique de l'Université Laval**.

This institution's collections are grouped according to four themes: the Universe, the Earth, Life and Man. The museum is now closed and its reopening date is not yet

known. The nearby **Pavillon Alexandre-de-Sève** and **La Laurentienne** are clearly more modern.

**Centre d'Accueil et de Renseignements de l'Université Laval (reception and information centre)** *(closed weekends, mid-Jun to mid-Aug 8:30am to noon, 1:30pm to 4pm, Fri 8:30am to noon, 1:30pm to 4pm; rest of the year 8am to 5pm; Pavillon Alphonse-Desjardins, room 1106, ☎656-3333).* Here, visitors can obtain information on campus activities. Finally, west of Avenue des Sciences-Humaines on Avenue de la Médecine is the **Musée de Géologie du Pavillon Adrien-Pouliot** *(free admission; every day 8:30am to 5pm; ☎656-2193),* exhibiting fossils and minerals from around the world.

*Cross the Vallon Highway to reach the Roger-Van den Hende Botanical Gardens.*

One of the most interesting gardens in Québec City is found on the university campus. **Jardin Roger-Van den Hende ★** *(free admission; early May to late Sep, every day 9am to 8pm; 2480 Boulevard Hochelaga, ☎656-3410)* is named after the Université Laval scientist who created it from scratch. Used for research and teaching, the garden is also open to visitors. The arboretum, herbacetum, rose garden and water garden are all worth a visit. Guided tours are also offered.

Exploring

*To return to the old part of Québec City, take Métrobus no. 800 or 801 in front of the **Maurice-Pollack** and **Alphonse-Desjardins** pavilions in the southern part of the campus, on the east side of the Vallon Highway. Note that nearly all the university buildings are connected by a series of long underground passageways that may be worth a visit for those interested in this kind of subterranean architecture.*

## Tour F: Saint-Roch

*(four hours)*

While Quebec City's wealthier classes lived on the promontory, the working class district lined both sides of Rivière Saint-Charles. There are no tourist attractions as such here, but the neighbourhood bustles with people going about their daily business. Saint-Roch, Saint-Sauveur and Limoilou are familiar names to the Québécois but unknown to visitors who seldom venture down to Basse-Ville. However, the Saint-Roch district, which lies at the foot of the northern cliff of Cap Diamant, has gone through a major revitalization process over the past few years. Overlooked by most travellers for a long time, this part of the city is slowly getting back on its feet, with several interesting businesses and shops now established here.

Originally settled by potters and tanners at the end of the French Regime, Saint-Roch slowly developed along Rue Saint-Vallier. Then, when the Napoleonic blockade forced Great Britain to rely on its colonies for its wood supply, huge shipyards were created on the banks of Rivière Saint-Charles. This attracted a large working-class population to Saint-Roch. A cholera epidemic in 1832 ravaged the area and almost a quarter of its inhabitants died. Floods then devastated it in both 1845 and 1866. The neighbourhood saw its largest industry disappear in a few years after France and Britain returned to normal relations and ships began using metal hulls (1860-1870).

This marked the beginning of a complete transformation that would make Saint-Roch one of the main industrial quarters in French Canada. A number of factories were created to produce goods for popular consumption (tobacco, shoes, clothing, furniture), in keeping with the tradition of 18th-century potters and tanners. Next to them, department stores such as Paquet, Pollack and the Syndicat de Québec all established themselves on Boulevard Charest, completing the district's commercial activities. Like the workers, factory and shop owners were French Canadians, a phenomenon that was rarely seen in Canada in those days.

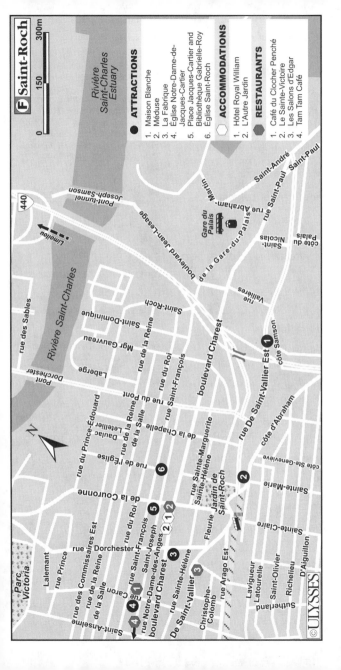

# F Saint-Roch

0   150   300m

● ATTRACTIONS

1. Maison Blanche
2. Méduse
3. La Fabrique
4. Église Notre-Dame-de-Jacques-Cartier
5. Place Jacques-Cartier and Bibliothèque Gabrielle-Roy
6. Église Saint-Roch

⬡ ACCOMMODATIONS

1. Hôtel Royal William
2. L'Autre Jardin

⬡ RESTAURANTS

1. Café du Clocher Penché
2. Le Sainte-Victoire
3. Les Salons d'Edgar
4. Tam Tam Café

© ULYSSES

However, in the early 20th century, the well-to-do who still lived here left Saint-Roch to settle in Haute-Ville, mainly on Grande Allée. Then, during the 1960s, commercial activity began to compete more and more with the suburbs and gradually declined; as a result, department stores and factories were forced to shut down and the neglected neighbourhood was all but forgotten for the next few decades.

In the mid-1990s, construction and revitalization projects began at a rather slow pace then took off at an unprecedented speed, completely transforming Saint-Roch. In 1992, the city launched a plan of action intended to give this former commercial centre a little of its old vitality, beginning with the creation of a lovely park on a site previously occupied by dilapidated buildings and weeds. The Jardin de Saint-Roch, an ideal place for a stroll, has caused residents and developers to regain an interest in the district. Several businesses (especially in the multimedia fjelds), schools such as the École des Arts Visuels de l'Université Laval and the École Nationale d'Administration Publique (ENAP), theatres and other cultural sites are now established in Saint-Roch. Today, the old neighbourhood is practically unrecognizable, making it a great place to explore.

*From Vieux-Québec, go down the Côte du Palais to leave the walled city, then turn left on Rue Saint-Vallier Est, which travels under the Dufferin-Montmorency Highway. This tour can easily be combined with the "Petit Champlain to Vieux-Port" tour, which ends at Rue De Saint-Vallier Est, as well as the nearby "Saint-Sauveur" and "Limoilou" tours.*

**Rue De Saint-Vallier Est** between Côte du Palais and Côte d'Abraham is a thoroughfare dating from the French Regime, located outside the boundaries of the historic quarter. It has been disfigured in many places, particularly by the construction of the Dufferin-Montmorency Highway ramps in 1970; nevertheless, it shows evidence of a very interesting past.

At number 870, you can see the ruins of the **Maison Blanche**, the secondary residence of Charles-Aubert de la Chesnaye, a wealthy merchant. The house was built in 1679 by architect Claude Baillif. In 1845, it was severely damaged by a fire and only half of it was salvaged. Today, only the arches and a few sections of wall remain from the original house.

A little further along are two cast-iron and wood staircases designed by Charles Baillairgé. One was constructed in 1883 and the other in 1889. Upon completion they connected the geographically and socially separate worlds of the city below and the city above. At number 715, a group of well-preserved buildings belongs to the Lépine-Cloutier Funeral Home, which has been in operation since 1845.

Wedged between Rue Saint-Vallier Est and Côte d'Abraham, **Méduse** *(541 Rue De Saint-Vallier Est, ☎640-9218, www. meduse.org)* houses various artists' associations that support and promote Québec culture. Encompassing restored houses and modern buildings that integrate the city's architecture, the complex is perched on the side of Cap Diamant, linking Haute-Ville and Basse-Ville. Associations in various fields such as photography, printmaking and video are installed here, as well as studios and galleries. Radio Basse-Ville, a community radio station, and L'Abraham-Martin bistro are also located on the premises. Running along the east side is a stairway which links Côte d'Abraham to Rue De Saint-Vallier Est.

At the foot of the stairway is **Îlot Fleuri**, a park where contemporary sculpture is exhibited, adding a bit of spice to this green space.

At the corner of Côte d'Abraham and Rue de la Couronne, you will find a rock garden with a waterfall known as the **Jardin de Saint-Roch**. The creation of this park seems to have launched the rejuvenation process of this neighbourhood. One could even say it marks the "entrance" to the neighbourhood.

*Cross Côte d'Abraham. At the opposite corner of the garden is the Édifice du Soleil, so named because it housed the headquarters of Québec City's major newspaper, Le Soleil, for many years.*

The section of Rue De Saint-Vallier Est between Rue Dorchester and Boulevard Charest is livelier now that a few friendly bars, restaurants and stores have sprung up.

*Turn right on Rue Dorchester.*

**La Fabrique** ★ *(295 Boulevard Charest Est at the corner of Rue Dorchester)* is located in the former Dominion Corset factory which, as its name indicates, was a manufacturer of corsets and brassieres. President Georges Amyot built this enormous factory between 1897 and 1911, creating jobs for the abundant workforce of young unmarried women. Because Amyot believed a married woman's place was in the home and not the factory, marriage ment immediate dismissal.

The former Dominion Corset factory was restored and renamed "La Fabrique" in 1993. It now houses an interpretation centre recounting Québec City's rich industrial past, the **Centre de développement urbain de Québec**, as well as the **École des arts visuels de l'Université Laval**. Take a look at the facade's complex brickwork, the clocktower and the water tower, elements that are reminiscent of American factory

**Exploring**

architecture of the end of the 19th century.

*Cross Boulevard Charest.*

**Boulevard Charest** was created in 1928 to relieve this neighbourhood's congested narrow streets, since the roads built between 1790 and 1840 were no longer able to handle commercial and industrial traffic. There are a few prominent buildings on Boulevard Charest which once were Québec City's department stores. Today they are all closed. At number 740 is the former Pollack store, dating from 1950. The back of the old Paquet store can still be found at the corner of Rue de l'Église, and at the corner of Rue de la Couronne, you can see the Syndicat de Québec, rebuilt in 1949 and shut down in 1981. The building was renovated and transformed into an office building in 2002.

*Head west on Boulevard Charest, to your left, and turn right on Rue Caron.*

**Église Notre-Dame-de-Jacques-Cartier** ★ *(corner of Rue Caron and Rue Saint-Joseph Est)* was originally the Saint-Roch Congregationalists' chapel. It was built in 1853 and expanded in 1875. In 1901, it brought together an entire parish. Its interior was richly decorated by Raphaël Giroux and includes lateral rood screens adorned with gold columns. At the back of the church is the stately embossed-stone presbytery constructed in 1902, but most noteworthy is its sloping steeple!

If you stroll around a bit, you'll see some of the **Saint-Roch workers' houses** ★, which are unique to Québec City's Basse-Ville. Compact and erected at the edge of the sidewalk, they are made of brownish brick or, occasionally, wood. They have sloping or mansard roofs and shuttered French windows. The architecture could be described as a kind of hybrid between North American working-class and French industrial-town architecture.

At the beginning of the 19th century, as Saint-Roch was rapidly developing, many wooden houses spring up, which were inspired by the French Regime's country houses. But the great fire of 1845 reduced the neighbourhood to ashes and changed the rules of the game. After the fire, brick or stone construction became mandatory and wood ornamentation was discouraged. These rules were softened at the end of the 19th century and several houses were then decorated with Victorian wood trim. But the face of Saint-Roch did not change significantly and has kept its quaint, old-time image to this day.

*Take Rue Saint-Joseph Est to the corner of Rue de la Couronne.*

This is the heart of Saint-Roch. In 1831, the creation of a marketplace was planned for this location but it was only in 1857 that two of its halls were actually built. One of them burned down in 1911 and the other was demolished around 1930 to create **Place Jacques-Cartier**. The statue of the famous explorer, which can be seen at the centre of the square, was a gift from the City of Saint-Malo, France.

At the far end, **Bibliothèque Gabrielle-Roy** *(Mon noon to 9pm, Tue-Fri 10:30am to 9pm, Sat-Sun noon to 5pm; 350 Rue Saint-Joseph Est, ☎529-0924)*, the municipal library, was named for one of French Canada's most famous writers. In her novels, this author describes the extreme poverty of people living in working-class neighbourhoods during the Depression. The library also offers special exhibition spaces to promote the work of contemporary artists.

The eastern section of **Rue Saint-Joseph** was once covered by a glass roof and was part of the Mail Centre-Ville, which is today limited to the eastern extremity of the street. Since the year 2000, the roof has been removed from a large part of the mall to transform it into a small-town shopping street, where cafés and shops make strolling a charming experience. You'll notice that this wind of revival has also affected the block that stretches west of the library, where a wide array of theatres, bookstores, inns and restaurants await you.

*Continue east on Rue Saint-Joseph by crossing Rue de la Couronne. You will soon see a church on your left.*

Surprisingly, none of the working-class neighbourhoods have kept their old churches. Fire and the rapidly-increasing population have meant that larger and more modern buildings have replaced the old churches. The first **Église Saint-Roch** ★ *(590 Rue Saint-Joseph Est)* was erected around 1811 and was replaced by two other buildings before the present church was built between 1916 and 1923 by architects Talbot and Dionne. It is an immense neo-Romanesque structure with two steeples and a rather austere interior; however, it features interesting stained-glass windows made by the Montréal firm Hobbs (around 1920). Stuck behind the Mail Centre-Ville, Église Saint-Roch was almost forgotten in the last few years. But the revitalization of Rue Saint-Joseph gave the church and its square a prime spot in the neighbourhood.

*Continue east on Rue Saint-Joseph.*

**Rue du Pont** was named as such when the first Pont Dorchester was inaugurated in 1789 at the north end of the street. The bridge crosses Rivière Saint-Charles and links Limoilou (see below) and the northern sector of Québec City, and has been rebuilt many times. You can still find remnants of the French Regime

Exploring

settlement east of Rue du Pont. This area, which reaches as far as the columns of the Dufferin-Montmorency Highway, is where the Récollet Fathers' Saint-Roch Hermitage was situated, giving its name to the area.

In 1692, after giving up their Saint-Sauveur monastery to Monseigneur de Saint-Vallier so that it could be turned into a hospital, the Récollets settled in the east where they built a hermitage (retreat) for their priests. The hermitage consisted of a large house with an adjoining chapel; both have since disappeared. Later, a small village was created and businesses were started, thus beginning to populate the area.

*Turn right on Rue du Pont to get to Boulevard Charest and go east on Boulevard Charest to return to Côte du Palais.*

## Tour G: Limoilou

*(half a day)*

As the winter of 1535 approached, Jacques Cartier, who was on his second exploration trip to Canada, had to find the proper spot to anchor his fleet before it was trapped by ice in the middle of the St. Lawrence River. He discovered a well-protected harbour in the bend of Rivière Saint-Charles and had a small log fort built. Towering

above it, a wooden cross with the coat of arms of François I was erected. And so, Limoilou became the first French settlement in Canada. However, after Jacques Cartier left, the fort disappeared. Today, the Cartier-Brébeuf National Historic Site marks the area.

In 1625, the territory was granted to the Jesuits. They created the Seigneurie de Notre-Dame-des-Anges here and had colonists settle and cultivate the land. It was only in the middle of the 19th century that Limoilou started to urbanize, taking advantage of the prosperity of Saint-Roch's shipyards on the other side of Rivière Saint-Charles.

Large estates began to appear, each with fields, warehouses, a working-class village and, on the outskirts, the owner's residence surrounded by a landscaped garden. However, little of this period now remains. It was only at the beginning of the 20th century that the present neighbourhood took shape and acquired its name. Limoilou refers to the Manoir de Limoilou near Saint-Malo, France, where Cartier retired after his numerous trips to New France.

*To get to Limoilou from Vieux-Québec, take bus no. 3 from Place d'Youville. It runs along Rue du Pont and then crosses Rivière Saint-Charles. Get off at the corner of 3e Rue, which you take on the right (going east).*

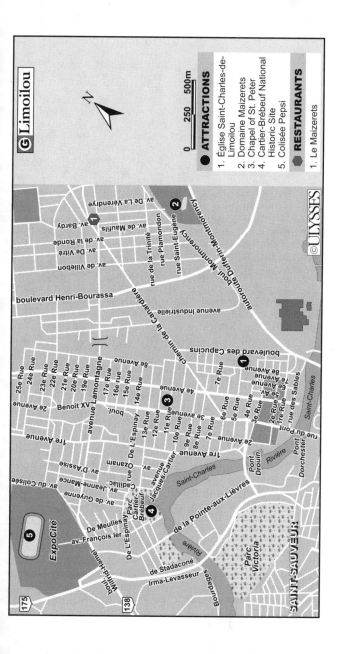

G Limoilou

ATTRACTIONS
1. Église Saint-Charles-de-Limoilou
2. Domaine Maizerets
3. Chapel of St. Peter
4. Cartier-Brébeuf National Historic Site
5. Colisée Pepsi

RESTAURANTS
1. Le Maizerets

© ULYSSES

Aboriginal Peoples called the river *Kabir Kouba*, meaning "river with many bends," and in 1535, Cartier renamed it "Rivière Sainte-Croix." The Récollets who settled on the southern banks in 1615 gave the river its present name, **Rivière Saint-Charles**, in honour of Pontoise priest Charles de Boves who had financed their establishment in New France. The river crosses the rich alluvial plane at the foot of Cap Diamant, going through the centre of Basse-Ville and isolating Limoilou from other working-class neighbourhoods. The river is made up of numerous loops that used to end in a swampy estuary, but now make up the Port de Québec and Bassin Louise.

During the Conquest of 1763, the Jesuits lost their right to teach in Canada. The last of them died in Québec City at the end of the 18th century, and the Notre-Dame-des-Anges seigneury was taken over by the King of England who redistributed the land. Around 1845, William Hedley Anderson created **Hedleyville** on his portion of land. It was the first Limoilou village to specialize in naval construction and the commerce of wood. Only a few of the buildings remain from the village, which was located between 1re and 3e Rues and between 4e and 7e Avenues. Number 699 3e Rue is the former **École d'Hedleyville** *(private, no visiting)*, constructed in 1863 to give the workers' children a

basic education. The school's architecture is not much different from the neighbourhood's wooden dwellings and was converted to housing quite a while ago.

Go to the end of 3e Rue, more precisely to the corner of Boulevard des Capucins, where you can admire, between the pillars of the Dufferin-Montmorency Highway, the view of the former **Anglo Canadian Paper Mills**, today the property of the Daishowa Company. This gigantic red-brick industrial complex looks like an impregnable stronghold and was erected in 1928 on the landfilled Rivière Saint-Charles estuary.

*Return to 8e Avenue and go north (turn right if you have gone as far as Boulevard des Capucins).*

Beautiful **Église Saint-Charles-de-Limoilou** ★ *(8e Avenue)* stands at the corner of 5e Rue, offering a pleasant perspective. The church and conventional buildings surrounding it were all erected on a strip of land that once belonged to Québec City's Hôtel-Dieu. Built with a typical neo-Romanesque facade (1917-1920), the nave of the Limoilou mother church has a double row of medieval-looking arches designed by architect Joseph-Pierre Ouellet. Its interior is representative of Québec City's parish churches which are generally narrower and taller than most churches in other Québec regions. In this manner, the influence of the

Notre-Dame de Québec Cathedral, a tall, narrow Baroque work from the mid-18th century, seems to have been felt locally right up until the Second World War.

Along 5e Rue are several of Limoilou's civic buildings, such as the beautiful Beaux-Arts fire station constructed in 1910 by the city of Québec. The city had annexed the formerly autonomous Limoilou municipality the previous year, making it part of Québec City.

*An option here is to explore the eastern part of Limoilou as far as Domaine Maizerets. Plan a good 30min walk to get there. Continue on 8e Avenue as far as Chemin de la Canardière and turn right. Turn right again on Avenue de la Vérendrye and go as far as Boulevard Montmorency.*

On **Domaine Maizerets** ★ *(free admission; every day 9am to 9pm; 2000 Boulevard Montmorency, ☎641-6335)* is the Maizerets house, one of the former summer residences of

the Séminaire de Québec. The first house was built in 1697 and has been expanded three times since. It was first known as the Domaine de la Canardière because of the innumerable ducks (*canards*) that nested on the nearby sandbars. The house was then given the name «Domaine de Maizerets» as a way of paying homage to Louis Ango de Maizerets, the Québec City seminary's superior at the time. The house, its farm and its park are a rare group of rural developments dating back to the 18th century in the Québec City region that are still intact. Its gardens, part of the Association des Jardins du Québec, are a pleasant spot to relax.

*To follow the main tour, go back to 8e Avenue and then turn left on 12e Rue where you will see the Chapel of St. Peter.*

The **Chapel of St. Peter** *(corner of 12e Rue and 3e Avenue)* bears witness to the Anglo-Saxon Anglican presence in

**Exploring**

Limoilou during the 1920s and 1930s. Most worshippers were managerial staff or owners of the nearby factories, and the Anglican bishop had this chapel built especially for them. However, their numbers were never sufficient enough to justify transforming the chapel into a large church.

The streets around the chapel are good examples of the **architecture of Limoilou houses**; their resemblance to those in Montréal is not accidental. In fact, Limoilou saw itself as a "modern" town—later a neighbourhood—modelling itself after other North American towns at the beginning of the 20th century. Developers from Montréal as well as the United States sold lots requiring Montréal-style constructions such as flat roofs, multi-level balconies, exterior metal staircases, parapets, alleyways and sheds. Even the shaded streets and avenues were given numbers instead of names, in all-American fashion.

*Continue along 12e Rue to 1re Avenue where you turn right and then left onto 13e Rue, which runs into Rue Cadillac and Rue de l'Espinay. This is the main entrance to the Cartier-Brébeuf National Historic Site.*

**Cartier-Brébeuf National Historic Site ★** *(free admission to the park, open year round; exhibit: $3.50, early May to early Sep every day 10am to 5pm, Sep every day 1pm to 4pm; 175 Rue de l'Espinay, ☎648-4038 or 800-463-6769)* is located near the spot where Jacques Cartier and his crew spent the winter of 1535-1536. The difficult conditions of this forced winter stay resulting in the death of 25 sailors are explained at the reception and interpretation centre. A scale model of Cartier's fort is also displayed there. One must remember that Cartier's plan was not to establish a colony on Canadian soil but rather to make more lucrative discoveries, such as a passage to China or minerals as precious as the gold of the Spanish colonies.

This historic site is a pleasant green space spread out around an inlet of Rivière Saint-Charles. Bike paths cross it, leading to the Vieux-Port and the Montmorency Falls. There was a time when this was the mouth of Rivière Lairet, but today it has been filled in. You can see a reconstructed **Iroquois Long House** showing Aboriginal living arrangements in the St. Lawrence Valley at the time of the first explorers. But Cartier is not the only person whose memory is honoured at this historic site. Saint Jean de Brébeuf (1593-1649), a Jesuit missionary martyred by the Iroquois, arrived here in 1625 to establish the Notre-Dame-des-Anges seigneury. A monument commemorating both men was inaugurated in 1889. The Cartier-Brébeuf National Historic Site has a pleasant walkway that runs along the meandering Rivère Saint-Charles to the south.

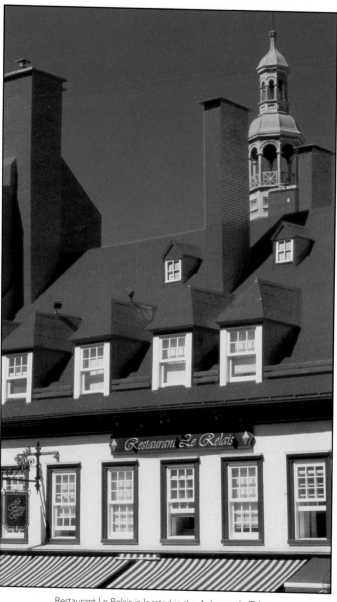

Restaurant Le Relais is located in the Auberge du Trésor,
the oldest inn in North America. - *Patrick Escudero*

The Promenade des Gouverneurs offers a stunning view of the St. Lawrence River.
- *Patrick Escudero*

Period buildings in Vieux-Québec. Note the typical small-paned windows.
- *Patrick Escudero*

*You can take Avenue Jeanne-Mance to get to Expocité. However, it is a good distance on foot and you must pass by a rather uninteresting area to get there. This excursion is particularly worthwhile if there are special events going on at the Centre de Foire (fairgrounds) during your visit. To return, take bus no. 12 going east to the corner of 1re Rue and Avenue Lamontagne (18e Rue), then transfer to bus no. 801 for Vieux-Québec.*

The **Colisée Pepsi** (formerly called the Colisée de Québec) is an indoor skating rink where the home-team favourites, the Québec Nordiques, used to play hockey. The Colisée was built in 1950 by an architect of Swiss origin, Robert Blatter, who is also responsible for several attractive international-style houses in Sillery. However, the Colisée's expansion and renovation during the 1970s was not a great success.

The Colisée is located at the centre of what is called **ExpoCité** *(250 Boulevard Wilfrid-Hamel, ☎691-7110)*. Very popular before the arrival of television, regional exhibitions were presented annually in various cities on the continent so that everyone could learn about recent discoveries and view fragments of an exotic, faraway world. These fairs also offered workers a place to relax and gave children a fun place to play. The Centre de Foire de Québec's new large functional pavilions are designed to receive the many exhibitions

and fairs that are of interest to the people of Québec City and its surrounding area.

ExpoCité includes the Colisée and the **Hippodrome de Québec** *(☎524-5283)* as well as some of the former pavilions that housed the annual provincial exhibitions presented here since 1892. The **Pavillon des Arts** (1913) and the **Palais Central** (1916) are two Beaux-Arts buildings that are reminiscent of the Chicago World's Fair pavilions of 1893.

# Tour H: Saint-Sauveur

*(half a day)*

Québec writer Roger Lemelin (1919-1994) has made the neighbourhood of his childhood and romances well known through his work. His novels *Au pied de la pente douce* (1944) and *Les Plouffe* (1948) have been made into television series and films. He describes the harsh, ordinary day-to-day life of the Saint-Sauveur people while showing both their short-comings and kind-heartedness. At the time, this working-class quarter of Basse-Ville located west of Saint-Roch was Québec City's poorest sector and had the highest rate of unemployment.

The history of Saint-Sauveur began in 1615 when the

Exploring

Récollets came to the banks of Rivière Saint-Charles. These reformed Franciscans had great plans for their land. They anticipated bringing 300 families from France who would settle in a town called "Ludovica." In 1621, they built the first stone church in New France. Unfortunately, when the Kirke brothers captured Québec City in 1629, the project was brought to a halt and, despite the return to French rule in 1632, the Récollets' colonisation project was never pursued any further. Only their monastery was rebuilt before being bought by the Bishop of Québec City to create the Hôpital Général (1693).

It was only after the great fire destroyed the neighbouring quarter of Saint-Roch (1845) that Saint-Sauveur became urbanized. In great confusion, hundreds of small wooden houses were built on meagre and often insalubrious land. In 1866 and again in 1889, major fires ravaged a good part of the neighbourhood, which nevertheless continued to attract a number of general workers. These days, Saint-Sauveur is known as a neighbourhood where the deep-seated spirit of Québec City can be found in its narrow streets and doll-like houses.

*Leaving Haute-Ville, take bus no. 2 from Place d'Youville. Get off at the corner of Boulevard Langelier and Boulevard Charest. Take Boulevard Langelier to the left, then turn right on Rue Arago.*

**Église Notre-Dame-de-Grâce** *(Rue Arago at the corner of Rue Colbert)* is situated at the foot of the Haute-Ville cliff. This eclectic late work (1925) was inspired by medieval architecture and built by Abbé Jean-Thomas Nadeau and notary Gérard Morisset. The latter also played an important role in saving Place-Royale many years later.

*Turn right on charming Rue Victoria.*

The small houses with mansard roofs on Rue Victoria and the surrounding streets give the neighbourhood a friendly village atmosphere. These dwellings were constructed on the tiniest plots of land by owners who wanted to fit a maximum number of families into a minimum space. At the beginning of the 20th century, some houses were expanded with extra storeys, along with balconies and richly-ornamented bay windows.

**Église Saint-Sauveur ★** stands at the north end of Rue Victoria. It was erected in 1867, re-using the original burnt walls of the first church built in 1851. Architect Joseph-Ferdinand Peachy designed a neo-Romanesque facade with a spire to give it a Baroque look. Abundantly decorated at the end of the 19th century, the interior has a slender nave and is surrounded by high lateral galleries. Note the windows by Beaulieu and Rochon (1897).

**Saint-Sauveur**

0 250 500m

N

© ULYSSES

● ATTRACTIONS

1. Église Notre-Dame-de-Grâce
2. Église Saint-Sauveur
3. Hôpital Général
4. Musée du Monastère des Augustines
5. École Technique
6. Moulin de l'Hôpital Général

*Cross the square in front of the church to get to Avenue des Oblats, turn right and go along to Rue De Saint-Vallier Ouest, where you turn left.*

This street is the heart of the Saint-Sauveur neighbourhood, with snack bars, Asian restaurants, second-hand dealers and workshops. There are also a few former residences of prominent personalities, which are adorned with balconies and towers. **Rue De Saint-Vallier** runs through several neighbourhoods in Basse-Ville as a winding path that ends at Bassin Louise.

*Take Rue de Carillon north, then turn right on Rue Elzéar-Bédard. Next, almost in front of you, take Avenue Simon-Napoléon-Parent, which was named after a mayor at the end of the 19th century. There are several interesting Second Empire and Queen Anne-style Victorian residences along this avenue leading to Parc Victoria.*

**Parc Victoria** was created in 1897 to provide the neighbourhoods of Saint-Roch and Saint-Sauveur with some green space, an element that had been missing until then. Pathways and rustic log structures were built and became very popular among city dwellers. But the park lost most of its appeal when the bend in Rivière Saint-Charles was filled in, since the river had almost completely encircled the park at that time. The construction of the Police Headquarters also

contributed to the transformation of this green space.

*Walk along Avenue Simon-Napoléon-Parent beside the park, then turn right on Avenue Saint-Anselme and right again on Avenue des Commissaires. Go around the walls of the Hôpital Général, because the entrance is at the end of Boulevard Langelier.*

The Récollets built the first stone church in New France in 1621 on the site of the **Hôpital Général ★★** *(260 Boulevard Langelier)*. Their plan was to bring 300 families from France and settle on the banks of Rivière Saint-Charles in a village called "Ludovica." Although this project never came through, the institution slowly grew and took root. The present chapel was built in 1673 and in 1682, the Récollets added an arched cloister to their monastery. A few elements remain and have been integrated into the subsequent additions.

In 1693, Monseigneur Jean-Baptiste de la Croix de Chevrières de Saint-Vallier, the second Bishop of Québec City, bought the monastery from the Récollets to establish a hospital. The Augustine Hospitaller Order of the Hôtel-Dieu took charge of the institution, which looked after destitute, disabled and elderly people. Today the Hôpital Général is a modern institution for long-term-care patients. However, a great deal of its past has been preserved—more, in fact, than

## Montcalm's Remains

In 1759, French general Marquis de Montcalm lost New France to the British during the Battle of the Plains of Abraham. He also lost his own life and was buried in the Ursulines monastery on Rue Donacona, in the heart of the fortified town. His remains stayed in the monastery chapel for 242 years, until 2001 when a funeral procession carried them to their new burial site. They now rest in a mausoleum that was recently built in his honour in the Hôpital Général cemetery. This is where soldiers from both camps were buried after the hospital's Augustine nuns tried to save them, in vain. A memorial was also built in memory of all the soldiers who died during the Seven Years' War.

any other institution of its kind in Québec City. There are many elements from the 17th and 18th centuries, such as the Récollets' cells, woodwork, dispensary cupboards and painted panelling. Fortunately, the hospital was never damaged by flames and only slightly by the Conquest bombardments, a rarity in Québec City.

It is not possible to visit these vestiges, but you can take a tour of the **Musée du Monastère des Augustines** *(free admission; Tue-Fri by appointment; ☎529-0931)* and the small Église Notre-Dame-des-Anges. This church was redecorated in 1770 by Pierre Émond and houses the preciously guarded tabernacle created in 1722 by François-Noël Levasseur. There are some beautiful paintings, such as *L'Assomption de la Vierge* by Frère Luc, painted here during the artist's visit to Canada in 1670, and several paintings by Joseph Légaré bought in 1824.

You can also visit the **Military Cemetery**, where many of the soldiers who died during the Battle of the Plains of Abraham are buried. There is also a mausoleum where the remains of the Marquis de Montcalm now rest, and nearby is the **Mémorial à la Guerre de Sept Ans ★**, along with a sculpture by Pascale Archambault named *Traversée sans retour*. This memorial honours the memory of the 1,058 soldiers who died

Exploring

between 1755 and 1760 and are buried here. In addition to French and British soldiers, French Canadians and Aboriginals who died trying to defend their land are also interred here.

*Take Boulevard Langelier, leaving the hospital and museum behind you.*

The **École Technique** *(310 Boulevard Langelier)*, or École des Métiers, is a good example of Québec City's Beaux-Arts architecture. This is a major architectural work by René Pamphile Lemay that was built between 1909 and 1911. The long red-brick and stone building had a 22m-high central tower that was unfortunately demolished around 1955.

The **Moulin de l'Hôpital Général** stands in the middle of a small park at the corner of Avenue Langelier and Rue Saint-François. This old windmill is the only one of about 20 to have survived the harshness of Québec's climate. Its stone tower was erected on earlier foundations in 1730 for the nuns and patients of the Hôpital Général. It milled grain until 1862, when a fire destroyed it completely. The mill was then integrated into an industrial building and was concealed so that it disappeared from view. Only in 1976 was the tower, or what remained of it, uncovered and given a new roof.

*To end this tour and return to Place D'Youville, take Rue Saint-François going east and continue for a while until you reach Rue Dorchester. At the corner of these two streets is a bus stop where you can take Métrobus nos. 800 or 801.*

## Tour I: Sillery to Cap-Rouge

*(half a day)*

This tour goes up and down along the cliff stretching from Cap Diamant to Cap-Rouge. It begins in Sillery, the affluent Québec City suburb, goes through **Sainte-Foy** (see p 113) and ends at the Cap-Rouge cliff. You will never be far from the river and at times will be able to enjoy magnificent panoramas. Note that all the cities you'll cross have merged with Québec City.

### Sillery

Sillery retains many traces of its colourful past and is influenced by the town's dramatic topography. There are actually two sections to Sillery, one at the base and the other at the top of a steep cliff which runs from Cap Diamant to Cap-Rouge. In 1637, the Jesuits built a mission in Sillery, on the shores of the river, with the idea of converting the Algonquins and Montagnais who came to fish in the coves upriver from Québec City. They named the fortified community in honour of the mission's benefactor, Noël Brûlart de Sillery, an aristocrat who had recently been converted by Vincent de Paul.

By the following century, Sillery was already sought after for its beauty. The Jesuits converted their mission into a country house, and the bishop of Samos built Sillery's first villa (1732). Following the British Conquest, Sillery became the favoured town of administrators, military officers and British merchants, all of whom built luxurious villas on the cliff in architectural styles that were fashionable in England at the time. The splendour of these homes and their vast English gardens were in stark contrast to the simple workers houses that were clustered at the base of the cliff. The occupants of these houses worked in the shipyards where a fortune was being made building ships out of wood coming from the Outaouais region to supply the British navy during Napoleon's blockade, which began in 1806. The shipyards, set up in Sillery's sheltered coves, had all disappeared before Boulevard Champlain, now running along the river's edge, was built around 1960.

*The tour begins at the entrance to Bois-de-Coulonge park, on Chemin Saint-Louis, which is the extension of Grande Allee just before it branches off towards the south and becomes Boulevard Laurier.*

The **Bois-de-Coulonge ★ ★** *(free admission; 1215 Chemin Saint-Louis, ☎528-0773)* borders Chemin Saint-Louis to the east. This English park once surrounded the residence of the lieutenant-governor of Québec. The stately home was destroyed in a fire in 1966, though some of its buildings survived, notably the guard's house and the stables. The Saint-Denys stream flows through the eastern end of the grounds at the bottom of a ravine, and marks the spot where British troops gained access to the Plains of Abraham, where a historic battle decided the future of New France. Today Bois-de-Coulonge, a member of the Jardins du Québec, features magnificent gardens and an attractive arboretum.

**Villa Bagatelle ★** *(free admission; Oct to Dec Wed-Sun 1pm to 5pm; Feb and March Sun 1pm to 5pm; Apr and May Wed-Sun 1pm to 5pm; Jun to Oct Tue-Sun 11am to 5pm; 1563 Chemin Saint-Louis, ☎654-0259)* was once home to an attaché of the British governor, who lived on the neighbouring property of Bois-de-Coulonge. Built in 1848, the villa is a good example of 19th-century Gothic Revival residential architecture, as interpreted by American Alexander J. Davis. The house and its Victorian garden were impeccably restored in 1984 and are now open to the public. There is an interesting information centre providing back-

Exploring

ground information on the villas and large estates of Sillery.

On Avenue Lemoine, which runs along the south side of Bagatelle, is the **Spencer Grange Villa**, built in 1849 for Henry Atkinson *(1321 Avenue Lemoine)*. During the Second World War, it was occupied by Zita de Bourbon-Parme, the dethroned Empress of Austria.

*Continue on Chemin Saint-Louis as far as the corner of Avenue Maguire and Côte de l'Église. Avenue Maguire is the neighbourhood's main shopping area. Turn left on Côte de l'Église.*

A short side trip leads to the **Cimetière de Sillery**, Sillery's Catholic cemetery, where René Lévesque, founder of the Parti Québécois and Premier of Québec from 1976 to 1984, is buried. To get there, turn right on Avenue Maguire, then left on Boulevard René-Lévesque Ouest. The cemetery is just a little further.

**Église Saint-Michel** ★ *(at the corner of Chemin du Foulon and Côte de l'Église)* was erected in 1852 by architect George Browne. Inside are five paintings from the famous Desjardins collection. These works originally hung in Parisian churches until they were sold in 1792 following the French Revolution and brought to Québec by Abbé Desjardins.

From the **Observatoire de la Pointe-à-Puiseaux**, opposite the church square, you can take a look at the vast panorama of the St. Lawrence River and its south shore. On the right are the bridges that link the north and south shores. The first, to the east, is the **Pont de Québec**, a cantilever bridge that was deemed an engineering marvel when it was first built. However, its construction was marked by a tragic event: the central span collapsed when workers were attempting to put it in place for the first time in August 1907. The other bridge with great white arches is named **Pont Pierre-Laporte** in memory of the provincial government minister who was abducted and killed by members of the Front de Libération du Québec (FLQ) during the 1970 October Crisis.

*Pont de Québec*

*At the foot of the hill, turn right on Chemin du Foulon, which takes its name from a mill that was used for carding and fulling wool in the old days.*

The **Maison des Jésuites de Sillery** ★★ *(free admission; Oct to Dec Wed-Sun 1pm to 5pm; Feb and March Sun 1pm to 5pm; Apr and May Wed-Sun 1pm to 5pm; Jun to Oct Tue-Sun 11am to 5pm; 2320 Chemin du Foulon, ☎654-0259)*, built of stone and covered with white plaster, occupies the former site of a Jesuit mission, a few ruins of which are still visible. In the 17th century, the mission included a fortified stone wall, a chapel and a priest's residence, as well as Aboriginal housing. As European illnesses such as smallpox and measles devastated the Aboriginal population, the mission was transformed into a hospice in 1702. At the same time, work began on the present house, a building with imposing chimney stacks. In 1763, the house was rented to John Brookes and his wife, writer Frances Moore Brookes, who immortalized it by making it the setting for her novel *The History of Emily Montague*, published in London in 1769. It was also during this time that the structure was lowered and the windows were made smaller, in the New England saltbox tradition. The house now has two storeys in front and one in back, covered with a catslide roof.

By 1824 the main building was being used as a brewery and the chapel had been torn down. The house was later converted into an office complex for various shipyards. In 1929, the Maison des Jésuites became one of the first three buildings designated as historic by the government of Québec. Since 1948, it has housed a museum detailing the 350-year history of the property.

*Continue along Chemin du Foulon then take Côte à Gignac up the embankment on the right. At the top of the hill turn right on Chemin Saint-Louis.*

**Domaine Cataraqui** ★ *(closed to the public for an undetermined time; 2141 Chemin Saint-Louis)* is the best-kept property of its kind still in existence in Sillery. It includes a large neoclassical residence, designed in 1851 by architect Henry Staveley, a winter garden and numerous outbuildings scattered across a beautiful restored garden. The house was built for a wood merchant named Henry Burstall, whose business operated at the bottom of the cliff on which the house stands. In 1935, Cataraqui became the residence of painter Henry Percival Tudor-Hart and his wife Catherine Rhodes. They sold the property to the Québec government to prevent it from being divided, as many others had been.

Exploring

*Head west now on Chemin Saint-Louis.*

**Maison Hamel-Bruneau** *(free admission; Tue-Sun 12:30pm to 5pm, Wed to 9pm; 2608 Chemin Saint-Louis, ☎641-6280)* is a beautiful example of Regency architecture, popular in the British colonies at the beginning of the 19th century. This style is characterized by hip roofs with flared eaves covering low wrap-around verandas. Graced with French windows, Maison Hamel-Bruneau has been carefully restored and transformed into a cultural centre.

*Turn left on Avenue du Parc to get to the Parc Aquarium du Québec.*

The "new" **Parc Aquarium du Québec** ★★★ *(children 12 and under who live in the new city of Québec and are accompanied by an adult can visit for free; annual passport: adults $25, children $9-$21; Jun to Sep every day adults $24, children $7-$16; Oct to May every day adults $15, children $5-$10; 1675 Avenue des Hôtels, ☎659-5264 or 888-659-5264, www.spsnq.qc.ca)*, which reopened in late 2002 after lengthy renovations, is a magnificent site. The "Pont de Québec" aquarium, as it was once known, was founded in 1959. Since then, it has welcomed over eight million visitors.

Now home to over 3,500 fish species, the Parc Aquarium du Québec features over 16ha of the St. Lawrence River and polar ecosystems. When you first walk in, you can attend a multimedia presentation that plunges you (virtually, of course) into the river to take you to the North Pole. Outside, all you have to do is follow the tours to meet various mammal species. You will also walk through a rocky valley along the shores of the St. Lawrence in a natural-like decor. Another must-see is the polar world of the North. In this reconstituted Arctic, polar bears and harp seals will undoubtedly impress you.

In addition, in the main building, you'll be transported from the marine universe of the Laurentian Plateau to the waters of the Northern Atlantic. Visitors will finally be able to head into laboratories, then to a huge circular basin where they can admire the sub-arctic Pacific Ocean in all its splendour: the Grand Océan, in which you'll be surrounded by 350,000 litres of water inhabited by 650 marine specimens. You can even watch feedings and handle small invertebrates, such as starfish and sea urchins. The Parc Aquarium du Québec features rest areas, play areas for children, food services (a restaurant with a panoramic terrace and a view of the St. Lawrence River and the bridges; daily and kids' menus), as well as two souvenir shops, one in the reception pavilion and the other in the main building's atrium.

*Take Chemin Saint-Louis west towards Cap-Rouge. This way, you won't be far from **Parc de la Plage Jacques-Cartier ★** (see p 161). In Cap-Rouge, take Rue Louis-Francœur to the right before turning left down Côte de Cap-Rouge.*

## Cap-Rouge

Jacques Cartier and the Sieur de Roberval tried to establish a French colony in Cap-Rouge in 1541. They named their encampments Charlesbourg-Royal and France-Roy. But the unfortunate souls who accompanied them, having no idea how cold Canada could get in January, built frail wood buildings with paper windows! Most died during the winter, victims of the cold or of scurvy, a disease caused by a lack of vitamin C. Those who survived returned to France in the spring.

A plaque has been placed at the **Site Historique de Cap-Rouge** *(at the end of Côte de Cap-Rouge)*, a historic site commemorating the first French colony in America. Cartier and Roberval had intended to make the site a base camp for expeditions heading out in search of a passage to the Orient.

# Tour J: Heading North

*(one day)*

The area covered by this tour is in fact crossed by several highways. The tour begins in Charlesbourg, one of the first areas to be populated in New France. From there, Route 369 will take you to Wendake, a village inhabited by the Huron-Wendat community. The same road will then take you west to Sainte-Catherine-de-la-Jacques-Cartier and Lac Saint-Joseph. From Wendake, you can also choose to follow Route 371, which reaches Saint-Gabriel-de-Valcartier and Tewkesbury. Or, from Charlesbourg, Route 73 will take you to Lac Beauport, Lac Delage and Stoneham. Route 175 heads north to Parc de la Jacques-Cartier. As you may already have noticed, this entire region is a paradise for those who love the great outdoors. For more information, consult the Outdoors chapter.

## Charlesbourg

In New France, seigneuries were usually shaped in long rectangles marked out in squares that ran up and down hills. Most of them were set up perpendicular to a significant

Exploring

waterway as well. Charlesbourg is the only real exception to this system, but what an exception! In 1665, while looking for different ways to populate the colony and assure its prosperity and security, the Jesuits developed an original plan to urbanize their land: the Notre-Dame-des-Anges seigneury. It is a huge square that was divided into angled plots of land converging towards the centre where the dwellings were situated. The houses faced a square defined by a road called the Trait-Carré, where there was a church, a cemetery and a community pasture. This concentric plan assured a better defence against the Iroquois and is still visible today in the old part of Charlesbourg. Two other initiatives of this kind, Bourg Royal to the east and Petite Auvergne to the south, did not have the same success, however, and little remains of them today.

The Notre-Dame-des-Anges seigneury was granted to the Jesuits in 1626, making it one of the first permanent settlements inhabited by Europeans in Canada. Despite this early settlement and original seigneurial design, few buildings built before the 19th century remain in Charlesbourg. The fragility of the early buildings and the push to modernize are possible explanations. Since 1950, Charlesbourg has become one of the main suburbs of Québec City and has lost much of its original character.

*It is best to park near the church and explore the Trait-Carré neighbourhood on foot. You can also take Métrobus no. 801 to get to Charlesbourg. This bus goes as far as the Jardin zoologique du Québec.*

### Église Saint-Charles-Borromée ★ ★ (135 80e Rue Ouest)

revolutionized the art of building in rural Québec. Architect Thomas Baillargé, influenced by the Palladian movement, showed particular innovation in the way he arranged the windows and doors of the facade, to which he added a large pediment. Construction of the church began in 1828 and the original design has remained intact since. The magnificent interior decor by Baillargé was done in 1833.

At the back of the choir, narrower than the nave, is the Arc de Triomphe-style retable, and in the centre is the tabernacle evoking St. Peter's Basilica in Rome. A 17th century painting by Pierre Mignard entitled *Saint Charles Borromée distribuant la communion aux pestiférés de Milan* (St. Charles Borromée giving communion to plague victims in Milan) also hangs there. Two beautiful statues by Pierre-Noël Levasseur, dating from 1742, complete the ensemble. When you step out, you can see the huge Second Empire-style 1876 presbytery, testament to the village priest's privileged status in the 19th century, and the Bibliothèque Municipale (municipal library) in the former Collège Saint-Charles (1904).

*Take 1re Avenue south then turn left on Rue du Trait-Carré Est, which leads to Chemin Samuel.*

**Maison Éphraïm-Bédard** *(free admission; Tue and Thu 1:30pm to 4pm; 7655 Chemin Samuel, ☎624-7745)* is one of the rare remaining houses in old Charlesbourg. The local historical society has been installed there since 1986 and presents an exhibition on the evolution of the Trait-Carré. Old maps and aerial photographs show the particular physical layout of Charlesbourg. Guided tours of the area are offered as well.

If you return to Rue du Trait-Carré Est, you can see **Maison Magella-Paradis** *(mid-Jun to mid-Aug Wed-Sun 10:30am to 5:30pm; mid-Aug to mid-Jun Fri 7pm to 9pm, Sat and Sun 1pm to 5pm; ☎623-1877)* at number 7970. Built in 1833, it occasionally hosts exhibitions. A little farther along at number 7985, **Maison Pierre-Lefevbre**, built in 1846, houses the **Galerie d'Art du Trait-Carré** *(free admission; Thu-Fri 7pm to 9pm, Sat-Sun 1pm to 5pm; ☎623-1877)*. Works by various artists are featured here.

*Turn right on 80e Rue Est. At the corner of Boulevard Henri-Bourassa is the Jesuits' old mill.*

The **Moulin des Jésuites** ★ *($2; Sep to mid-Jun Sat and Sun 10am to 5pm; mid-Jun to Sep Wed-Sun 10am to 6pm; 7960*

*Boulevard Henri-Bourassa, ☎624-7720)*. This pretty rough-cast rubble stone mill, is the oldest building in Charlesbourg. It was built in 1740 by the Jesuits who were the landowners at the time. After several decades of neglect, the two-storey building was restored in 1990 and now houses the **Centre d'Interprétation du Trait-Carré** and a tourist bureau. Concerts and exhibits are also presented here.

*To get to the zoo, take the Autoroute Laurentienne (Laurentian Highway-73) north and exit at Rue de la Faune.*

The "new" **Jardin zoologique du Québec** ★★★ *(children 12 and under who live in the new city of Québec and are accompanied by an adult can enter for free; annual passport: adults $25, children $9-$21; Jun to Sep every day adults $24, children $7-$16; Oct to May every day adults $10, children $3-$8; 9300 Rue de la Faune, ☎622-0312 or 888-622-0312, www.spsnq.qc.ca)*, which reopened in June 2003 after two years of renovations, is simply wonderful. The "Zoo de Québec," as it was once known, was established in 1931, and by 1997, the site, consisting of a vegetation and animal garden, had welcomed its 15-millionth visitor. Throughout its unique landscape, which highlights decorative horticulture thanks to a marsh, a pond and a fountain, you'll enjoy a collection specializing in bird fauna, in addition to 750 animals belonging to 300 different species. Several short tours will take adults and children to the wide array of sectors they can discover: the pond gardens, the fountain garden, the conservatory (home to rare species from such places as Africa), the Africa trails, the garden of fragrances, the garden of flight, the Indo-Australian hothouse (covering 2,400m², with tropical fauna and flora), the Grande Place (which presents shows featuring birds of prey), the river gardens, the farm and the forest (home to white-tailed deer). It is even possible to watch the animals being fed at specific times. The Jardin zoologique du Québec also features a great restaurant under an atrium next to an outdoor terrace; children's menus are available, as are daily specials. Visitors can also peruse two souvenir shops, one at the entrance, in the reception pavilion, the other in the main building's atrium.

*Take Autoroute Laurentienne (73), this time going south to return to the vicinity of 80e Rue, which becomes Boulevard Saint-Joseph. Take Boulevard Saint-Joseph going west until it becomes Boulevard Bastien.*

## Wendake

Forced off their land by the Iroquois in the 17th century, 300 Huron families moved to various places around Québec before settling in 1700 in Jeune-Lorette, today known as Wendake. Visitors will be charmed by the winding roads of this village, located on the banks of the Rivière Saint-Charles. The museum and gift shop provide a lot of information on the culture of this peaceful and sedentary people.

The **Église Notre-Dame-de-Lorette ★** *(140 Boulevard Bastien)*, the Huron-Wendat church completed in 1730, is reminiscent of the first churches of New France.

This humble building with a white plaster facade conceals unexpected treasures in its chancel and sacristy. Some of the objects on display were given to the Huron-Wendat community by the Jesuits, and come from the first chapel in Ancienne-Lorette (late 17th century). Among the works are several statues by Noël Levasseur created between 1730 and 1740, an altar face depicting an Aboriginal village by Huron-Wendat sculptor François Vincent (1790) and a beautiful *Vierge à l'enfant* (Madonna and Child) sculpture by a Parisian goldsmith (1717). In addition, the church features a reliquary that was made in 1676, chasubles from the 18th century and various liturgical objects by Paul Manis (1715). However, the most interesting element remains the small, Louis XIII-style gilded tabernacle on the high altar sculpted by

Levasseur in 1722. The Tsawenhohi House offers guided tours.

**Onhoüa Chetek8e ★** *($9; &; May to mid-Oct every day 9am to 5pm; mid-Oct to May every day 10am to 4pm; 575 Rue Stanislas-Koska, ☎842-4308, www.huron-wendat.qc.ca)* is a replica of a Huron-Wendat village from the time of early colonization. The traditional design includes wooden longhouses and fences. Visitors are given an introduction to the lifestyle and social organization of the ancient Huron-Wendat nation. Various Aboriginal dishes are also served at the renowned **Nek8arre** restaurant (see p 223) and are worth a taste.

**Maison Tsawenhohi** *(May to late Oct every day 10am to 5pm, reservations required the rest of the year; 75 Chef Nicolas Vincent Tsawenhohi, ☎845-0700)*, whose Huron-Wendat name means "He who sees clearly," was purchased in 1804 by Grand Chief Nicolas Vincent Tsawenhohi. It is now part of the Huron-Wendat nation's heritage and houses an interpretation centre on traditional customs and a crafts shop where you can watch artisans at work. Moose hair, porcupine quills, leather and birch bark are used to make baskets, moccasins, snowshoes and "water drums" (which actually contain water). In summer, guide services are offered to visit the village's historic sector.

**Parc de la Falaise et de la Chute Kabir Kouba** (see p 161).

## Sainte-Catherine-de-la-Jacques-Cartier

From Wendake, you can reach the **Lac Saint-Joseph region**, to the northwest. This is a popular resort area for Québec City residents who swim and practice watersports in this lake all summer long and enjoy, among other things, its beach (see p 161).

Before reaching Lac Saint-Joseph, you'll pass Sainte-Catherine-de-la-Jacques-Cartier and the **Station Touristique Duchesnay ★** (see p 161), a lovely park that, come wintertime, features the famous **Ice Hotel ★** *(guided tour $14, every day, hourly from 10am to 8pm; ☎875-4522 or 877-505-0423, www.hoteldeglace.qc.ca)*. The Québec Ice Hotel (see p 188), a spectacular, Swedish-inspired structure, is unique in North America and definitely one of the region's "hottest" attractions. Its lifespan is obviously limited (early Jan to late March), but every year, builders return to the site to erect this stunning complex using several tonnes of ice and snow. And not only is the ice used for building, it also serves as decoration! The hotel houses an art gallery showcasing unusual snow and ice sculptures, as well as an exhibit room, a small movie theatre, a chapel and a bar where vodka

Exploring

is served in ice glasses. You'll be simply amazed!

## Lac Beauport

*From Charlesbourg, take Route 73, which eventually branches off towards Lac Beauport.*

Lac Beauport is a resort site that is popular throughout the year. A downhill-skiing resort, **Le Relais** (see p 169), has even been created here. Around the lake, summer visitors can enjoy lovely beaches.

Route 73 becomes Route 175 and runs along the resort towns of **Lac-Delage** and **Stoneham**, which is home to another ski resort (see p 169). A bit further, it provides access to **Parc national de la Jacques-Cartier** (see p 162) and the **Réserve Faunique des Laurentides**.

*To return to Québec City, head south on Route 175.*

## Tour K:
## Côte-de-Beaupré
## and Île d'Orléans

*(one to two days)*

This long, narrow strip of land nestled between the St. Lawrence River and the undeveloped wilderness of the Laurentian massif, is the ancestral home of many families whose roots go back to the beginning of the colony. It illustrates how the spread of the population was limited to the riverside in many regions of Québec, and recalls the fragility of development in New France. From Beauport to Saint-Joachim, the colony's first road, the Chemin du Roy (king's road) built under orders from Monseigneur de Laval during the 17th century, follows the Beaupré shore. Along this road, houses are built in a style characterized by a raised main floor covered in stucco, long balconies with intricately carved wood balusters and lace-curtained windows.

As for Île d'Orléans, it is a 32km-by-5km island in the middle of the St. Lawrence River, downstream from Québec City. The island is close to the hearts of this region's inhabitants. You will quickly understand why when you visit the island and see the superb countryside, as well as Québec's heritage treasures that appear along Chemin Royal.

## Beauport

Three types of urban development have shaped Beauport over the course of its history. Originally an agricultural settlement, in the 19th century it became an important industrial town, evolving into one of

Québec City's main suburbs in the 1960s, before merging with the city in 2002. In 1634, the Beauport seigneury from which the present city grew was granted to Robert Giffard, a doctor and surgeon from the Perche region of France. During the next few years he enthusiastically set about building a manor house, a mill and a small village, establishing one of the largest seigneuries in New France. Unfortunately, wars and fires have claimed several of these buildings.

The large white house known as **Manoir Montmorency** *(2490 Avenue Royale, ☎663-3330)* was built in 1780 for British governor John Haldimand. At the end of the 18th century, the house became famous as the residence of the Duke of Kent, son of George III and father of Queen Victoria. The manor, which once housed a hotel, was severely damaged by fire in May 1993. It has been restored according to the original plans and now features an informa-

tion centre, a few shops and a restaurant (see p 224) which offers an exceptional view of the Montmorency Falls, the St. Lawrence River and Île d'Orléans. The small Sainte-Marie chapel on the property and the gardens are open to the public.

The Manoir Montmorency is nestled in the **Parc de la Chute Montmorency ★★** *(parking $8.25, free in winter, cablecar $7.50 return; accessible all year; for opening hours and parking ☎663-2877, www.sepaq.com).* Rivière Montmorency, with its source in the Laurentians, flows peacefully until it reaches a sudden 83m drop and tumbles into a void, creating one of the most impressive natural phenomena in Québec. One and a half times the height of Niagara Falls, the Montmorency Falls flow at a rate that can reach 125,000 litres-per-second during spring thaw. To take in this magnificent spectacle, a park has been created and a tour of the falls is offered. From the manor, follow the pretty

**Exploring**

*Manoir Montmorency*

cliff path, where you'll find the Baronne lookout. You'll soon reach two bridges, the *Pont Au-dessus de la Chute* and the *Pont Au-dessus de la Faille*, which cross the falls and the fault respectively and offer spectacular views. Once in the park you'll find picnic tables and a playground. The bottom of the falls can be reached by the 487-step panoramic staircase or the trail. The cable car provides a relaxing and picturesque way to get back to the top. During winter, mist freezes into ice cones called "sugar-loaves" that adventurous souls can climb.

Samuel de Champlain, the founder of Québec City, was impressed by the falls and named them after the viceroy of New France, Charles, duc de Montmorency. During the 19th century, the falls became a fashionable leisure area for the well-to-do of the region who would arrive in horse-drawn carriages or sleighs.

The lower part of the park, situated opposite the falls, is accessible via a long wooden staircase or by cable car. To reach the lower part of the park by car, you must make a complicated detour: continue along Avenue Royale, turn right on Côte de l'Église, then right again on Highway 40. The parking lot is on the right. To get back to Avenue Royale, take Boulevard Sainte-Anne west, Côte Saint-Grégoire and finally Boulevard des Chutes to the right.

*Take Boulevard Sainte-Anne (Highway 138) going east or take Chemin Royal, which travels through the bucolic countryside and pretty villages.*

## Château-Richer

Château-Richer is charming and picturesque, highlighted by the striking situation of the church on a promontory. Hundred-year-old root cellars and stone ovens are visible from the road and are still used occasionally. Throughout the village, small wooden signs have been posted in front of historical buildings, indicating any distinctive architectural features and when they were built.

The superb Petit-Pré windmill, which dominates the river of the same name on the edge of Chemin Royal, is where you will find (since 2001) the **Corporation du Moulin du Petit-Pré** (*$6; late Jun to mid-Oct every day 10am to 5pm; 7007 Avenue Royale,* ☎824-7007), which organizes guided tours in period costumes. The windmill was rebuilt after the Conquest, modeled after the windmill that had been built by the Séminaire de Québec in 1695. It is the oldest wheat windmill in North America and the visitors can get a glance at the milling process. Since the early 1990s, beautiful vines grow behind the windmill. Inside, a shop sells regional products and flour that has been ground on-site.

The **Centre d'Interprétation de la Côte-de-Beaupré** ★ *($5; summer every day 10am to 5pm, rest of the year Mon-Fri 10am to 4:30pm; 7976 Avenue Royale, ☎824-3677)*, which used to be housed in the Petit-Pré windmill, was moved to a new locale in the heart of the village. Now occupying a four-storey former school, the centre features a permanent exhibit on the history and geography of Côte-de-Beaupré, as well as temporary exhibits.

For those who are curious about bees and honey, here's an interesting little museum: the **Musée de l'Abeille** *(free admission; "bee safari" $3.50; late Jun to mid-Oct every day 9am to 6pm, mid-Sep to late Jun 9am to 5pm; 8862 Boulevard Sainte-Anne, ☎824-4411, www.musee-abeille.com)* offers a brief look into the lives of these tireless workers. Visitors can stroll through at their leisure or receive an introduction to the art of beekeeping by participating in a "bee safari." A beekeeper explains the steps involved in making honey and mead (honey wine). There is also a pastry shop and a gift shop.

*To reach Sainte-Anne-de-Beaupré, you can take Boulevard Sainte-Anne (Route 138) eastbound, or Chemin Royal, which travels through the countryside and its quaint villages.*

## Sainte-Anne-de-Beaupré

This long, narrow village is one of the largest pilgrimage sites in North America. In 1658, the first Catholic church on the site was dedicated to Saint Anne after sailors from Brittany, who had prayed to the Virgin Mary's mother, were saved from drowning during a storm on the St. Lawrence River. Soon, a great number of pilgrims began to visit the church. The second church, built in 1676, was replaced in 1872 by a huge temple, which was destroyed by fire in 1922. Finally, work began on the present basilica which stands at the centre of a virtual compound of chapels, monasteries and facilities as varied as they are unusual. Each year, Sainte-Anne-de-Beaupré welcomes more than a million pilgrims, who stay in the hotels and visit the countless souvenir boutiques, of perhaps questionable taste, along Avenue Royale.

The **Basilique Sainte-Anne-de-Beaupré** ★★★ *(the information counter is loctated near the entrance; every day 8:30am to 5pm; 10018 Avenue Royale, ☎827-3781)*, towering over the small, metal-roofed wooden houses that line the winding road, is surprising not only for its impressive size, but also for the feverish activity it inspires all summer long. The church's granite exterior, which takes on a different colour depending on

Exploring

the lighting, was designed in the French Romanesque Revival style by Parisian architect Maxime Roisin, assisted by Quebecer Louis Napoléon Audet. Its spires rise 91m high, while the nave is 129m long and the transepts over 60m wide. The copper-gilded wooden statue sitting atop the church's facade was taken from the 1872 church.

The basilica's interior is divided into five naves, supported by heavy columns with highly sculpted capitals. The vault of the main nave is adorned with sparkling mosaics designed by French artists Jean Gaudin and Auguste Labouret, recounting the life of Saint Anne. Labouret also created the magnificent stained glass found all along the perimeter of the basilica. The left transept contains an extraordinary statue of Saint Anne cradling Mary in her right arm. Her tiara reminds visitors that she is the patron saint of Québec. In a beautiful reliquary in the background, visitors can admire the Great Relic, part of Saint Anne's forearm sent over from the San Paolo Fuori le Mura in Rome. Finally, follow the ambulatory around the choir to see the ten radiant chapels built in the 1930s, whose polychromatic architecture is inspired by the Art Deco movement. The Basilica is open all year.

Materials retrieved after the demolition of the original church in 1676 were used to build the **Chapelle Commé-morative ★** *(free admission; May to mid-Sep, every day 8am to 8pm; mid-Sep to mid-Oct every day 8am to 5pm; Avenue Royale,* ☎*827-3781)* in 1878. The stee-ple (1696) was designed by Claude Baïliff, an architect whose numerous other pro-jects in 17th-century New France have all but disappeared because of war and fire. Inside, the high altar comes from the original church built under the French Regime. It is the work of Jacques Leblond dit Latour (1700). The chapel is adorned with paintings from the 18th century. The water from the Fontaine de Sainte-Anne, at the foot of the chapel, is said to have healing powers.

The **Scala Santa ★** *(free admis-sion; May to mid-Sep, every day 8am to 8pm; mid-Sep to mid-Oct every day 8am to 5pm; to the right of the Chapelle Commémo-rative)*, an unusual yellow-and-white wooden building (1891), covers a staircase which pil-grims climb on their knees while reciting prayers. It is a replica of the Scala Santa, the sacred staircase conserved in Rome at San Giovanni in Laterano that Christ climbed to get to the court of Pontius Pilate. An image of the Holy Land is inlaid in each riser.

The **Chemin de la Croix** *(be-hind the Chapelle du Souvenir)* is located on the side of the hill and leads to the **Monastère des Laïcs**. The Chapelle de Saint-Gérard is worth a short visit.

The life-size statues were cast in bronze at Bar-le-Duc, France.

The **Cyclorama de Jérusalem** ★★ *($7; May to Oct every day 9am to 6pm, Jul and Aug every day 8am to 8pm; 8 Rue Régina, near the parking lot, ☎827-3101).* This round building with Oriental features houses a 360° panorama of Jerusalem on the day of the crucifixion. This immense *trompe l'œil* painting, measuring 14m by 100m, was created in Chicago around 1880 by French artist Paul Philippoteaux and his assistants. A specialist in panoramas, Philippoteaux produced a work of remarkable realism. It was first exhibited in Montréal before being moved to Sainte-Anne-de-Beaupré at the very end of the 19th century. Very few panoramas and cycloramas, so popular at the turn of the century, have survived to the present day.

The **Musée de Sainte Anne** ★ *($4; early Jun to early Sep every day 9am to 5pm; 9803 Boulevard Sainte-Anne, ☎827-6873)* is dedicated to sacred art honouring the mother of the Virgin Mary. These interestingly diverse pieces were acquired over many years from the basilica and are now put on display for the public. Sculptures, paintings, mosaics, stained-glass windows and goldworks are dedicated to the cult of Saint Anne, as are written works expressing prayers or thanks for favours obtained. The history of the pilgrimages to Sainte-Anne-de-Beaupré is also explained. The exhibition is attractively presented and spread over two floors.

To learn more about Québec folklore, go to the **Atelier Paré** *(free admission; mid-May to mid-Oct every day 9am to 5:30pm, mid-Oct to mid-May Wen-Fri 1pm to 4pm, Sat-Sun 10am to 4pm; 9269 Avenue Royale, ☎827-3992).* All the works presented at this woodsculpting museum are inspired by the fascinating world of local legends.

*You can follow Route 138 to the **Réserve Nationale de Faune du Cap Tourmente** ★ (see p 162), or take Route 360 Est to **Station Mont-Sainte-Anne** ★ (see p 162) and the **Grand Canyon des Chutes Sainte-Anne** (see p 163). Continuing further east on this highway, you will approach the magnificent Charlevoix region that you can visit with the **Ulysses Travel Guide Québec**. To continue the present tour on Île d'Orléans, take route 138 west and you will soon see signs for the bridge that leads to the island.*

## Île d'Orléans

Île d'Orléans is synonymous with old stones. In fact, of all Québec's regions, it is the most evocative of life in New France. When Jacques Cartier arrived in 1535, the island was covered in wild vines which inspired its first name: «Île Bacchus.» However, it was soon renamed in homage to the Duc d'Orléans. With the exception of Sainte-Pétronille, all of the parishes on the island were established during the 17th century. The colonization of the entire island followed soon after. In 1970, the government of Québec declared Île d'Orléans a historic district. The move was made in part to curb down the development that threatened to turn the island into yet another suburb of Québec City, and also as part of a widespread movement among the Québécois to protect the roots of their French ancestry by preserving old churches and houses. Since 1936, the island has been linked to the mainland by a suspension bridge, the Pont de l'Île. Île d'Orléans is also known as the country of Félix Leclerc (1914-1988), the most famous Québec poet and *chansonnier*.

This tour around Île d'Orléans will allow you to enjoy its many charms: its old buildings dating from the French Regime, the small chapels that line the road, its large fields that seem to plunge into the river, its orchards... Depending on the season, you may also be able to pick fruit (see p 166). Don't be surprised if, along the way, you see enclosed llamas or ostriches. Barely 15 years ago, this island only had old-fashioned black and white cows, but today, new kinds of farming have developed, multiplying the number of discoveries you can make here!

*Begin the tour of the island by taking Chemin Royal to the right on top of the hill by the bridge.*

# ★
# Sainte-Pétronille

Paradoxically, Sainte-Pétronille was the site of the first French settlement on Île d'Orléans and is also its most recent parish. In 1648, François de Chavigny de Berchereau and his wife Éléonore de Grandmaison established a farm and a Huron-Wendat mission here. However, constant Iroquois attacks forced the colonists to move further east to a spot facing Sainte-Anne-de-Beaupré. It was not until the middle of the 19th century that Sainte-Pétronille was consolidated as a village, as its beautiful location began attracting numerous summer visitors. Anglophone merchants from Québec City built beautiful second homes here, many of which are still standing along the road. A word to music lovers: chamber music concerts are presented at the Église de Sainte-Pétronille on Sundays in the summer.

During her life, Éléonore de Grandmaison had four husbands. After the death of François de Chavigny, she married Jacques Gourdeau who gave his name to the estate, his wife's property. Overlooking the river from the top of a promontory, **Manoir Gourdeau** (*137 Chemin Royal*) has been given this name even though the house's construction date does not quite coincide

*Historic Québec house*

with the time the couple was together. The long building was very likely built at the end of the 17th century but has been considerably expanded and changed since then.

*Turn right on Rue Horatio-Walker, which leads to the river banks and a promenade.*

The street is named after **Maison Horatio-Walker** ★ *(11 and 13 Rue Horatio-Walker)*. The red-brick building and the stucco house beside it were, respectively, the workshop and residence of painter Horatio Walker from 1904 to 1938. The British-born artist liked the French culture and meditative calm of Île d'Orléans. His workshop, designed by Harry Staveley, remains a good example of English Arts and Crafts architecture.

*Return to Chemin Royal.*

The Porteous family, of English origin, settled in Québec City at the end of the 18th century. In 1900, they built the **Domaine Porteous** ★ *(253 Chemin Royal)*. This vast country house surrounded by superb gardens was christened "La Groisardière." Designed by Toronto architects Darling and Pearson, the house revived certain aspects of traditional Québec architecture. The most notable of these is the Louis XV-inspired woodwork, and the general proportions used in the design of the house, which are similar to the Manoir Mauvide-Genest in Saint-Jean. Inside are many re-mounted paintings by William Brymner and Maurice Cullen depicting countryside scenes on Île d'Orléans. The building also incorporates Art Nouveau features. The property, which today belongs to the Foyer de Charité Notre-Dame-d'Orléans, a seniors'

Exploring

residence, was expanded between 1961 and 1964 when a new wing and a chapel were added.

Sainte-Pétronille's wharf dates back to 1855 and offers a magnificent view of Québec City. Next to it is **l'Auberge La Goéliche** (see p 191).

*After your tour of this tip of the island, head towards Saint-Laurent by Chemin Royal. You will then cross a forest of red oaks.*

### Saint-Laurent-de-l'Île-d'Orléans

Until 1950, Saint-Laurent's main industry was the manufacturing of *chaloupes* (barges), boats and sailboats that were popular in the United States and Europe. Though production of these boats has ceased, some traces of the industry, such as abandoned boatyards, can still be seen off the road near the banks of the river. The village was founded in 1679 and still has some of its older buildings, such as the beautiful **Maison Gendreau** built in 1720 *(2387 Chemin Royal, west of the village)* and the **Moulin Gosselin**, which was turned into a restaurant *(758 Chemin Royal, east of the village)*.

The **Parc Maritime de Saint-Laurent** ★ *($3; mid-Jun to early Sep every day 10am to 5pm; 120 Chemin de la Chalouperie, ☎828-9672)* has been developed on the site of the Saint-Laurent shipyard. Here you can

visit the Godbout *chalouperie* workshop, a family business established around 1840. They have a collection of nearly 200 craftsmen's tools. A path behind the building leads to the water where you can rent a small boat and go on a ride.

### ★★
### Saint-Jean-de-l'Île-d'Orléans

In the mid-19th century, Saint-Jean was the preferred homebase of nautical pilots who made their living guiding ships through the difficult waters and rocks of the St-Lawrence River. Some of their neoclassical and Second Empire houses can still be seen along Chemin Royal, and provide evidence of the privileged place that was held by these seamen who were indispensable to the success of commercial navigation.

The most impressive manor from the French Regime still standing is in Saint-Jean. **Manoir Mauvide-Genest** ★★ *($5; early May to late Oct every day 10am to 5pm; 1451 Chemin Royal, ☎829-2630)* was built in 1734 for Jean Mauvide, the royal doctor, and his wife Marie-Anne Genest. This beautiful stone building is coated with white roughcast in traditional Norman architectural style. The property officially became a seigneurial manor in the middle of the 18th century, when Mauvide, who had become rich doing business in the Caribbean, bought the southern half of the Île d'Orléans seigneury.

In 1926, Camille Pouliot, a descendant of the Genest family, bought the manor house. He then restored it, adding a summer kitchen and a chapel and later transformed the house into a museum, displaying furniture and objects from traditional daily life. Pouliot was one of the first people to be actively interested in Québec's heritage. The manor was bought back in 1999 and its new owners have begun major works to renovate and embellish the site. Here, you can enjoy a lovely guided tour accompanied by characters in period costumes and explore the three floors of the manor, which was restored in the tradition of the era to evoke the daily life of a domain under the French Regime. The tour lasts 1hr 15min. The Restaurant du Manoir serves Nouvelle-France inspired cuisine in a historic setting.

## ★
## Saint-François-de-l'Île-d'Orléans

This, the smallest village on Île d'Orléans, retains many buildings from its past. Some, however, are far from the Chemin Royal and are therefore difficult to see from the road. The surrounding countryside is charming and offers several pleasant panoramic views of the river, Charlevoix and the coast. The famous wild vine that gave the island its first name, Île Bacchus, can also be found in Saint-François.

As you leave the village, you will find an **observation tower ★** which provides excellent views to the north and east. Visible are the Îles Madame and Au Ruau, which mark the meeting point of the fresh water of the St. Lawrence River and the salt water of the gulf. Mont Sainte-Anne's ski slopes, Charlevoix on the north shore and the Côte-du-Sud seigneuries on the south shore can also be seen in the distance.

The **Parc des Bisons de l'île d'Orléans ★ ★** *(adults $11, children $4-$6; $3 for a guided tour aboard a panoramic vehicle, late Jun to early Sep, departures at noon and 3:30pm, lasts 45min; mid-May to late Oct 10am to 6pm, early Nov to mid-March 10am to 3pm; 156 Chemin Royal, ☎829-1234, www.parcdesbisons.com)* is a unique concept that allows you to observe the magnificent animal that is the bison from up close. In both a natural setting (three lakes outfitted for canoeing, kayaking, pedal-boating and inflatable rafts) and a ranch (120ha pasture), the Parc des Bisons features the largest bison herd in Québec, with over 400 animals. When you first arrive, you can enjoy a taste of products based on bison meat and a video about the bison, one of the rare mammals to have survived the ice age. You can then explore the park (along a 4km dirt road with interpretation panels on the edge of the lakes) in your own vehicle or take part in the motorized guided tour (the guide-interpreter's comments on the

Exploring

history of the bison are quite interesting), or even take the footpath (45min return trek, accessible to wheelchairs) that leads to an elevated site where you can admire a panoramic view of the surroundings (Mont Sainte-Anne, Cap Tourmente and the bison park). In addition, there is a museum that is home to a family of naturalized bison and mural frescoes, as well as a mini-farm, a log building for food services, picnic areas and a souvenir shop. Finally, Le Bison Futé, the park's restaurant, serves several excellent dishes made from bison meat (sampling menus are offered at the reception, where there is also a meat counter).

## ★
## Sainte-Famille

The oldest parish on Île d'Orléans was founded by Monseigneur de Laval in 1666, in order to establish a settlement across the river from Sainte-Anne-de-Beaupré for colonists who had previously settled around Sainte-Pétronille. Sainte-Famille has retained many buildings from the French Regime. Among them is the town's famous church, one of the greatest accomplishments of religious architecture in New France, and the oldest two-towered church in Québec.

*Chapel in Sainte-Famille*

The beautiful **Église Sainte-Famille ★★** *(3915 Chemin Royal)* was built between 1743 and 1747 to replace the original church built in 1669. Inspired by the Église des Jésuites in Québec City which has since been destroyed, Father Dufrost de la Jemmerais ordered the construction of two towers with imperial roofs, which explains the single steeple sitting atop the gable. Other unusual elements such as the five alcoves and the sundial by the entrance (which has since been destroyed) made the building even more unique. In the 19th century, new statues were installed in the alcoves and the imperial roofs gave way to two new steeples, bringing the total number of steeples to three.

Although modified several times, the interior decor retains many interesting elements. Sainte-Famille was a wealthy parish in the 18th century, thus allowing the decoration of the church to begin as soon as the frame of the building was finished. In 1748, Gabriel Gosselin installed the first pulpit, and in 1749 Pierre-Noël Levasseur completed construction of the high altar's present tabernacle. Louis-Basile David, inspired by the Quévillon school, designed the beautiful coffered vault in 1812. Many paintings adorn the church, such as *La Sainte Famille* (The Holy Family), painted by Frère Luc during his stay in Canada in 1670, the *Dévotion au Sacré Coeur de Jésus* (Devotion to the Sacred Heart of Jesus, 1766)

and *Le Christ en Croix* (Christ on the Cross), by François Baillargé (1802). The church grounds offer a beautiful view of the coast.

Most of the French Regime farmhouses on Île d'Orléans were built a good distance from the road. Today these properties are much sought after and their owners guard their privacy jealously, which makes any visiting unlikely. Fortunately, a foundation has been set up by residents so that **Maison Drouin ★★** *($3; late Jun to mid-Oct every day 11am to 6pm; ☎829-0330)* is open every summer to visitors. It is one of the oldest houses on the island and in Québec, dating from the 17th century. It stands by a bend on Chemin Royal and was build with large fieldstones and wooden beams. You will learn about its history from guides dressed in period costumes acting out the daily life of its former inhabitants. The three rooms on the ground floor, as well as the upstairs, recall the environment of the first colonists. Antique furniture and tools are also displayed to help illustrate pioneer life, making it a lovely place to visit.

### Saint-Pierre-de-l'Île-d'Orléans

The most developed parish on Île d'Orléans had already lost some of its charm before the island was declared a historic site. Saint-Pierre is particularly important to the people of Québec, since it was the home

Exploring

of renowned poet and singer Félix Leclerc (1914-1988) for many years. The singer and songwriter, who penned *P'tit Bonheur* was the first musician to introduce Québécois music to Europe. He is buried in the local cemetery.

In addition, at the end of the village is a site honouring the poet's memory, **Espace Félix-Leclerc** *($4; mid-Feb to mid-Dec every day 9am to 6pm; 682 Chemin Royal, ☎828-1682)* includes a wide array of interesting features: a building housing an exhibit on the life and work of Félix Leclerc, a *boîte à chansons* (a music venue for singer-songwriters) where young and old alike can belt out Leclerc's famous tunes or come up with some new ones of their own, and hiking trails to explore the heart of the island, as Leclerc did so many times. The site covers 50ha on both sides of the road, from the sand bars to the centre of the island, knows as the *mitan*. There is also a small café and picnic tables, so plan to stay a while!

**Église Saint-Pierre ★** *(1249 Chemin Royal)*, a lowly building erected in 1716, is the oldest village church still standing in Canada. The church is also a rare survivor of this kind of architecture, which was widespread in New France. It only has one portal and an oculus window on the facade. Most of these little churches with pointed roofs were destroyed in the 19th century and replaced with more elaborate

structures. Pillaged during the Conquest, the interior of Église Saint-Pierre was rebuilt at the end of the 18th century. Note the altars by Pierre Émond (1795), embellished with the papal coat of arms. The paintings above the altars are by François Baillairgé.

This church was abandoned in 1955 when the larger nearby church was inaugurated. However, when it was threatened with demolition it was taken over by the Québec government.

Conserved intact, it displays furnishings no longer found in most Québec churches, such as a central stove with a long iron stovepipe. The pews have doors which allowed these closed spaces to be reserved as private property; in winter, the owners kept warm with hot bricks and furs.

*The tour is now over. At the traffic light, turn right, go down the hill and return to Québec City on Autoroute 138 Ouest.*

# Children's Favourite Attractions

Here are a few sights and activities that will entertain children during their visit to Québec City:

The **Musée de la Civilisation** always features an exhibit or two that will please children of all ages. Family workshops are often scheduled on weekends.

The **Centre d'Interprétation de Place-Royale** features a playroom where both young and old can dress up in period costumes and act up a storm...

At the **Musée du Québec**, creativity abounds! On weekend afternoons, children can take part in arts and crafts related to the current exhibit, like sculpting or drawing. A fun time is guaranteed!

The **Parc Aquarium du Québec** and the **Jardin zoologique du Québec** offer multimedia experiences, interactive games and field trips. The Parc Aquarium takes you on a discovery of various ecosystems, from the St. Lawrence Valley to the Artic, allowing you to get acquainted with several impressive mammals like the walrus and the polar bear, while the Jardin zoologique du Québec introduces you to animals from all over the world.

Several historic sites offer tours guided by characters in period costume. This type of activity is usually a hit with children who love stories.

Sound-and-light shows, such as *Québec Expérience* and *Feux Sacrés*, which light up the basilica-cathedral, are also quite popular with kids.

Watch out for festivals! The **Carnaval de Québec**, the **Festival d'Été** and the **Fêtes de la Nouvelle-France** always have activities for children. In addition, even when there are no festivals, the Vieux-Québec area (Place-Royale, Terrasse Dufferin, Place de l'Hôtel de Ville, etc.) is usually animated by street performers in the summer.

And don't forget the round-trip ferry ride to Lévis!

Exploring

# Outdoors

# Québec City is certainly
a choice destination for outdoor enthusiasts.

The greater Québec City region has many rich and varied natural attractions, as well as numerous beautiful parks that are scattered throughout the area as well as within the city itself.

Québec City's most beautiful gardens are grouped together by an association called **Association des Jardins du Québec** *(82 Grande Allée Ouest, ☎647-4347, www. associationdesjardinsduquebec. com)*. These gardens are a treasure to explore that need to be preserved. They are open to the public, whether to learn more about horticulture and botany or simply to stroll around and enjoy their beauty. There are eight of these gardens in Québec City, namely the **Parc des Champs-de-Bataille** (see p 106), **Jardin Roger-Van den Hende** (see p 117), **Domaine Maizerets** (see p 127), **Maison Henry-Stuart** (see p 104), **Bois-de-Coulonge** (see p 135),

**Jardin Zoologique de Québec** (see p 141), **Parc Aquarium du Québec** (see p 138) and **Villa Bagatelle** (see p 135).

If you feel so inclined during your stay, you will certainly get a chance to participate in several outdoor activities. To find the right equipment, you can consult our list of stores in the Shopping chapter, p 249.

Here is a general overview of the many possibilities to you can take advantage of.

## Parks

### Tour C: Grande Allée

The **Parc des Champs-de-Bataille** (see p 106), better known as the Plains of Abraham, is Québec City's undisputed king of parks. This immense green space covers some 100ha and stretches all the way to Cap Diamant, which slopes down to the river. It is a magnificent place for local residents to enjoy all sorts of outdoor activities. Strollers and picnickers abound during the summer, but there is more than enough space for everyone to enjoy a little peace and quiet.

### Tour G: Limoilou

With its big trees and lawns, **Domaine Maizerets** (*free admission; 2000 Boulevard Montmorency,* ☎691-2385) is the perfect place for a leisurely stroll. Gardening buffs will love the arboretum and the landscaping; the Domaine also belongs to

the Association des Jardins du Québec. In the heart of the arboretum is a butterfly aviary. Weather permitting (it is closed when it rains), visitors can walk into this world of butterflies, which features some 30 species from eastern Canada. Not only will you be amazed, but you will also learn about the different stages of their development. A number of historic buildings can also be found here, including the **château** (see p 127) that houses a small exhibition on the history of the estate. All sorts of outdoor activities can be enjoyed here in both summer and winter. Outdoor concerts, plays and conferences on ornithology and other subjects are held at the Domaine Maizerets all year round.

**Parc Cartier-Brébeuf** (see p 128) is a small park on the banks of Rivière Saint-Charles. It has been redesigned to make it a pleasant spot for people to enjoy a stroll. Cement walls used to contain the river but it is now free of this yoke, at least in this area, and is adorned with aquatic plants. Flowers and decorative trees also embellish the park.

## Tour I: Sillery to Cap-Rouge

On the shores of the river, at the limits of what used to be the towns of Sainte-Foy and Cap-Rouge, **Parc de la Plage-Jacques-Cartier ★** *(Apr to Nov; Chemin de la Plage-Jacques-Cartier)* allows residents to fully enjoy the St. Lawrence River. Indeed, there didn't use to be many places where they could leisurely stroll on the riverbanks and admire the water, the tides, the birds and the boats, but today, this beach allows everyone to appreciate the majesty of this important life source.

## Tour J: Heading North

**Parc de la Falaise et de la Chute Kabir Kouba** *($5; Wendake, ☎842-0077, www.chutekabirkouba.com)* has several short paths running along the cliff about 40m above Rivière Saint-Charles. The Aboriginal people called this river *Kabir Kouba*, which means "the river with many twists and turns."

About 45km from Québec City, on the shores of the region's largest lake, Lac Saint-Joseph, the **Station Touristique Duchesnay ★** *(parking fee from mid-May to late Nov; 143 Route Duchesnay, Ste-Catherine-de-la-Jacques-Cartier, ☎875-2122 or 877-511-5885, www.sepaq.com/duchesnay)* allows visitors to familiarize themselves with the Laurentian forest. Located on an area of 90km², this centre is dedicated to researching the fauna and flora of our forests and is now one of Sépaq's tourism and recreation centres. Long famous for its cross-country ski trails, it is also ideal for practicing all kinds of outdoor activities, such as hiking on its 52.3km maintained footpaths, 15km of which are part of the Trans-Québec hiking path. There are also ample opportunities for watersports. The Jacques-Cartier–Portneuf bike path also traverses Duchesnay. In addition, you will find an interpretation centre that hosts various educational and awareness-raising activities. The installations have been entirely renovated to offer visitors comfortable lodging and dining. In winter, the site is home to the **Ice Hotel** (see p 143).

On the shores of Lac Saint-Joseph, in the village of Fossambault-sur-le-Lac, stretches the **Plage Lac Saint-Joseph** *($10 for the day; every day mid-Jun to mid-Sep; 7001 Route de Fossambault, ☎875-2242 or 877-527-5243, www.quebeccamping.com)*. You're not dreaming: this is a real beach, complete with palm trees (imported from Florida annually)! In addition to swimming, you can enjoy a wide array of water activities here. Note, however, that the beach attracts a large crowd on hot summer days.

**Outdoors**

The **Station Touristique Stoneham** *(fees vary according to the activities; Stoneham, ☎848-2411 or 800-463-6888, www.ski-stoneham.com)* welcomes visitors year-round. In the winter there are 32 ski runs. In the summer, paths are at the disposal of hikers, mountain-bikers and horseback riders.

Throughout the year, hordes of visitors come to **Parc national de la Jacques-Cartier ★ ★ ★** *($3.50; Highway 175 N., Km 74, ☎848-3169 or 800-665-6527, in winter 528-8781)*, located in the Réserve Faunique des Laurentides, 40km north of Quebec City. The area is called «Vallée de la Jacques-Cartier», after the river of the same name that runs through it, winding between steep hills. As a result of the microclimate caused by the river being hemmed in on both sides, the site is suitable for a number of outdoor activities. The vegetation and wildlife are abundant and diverse. The winding and well-laid-out paths sometimes lead to interesting surprises, like a moose and its offspring foraging for food in a marsh. Before heading out to discover all the riches the site has to offer, you can get information at the nature centre's reception area. Campsites (see p 188), chalets and equipment are all available for rent.

At the park, specialists organize **moose observation safaris** *(22$; ☎418-848-2422 for reservations; the activity lasts 4h30)* from mid-September to mid-

October as well as at **sunset rabaska canoe animal-watching tour** *($10, 12 years old and up; ☎848-2422 for reservations)* during summer, introducing visitors to the animals in their natural habitat..

## Tour K: Côte-de-Beaupré and Île d'Orléans

**Parc de la Chute-Montmorency ★ ★** (see p 145).

The **Cap-Tourmente National Wildlife Area ★ ★ ★** *($6; early Jan to Nov; 570 Chemin du Cap-Tourmente, Saint-Joachim, ☎827-3776)* is located on pastoral, fertile land. Each spring and autumn its sandbars are visited by countless snow geese that stop to gather strength during their long migration. The reserve also has bird-watching facilities and naturalists on hand to answer your questions about the 300 species of birds and 45 species of mammals you might encounter on the hiking and walking trails that cross the park.

**Station Mont-Sainte-Anne ★ ★** *(2000 Boulevard Beaupré, Beaupré, ☎827-4561, www.mont-sainte-anne.com)* covers 77km$^2$ and includes the 800m-high Mont Sainte-Anne, one of the most beautiful downhill-ski sites in Québec. There are a few hotels close to the ski hill and the park. Various other activities are also offered, since the park has

200km of mountain-bike and cross-country ski trails. Sports equipment can be rented on site.

The **Grand Canyon des Chutes Sainte-Anne** *($79; early May to late Jun and early Sep to late Oct, every day 9am to 4:30pm; late Jun to early Sep 9am to 5:45pm; 206 Route 138, Beaupré, ☎827-4057, www.canyonste-anne.qc. ca)* is where rushing Rivière Sainte-Anne carves a deep path through the hills near Beaupré and plunges 74m into a large 22m pothole formed by the resulting water current. Visitors can take in this impressive site from lookouts and a suspension bridge.

# Outdoor Activities

## Hiking

### Tour J: Heading North

The **Station Touristique Stoneham** *(free admission; Stoneham, ☎848-2411 or 800-463-6888, www.ski-stoneham. com)* welcomes hikers with a few trails, one of which goes as far as the Parc de la Jacques-Cartier.

The 100km of paths in **Parc national de la Jacques-Cartier**

*($3.50; mid-May to mid-Oct; Hwy. 175 N., ☎848-3169 or 800-665-6527, www.sepaq.com)* are among the favourites for hikers in this region. Wether easy-going or abrupt, they will allow you to discover the hidden corners of the forest, as well as superb views of the valley and the river.

### Tour K: Côte-de-Beaupré and Île d'Orléans

At the **Cap-Tourmente National Wildlife Area** *($6 Saint-Joachim, ☎827-3776)* you can, if your legs are up to it, climb the 20km of trails that lead to a magnificent view of the river and its surroundings. You can also use the wooden sidewalks (adapted for people with disabilities) for an equally enjoyable walk.

**Station Mont-Sainte-Anne** *($2.60; Hwy. 360, Beaupré, ☎827-4561, www.mont-sainte-anne.com)* has 32km of hiking trails.

## Cycling

Québec City is developing its cycling infrastructure. Today, more than 100km of cycling paths stretch out around the city and its surroundings. Consult the Ulysses Travel Guide *Le Québec cyclable* to obtain maps of these trails.

Outdoors

A bike path called the **Corridor des Cheminots** (☎641-6415) enables cyclists and other sports enthusiasts to travel 22km through various municipalities to Val-Bélair, not far from the beginning of the Jacques-Cartier–Portneuf path (see below).

Some noteworthy bike paths have existed for a number of years, such as the one that leads to Beauport or the one that runs along Rivière Saint-Charles. The many marked or shared routes make Québec City and its neighbouring communities enjoyable places to discover by bicycle.

The **Promo-Vélo** association (C.P. 700, Succ. Haute-Ville, Québec, G1R 4S9, ☎522-0087) offers a great deal of information on the various kinds of tours available in the region. Furthermore, this organization publishes a map of bike paths in the Québec City region.

### Bicycle Rentals

You can rent mountain bikes at Station Mont-Sainte-Anne and in Parc de la Jacques-Cartier (see above).

**Cyclo Services**
*$20/day*
Marché du Vieux-Port
160 Rue Quai St-André
☎692-4052
Cyclo Services also organizes excursions in the city and its surrounding area.

**Vélotek**
*$30/day*
463 Rue Saint-Jean
☎648-6022

### Bicycle Repairs

**Vélotek**
463 Rue Saint-Jean
☎648-6022
They also rent bicycles (see above).

**Le Vélomane**
957 Avenue Royale, Beauport
☎663-3930

### Tour K: Côte-de-Beaupré and Île d'Orléans

A bicycle path runs from the Vieux-Port of Québec City to the Parc de la Chute Montmorency, passing through Beauport on the way. Also, roads such as the Chemin du Roy, on the Côte de Beaupré and Île d'Orléans (bike rentals at the Le Vieux-Presbytère guesthouse, see p 191), are meant to be shared by motorists and cyclists. Caution is always in order, but these trips are definitely worth the effort.

**Station Mont-Sainte-Anne**
($8.70; late May to mid-Oct, 9am to 5pm; Beaupré, ☎827-4561, www.mont-sainte-anne.

*com)* has about 150km of trails to offer mountain-bike enthusiasts. Pedal your way to the top of the mountain or rush down the slopes after riding up in the cable car with your bicycle ($13). There are more than 20 trails with most evocative names, such as *La Grisante* (the exhilarating one) or *La Vietnam.* This is a well-known biking spot: **World Cup Mountain Bike** (see p 237) races are held here every year.

The **Station Touristique Stoneham** *(free admission; Stoneham, ☎848-2411 or 800-463-6888, www.ski-stoneham. com)* also has a few mountain-bike trails.

### Tour J: Heading North

Following the route of some old railway lines, the **Piste Jacques-Cartier–Portneuf** *($5; 100 Rue Saint-Jacques, C.P. 238, St-Raymond, ☎337-7525)* crosses through the Réserve Faunique Portneuf and the Station Forestière Duchesnay (where you can park your car and rent bicycles), and borders some lakes. It is 68km long, stretching from Rivière-à-Pierre to Saint-Gabriel-de-Valcartier. Its magical setting and safe riding conditions have already attracted many cyclists. In winter, the path is used for snowmobiling.

In **Parc national de la Jacques-Cartier** *($3.50; mid-May to mid-Oct; Hwy. 175 N., ☎848-3169)* trails are available for both hikers and mountain-biking

enthusiasts. Bike rentals are available.

## Cruises

**Croisières AML** *(tickets sold at 124 Rue St-Pierre, ☎692-2634 or 800-563-4643, www.croisieres aml.com)* organizes cruises all summer, offering a great view of Québec City and its surroundings from a different angle. One of the ships owned by this company is the ***M/V Louis-Jolliet*** *($25; departures 11am, 2pm and 4pm)*, which sails from Québec City, its port of registry. Day cruises last 1hr 30min and go as far as the Montmorency Falls. At night, you can go up to Île d'Orléans and enjoy dinner in one of the ship's two dining rooms. These evening cruises last a few hours and feature musicians and dancing.

**Croisières du Groupe Dufour** *(22 Quai Saint-André, ☎800-463-5250, www.familledufour. com)* take passengers to the lovely Charlevoix region, to Pointe-au-Pic, Île-aux-Coudres and even to the heart of the breathtaking Saguenay fjord, among other destinations, aboard a big modern catamaran.

**Outdoors**

## In-Line Skating

On the **Plains of Abraham** in front of the Musée du Québec is a large paved rink for in-line skating. Scores of children and adults wearing protective helmets can be seen blading around the track on fine summer days. Equipment rentals are available at a small stand by the rink. This is the only spot on the Plains of Abraham where skating is allowed.

## Jogging

Again, the place to go is the **Plains of Abraham**. The big flat track in front of the Musée du Québec is a good place for a run, though people also go jogging on the paved streets and trails.

## Fruit-Picking

### Tour K: Côte-de-Beaupré and Île d'Orléans

From strawberries and raspberries to corn, leaks and apples, the harvests follow one another all summer long, continuously changing the look of the surrounding countryside. On **Île d'Orléans**, farmers open their doors to anyone, parents and children alike, who wishes to spend a day playing in an orchard or a field. Learn the secrets of picking and enjoy the fruits of your labour!

## Bird-Watching

### Tour K: Côte-de-Beaupré and Île d'Orléans

One of the best places in the region for bird-watching is definitely the **Cap-Tourmente National Wildlife Area** *($6; 570 Chemin du Cap-Tourmente, Saint-Joachim, ☎827-3776).* During spring and autumn, the thousands of migrating snow geese that overtake the area are a fascinating sight to behold. Any questions you might have after seeing these creatures up close and in such great numbers can be answered here. The reserve is home to 280 avian species. They are attracted here throughout the year by a number of bird houses and feeders.

## Rafting

### Tour J: Heading North

In spring and summer, Rivière Jacques-Cartier gives adventurers a good run for their money. Two longstanding companies offer well-supervised rafting expeditions with all the necessary equipment. At **Village Vacances Valcartier** (*$56, including wet suit rental; reservations must be made at least two days ahead; 1860 Boulevard Valcartier, St-Gabriel-de-Valcartier, ☎844-7238 or 888-384-5524, www.valcartier.com*), an 8km ride delivers a lot of excitement.

With **Excursions Jacques-Cartier** (*860 Avenue Jacques-Cartier, Tewkesbury, ☎848-7238*), you can also experience some very exciting runs.

## Golf

### Tour J: Heading North

The **Royal Charlesbourg** (*$36 Mon-Thu, $45 Fri-Sun; 2180 Chemin de la Grande-Ligne, Charlesbourg, ☎841-3000*) is an 18-hole golf course located far from the hustle and bustle of the city.

The **Mont-Tourbillon** 18-hole golf course (*$36 Mon-Thu, $45 Fri-Sun; 55 Montée du Golf, Lac-Beauport, ☎849-4418 or 866-949-4418, www.monttourbillon.com*) is a great place to enjoy this sport.

### Tour K: Côte-de-Beaupré and Île d'Orléans

Station Mont-Sainte-Anne's golf course, **Le Grand Vallon** (*$69 Mon-Thu, $80 Fri-Sun; 100 Rue Beau-Mont, Beaupré, ☎827-4653 or 888-827-4579, www.mont.sainte.anne.com*), offers a par 72 course with several sand traps and four lakes, and is known as one of the most interesting courses in eastern Canada.

## Ice Skating

### Tour A: Vieux-Québec

Each winter, an ice rink is laid out on **Terrasse Dufferin**, enabling skaters to swirl about at the foot of Château Frontenac with a view of the icy river. You can don your gear at the kiosk (*$2; mid-Dec to mid-Mar, every day 11am to 11pm; ☎694-9487*), which also rents out skates (*$3/day*).

### Tour D: Saint-Jean-Baptiste

On beautiful winter days, Place d'Youville is turned into a magical place, with skaters, snow, frost-covered Porte-Saint-Jean, the illuminated Capitole and Christmas decorations hanging from lampposts. In the centre of the square is a skating rink with music, and even if you don't feel like joining in the ice waltz, you can still enjoy the sights. The skating rink opens early in the season, around the end of October, and shuts down in late spring, ensuring that Québec City residents can skate for as long as possible! There are restrooms for skaters *(free admission; Mon-Thu noon to 10pm, Fri-Sun 10am to 10pm; ☎641-6256)*.

### Tour G: Limoilou

A lovely skating rink winds beneath the trees of **Domaine Maizerets** *(free admission; 2000 Boulevard Montmorency, ☎641-6335)*. There's a small chalet nearby where you can take off your skates and warm up next to a wood stove. Skate rentals are available *($4; mid-Dec to mid-Mar, every day 10am to 9pm)*.

Once it has iced over, **Rivière Saint-Charles** is turned into a natural skating rink that, weather permitting, winds 2km between the neighbourhoods of Limoilou and Saint-Roch, in Basse-Ville. There is a heated place to rest *(free admission, skate rentals $5/hour; Mon-Thu noon to 10pm, Fri-Sun 10am to 10pm; 25 Rue de la Pointe-aux-Lièvres, ☎691-5488)*.

## Cross-Country Skiing

### Tour C: Grande Allée

The snow-covered **Plains of Abraham** provide an enchanting setting for cross-country skiing. Trails crisscross the park from one end to the other, threading their way through the trees or leading across a headland with views of the icy river. All this right in the heart of the city!

### Tour G: Limoilou

Some extremely pleasant cross-country ski trails can also be found at **Domaine Maizerets** *(free admission; 2000 Boulevard Montmorency, ☎641-6335)*. At the starting point, there is a little heated chalet with a wood-burning stove. Equipment rentals *($4; mid-Dec to mid-Mar every day 10am to 4pm)* are available.

### Tour J: Heading North

In winter, **Station Touristique Duchesnay** *($9.60; 143 Route Duchesnay, Sainte-Catherine-de-la-Jacques-Cartier, ☎875-2122 or 877-511-5885, www.sepaq. com/duchesnay)* is very popular among skiers in the area. This great forest boasts 188.5km of well-kept trails and many little crested tits and other bird species that don't mind the cold! Nestled in the heart of the

Réserve Faunique des Laurentides, **Camp Mercier** *($9.60; late Nov to mid-Apr, every day 8:30am to 4pm; Hwy. 175 N., Réserve Faunique des Laurentides, ☎848-2422 or 800-665-6527, www.sepaq.com)* is criss-crossed with 190km of well-maintained trails in an extremely tranquil landscape. Given its ideal location, you can ski here from fall to spring. Long routes (up to 42km) with heated huts offer some interesting opportunities. There are also cottages for rent that can accommodate from two to 14 people.

### Tour K: Côte-de-Beaupré and Île d'Orléans

The **Station Mont-Sainte-Anne** *($16.50; Mon-Fri 9am to 4pm, Sat and Sun 8:30am to 4pm; 2000 Boulevard Beau-Pré, Beaupré, ☎827-4561 or 800-469-1568 for accommodations, www.mont-sainte-anne.com)* has 212km of well-maintained cross-country ski trails with some heated huts set up along the way. Ski equipment can be rented *($20/day)*.

## Snowshoeing

Snowshoeing, a sport that regained its popularity when smaller, lighter models of snowshoes began to appear on the market, can be practiced in most of the region's cross-country skiing centres. The **Station Écotouristique Duchesnay** (see above), the **Mont-Sainte-Anne resort** (see above), as well as **Parc national de la Jacques-Cartier** (see above) are some of the nicer sites.

## Downhill Skiing and Snowboarding

### Tour J: Heading North

**Le Relais** *($30/day; 1084 Boulevard du Lac, ☎849-1851, www.skirelais.com)* has 25 downhill skiing trails, all of which are lit for night skiing.

The **Station Touristique Stoneham** *($40.90; Stoneham, ☎848-2411 or 800-463-6888, www.ski-stoneham.com)* welcomes visitors year-round. In the winter there are 32 runs, 16 of which are lit at night.

### Tour K: Côte-de-Beaupré and Île d'Orléans

**Mont-Sainte-Anne** *($50.45; 2000 Boulevard Beau-Pré, Beaupré, ☎827-4561, www. mont-sainte-anne.com)* is one of the biggest ski resorts in Québec. Among its 63 runs, some reach 625m in height and 15 are lit for night skiing. It's equally a delight for snowboarders. Equipment rentals are also available.

**Outdoors**

Located 15min away from Station Mont-Sainte-Anne via Route 138, **Le Massif** *($45.20; Petite-Rivière-Saint-François, ☎632-5876 or 877-536-2774, www.lemassif.com)* may be a bit outside this tour, but it's one of the best ski resorts in the province of Québec. Firstly, because Le Massif features the highest vertical drop in eastern Canada (770m), and secondly, because every winter it receives a great deal of snow, which, aided by artificial snow, creates ideal ski conditions. Then there's the amazing natural setting! The mountain, which almost plunges into the river, offers a stunning panorama. There are 42 runs for all types of skiers, and a cozy chalet awaits you at the summit.

---

## Tobogganing and Waterslides

### Tour A: Vieux-Québec

During winter, a hill is created on **Terrasse Dufferin**, which you can slide down on a toboggan. First purchase your tickets at the little stand in the middle of the terrace *($2/ride; late Dec to mid-Mar, every day 11am to 11pm; 694-9487)*, then grab a toboggan and climb to the top of the slide. Once you get there, make sure to take a look around: the view is magnificent!

### Tour C: Grande Allée

The hills of the **Plains of Abraham** are wonderful for sledding. Bundle up and follow the kids pulling toboggans to find the best spots!

### Tour J: Heading North

Winter or summer, **Village Vacances Valcartier** *(waterpark during summer $24.34; winter slide $17.40; 1860 Boulevard Valcartier, Saint-Gabriel-de-Valcartier; take Route 371 N. from Quebec City; ☎844-2200 or 800-384-5524, www.valcartier. com)* is the undisputed authority when it comes to slides. It is an outdoor-activity centre that offers a full range of facilities. In the summer, waterslides and a wave pool draw huge crowds. In winter, ice slides will help you forget the cold for a little while. There is also snow rafting and skating on a 2.5km-long ice rink that snakes through the woods. A restaurant and bar are also included on the premises.

# Accommodations

## Québec City has
all kinds of accommodations to offer: two youth hostels and plenty of bed and breakfasts, inns and luxury hotels.

You will certainly find a suitable place to stay, whether it is for one night or one week.

Although comfort may be a little rudimentary in the smaller inns, most hotels offer very comfortable conditions and offer many services. There are quite a few bed and breakfasts in Québec City. They are reasonably priced and offer the advantages of a home-style atmosphere. In Québec, bed and breakfasts are known as *gîtes du passant*. These establishments are members of the Fédération des Agricotours du Québec and must conform to their regulations and standards to ensure a high level of quality. The *Ulysses Inns and Bed & Breakfasts in Québec* travel guide is available and lists the various accommodations and services for each Québec region.

**Hospitalité Canada Tours** is a free telephone service operated by the **Maison du Tourisme de Québec** (*12 Rue Sainte-Anne;* ☎*800-665-1528*). Depending on what kind of accommodations you're looking for, the staff can suggest various establishments belonging to the network and even make reservations for you.

## Rates

Rates may vary from one season to another. Rooms are more expensive during the summer or high season, and the weeks of the **Festival d'été de Québec** (Summer Festival) in July and **Carnaval de Québec** in February are the busiest of the year. We recommend that you reserve well in advance if you plan to visit Québec City during these periods.

The prices mentioned in this guide are for a standard room for two people in high season, unless otherwise indicated.

| $ | less than $60 |
|---|---|
| $$ | $60 to $100 |
| $$$ | $101 to $150 |
| $$$$ | $151 to $225 |
| $$$$$ | more than $225 |

However, room prices may also vary within the same hotel. Furthermore, many hotels and inns offer considerable discounts to employees of corporations or members of automobile clubs (CAA, AAA). Be sure to ask about corporate and other discounts, as they are often very easy to obtain.

The following accommodations are classified according to price starting with the least expensive. Remember to add the 7% federal tax and the 7.5% Québec sales tax to the given rate when making your calculations. The federal tax is refundable to non-residents (see p 50). A non-refundable tax called "Taxe Spécifique sur l'Hébergement" (accommodation tax) is also applied to accommodation costs. The amount is $2 per night, regardless of the total bill or the type of accommodation.

## Symbols in this Guide

The various services offered by each establishment are indicated with a small symbol, which is explained in the legend in the opening pages of this guidebook. By no means is this an exhaustive list of what the establishment offers, but rather the services we consider to be the most important.

Please note that the presence of a symbol does not mean that all the rooms have this service; you sometimes may have to pay extra to get, for example, a whirlpool tub. And likewise, if the symbol is not attached to an establishment, it means that the establishment cannot offer you this service. Please note that unless otherwise indicated, all hotels in this guide offer private bathrooms.

### The Ulysses Boat

The Ulysses boat pictogram is awarded to our favourite accommodations and restaurants. While every establishment recommended in this guide was included because of its high quality and/or uniqueness, as

# **Ulysses' Favourites**

**For history buffs:**
>  Auberge Baker (p 189)
>  Château Frontenac (p 179)
>  Hôtel Clarendon (p 178)
>  Le Vieux-Presbytère (p 191)

**For the view:**
>  Château Bellevue (p 178)
>  Château de Pierre (p 177)
>  Château Frontenac (p 179)
>  Hôtel Dominion 1912 (p 180)
>  Hôtel Loews Le Concorde (p 183)
>  La Goéliche (p 191)

**For the décor:**
>  Auberge Saint-Antoine (p 181)
>  Auberge Saint-Pierre (p 180)
>  Hôtel Dominion 1912 (p 180)
>  Hôtel du Capitole (p 184)
>  Hôtel Germain-des-Prés (p 185)

**For the warm welcome:**
>  Auberge du Quartier (p 182)
>  Auberge du Petit Pré (p 189)

**For the peace and quiet:**
>  Château Bonne-Entente (p 185)
>  Chaumière Juchereau-Duchesnay (p 187)
>  Le Canard Huppé (p 192)

**For the friendly atmosphere:**
>  Auberge de la Paix (p 174)
>  B&B Café Krieghoff (p 181)
>  Hôtel Belley (p 179)
>  L'Autre Jardin (p 186)

**For business people:**
>  Hôtel Loews Le Concorde (p 183)
>  Hilton Québec (p 184)
>  Hôtel Royal William (p 186).

well as its value for the money, every once in a while we come across an establishment that absolutely wows us. These, our favourite establishments, are awarded a Ulysses boat. You'll find boats in all price categories: next to exclusive, high-priced establishments, as well as budget ones. Regardless of the price, each of these establishments offers the most for your money. Look for them first!

# Tour A: Vieux-Québec

### Auberge de la Paix
*$ bkfst incl.*
*$3 bedding surcharge for the first night if you don't bring your own*
*sb, K*
31 Rue Couillard
☎694-0735
Behind its lovely white facade in Vieux-Québec, Auberge de la Paix offers a youth-hostel atmosphere. It has 60 beds in rooms able to accommodate from two to eight people, as well as a kitchenette and a living room. This inn lives up to its name by providing a friendly and fun place to relax. In the summer, a lovely garden is filled with flowers. Children are welcome!

### Manoir LaSalle
*$*
*pb/sb, K*
18 Rue Sainte-Ursule
☎692-9953
Manoir LaSalle is a small hotel with 11 rooms, one of which has a private bathroom. This red-brick building is exemplary of the architectural style of some of the first homes built in the city. Visitors must not be allergic to cats.

### La Maison Demers
*$-$$ bkfst incl.*
68 Rue Ste-Ursule
☎692-2487 or 800-692-2417
This beautiful home dating from 1898 is filled with charmingly mismatched furnishings and travel souvenirs. The reception is warm and charming, and both gay travellers and families are welcome.

### Auberge Saint-Louis
*$$ bkfst incl.*
*pb/sb, ℜ, ≡*
48 Rue Saint-Louis
☎692-2424 or 888-692-4105
≈692-3797
Located on busy Rue Saint-Louis, Auberge Saint-Louis is a small, pleasant hotel. Room prices vary according to included amenities. The less expensive rooms do not have private bathrooms. The hotel is well maintained.

### Auberge Internationale de Québec
*$$*
*pb/sp*
19 Rue Ste-Ursule
☎694-0755
*from Montréal*
☎(514) 252-3117
The Auberge Internationale de Québec is a youth hostel with 280 beds for young people. The rooms can accommodate from two to five people, the dormitories from four to 12, and there are also private double rooms.

### Maison Sainte-Ursule
*$$*
*pb/sb*
40 Rue Ste-Ursule
☎694-9794
≈694-0875
Maison Sainte-Ursule is a small, charming house with green shutters. Unfortunately, its rooms are oddly shaped and dark. In low season, though, prices are quite affordable.

# A Vieux-Québec

N

**ACCOMMODATIONS**

1. Auberge de la Chouette
2. Auberge de la Paix
3. Auberge du Trésor
4. Auberge Internationale de Québec
5. Auberge Saint-Louis
6. Au Jardin du Gouverneur
7. Au Petit Hôtel
8. Château Bellevue
9. Château de Léry
10. Château de Pierre
11. Château Frontenac
12. Hôtel Acadia
13. Hôtel Cap-Diamant
14. Hôtel Clarendon
15. Hôtel du Vieux-Québec
16. Hôtel Saint-Anne
17. La Maison Demers
18. Le Clos Saint-Louis
19. Maison du Fort
20. Maison Sainte-Ursule
21. Manoir LaSalle
22. Manoir Victoria
23. Marquise de Bassano

© ULYSSES

## Au Petit Hôtel
*$$*
3 Rue des Ursulines
☎*694-0965*
Located in the heart of Vieux-Québec, this large red-and-yellow house with a green roof, tucked away on Rue des Ursulines, offers 16 rooms that inspire happiness and tranquility. Parking.

## Auberge de la Chouette
*$$*
≡, ℜ
71 Rue D'Auteuil
☎*694-0232*
Occupying two floors above the **Apsara** (see p 200) restaurant, Auberge de la Chouette's 10 rooms are simply decorated and furnished with antiques. The Vietnamese family that manages the restaurant and the inn will welcome you with a smile. No smoking.

## Marquise de Bassano
*$$-$$$ bkfst incl.*
*sb*
15 Rue des Grisons
☎*692-0316 or 877-692-0316*
*www.marquisedebassano.com*
Vieux-Québec has been home to some colourful characters throughout its history. At the corner of the Rue des Grisons and Avenue Sainte-Geneviève is a small Victorian house which, it is said, was built for one such character. The dark panelling that decorates the inside surely guards some secrets of the Marquise de Bassano. The house has been transformed into a welcoming bed and breakfast, with charming rooms and a cheerful sitting room with a piano and a fireplace. During breakfast, which sometimes lasts into the afternoon, the young hosts take pleasure in animating the discussions. Parking is available. No smoking.

## Au Jardin du Gouverneur
*$$-$$$ bkfst incl.*
≡
16 Rue Mont-Carmel
☎*692-1704*
≈*692-1713*
Au Jardin du Gouverneur is a charming little hotel set in a small blue and white house opposite Parc des Gouverneurs. The rooms are spacious but there is nothing special about the decor. No smoking.

## Hôtel Acadia
*$$-$$$$*
*pb/sb*, ⊛, ≡, *K*, ℝ
43 Rue Ste-Ursule
☎*694-0280 or 800-463-0280*
≈*694-0458*
*www.hotelacadia.com*
A number of old houses on Rue Sainte-Ursule have been transformed into hotels. Among these, Hôtel Acadia stands out with its large, white facade. In the basement are luxury suites with stone walls and beautiful woodwork. Rooms have wireless Internet access. Hôtel l'Ermitage across the street is under the same administration.

## Hôtel du Vieux-Québec
*$$$ bkfst incl.*
≡, ⊛, 🐾
1190 Rue St-Jean
☎*692-1850 or 800-361-7787*
≈*692-5637*
*www.hvq.com*
Hôtel du Vieux-Québec is a modern establishment that

The Château Frontenac and the Fortifications. - *Philippe Renault*

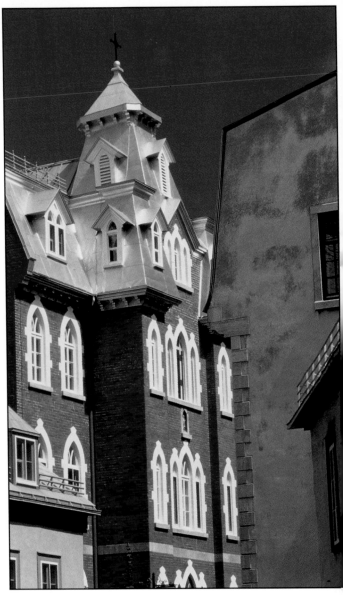

The Musée Bon-Pasteur, located in an eclectic brick structure built around 1887.
- *Patrick Escudero*

exudes the kind of cool ambiance that is often associated with modernism. Although the decor is not extravagant, it is quite comfortable and friendly. The rooms are spacious and offer Internet access. Pets are welcome.

### Château de Léry
**$$$**
≡, ⊛, K
8 Rue de la Porte
☎692-2692 or 800-363-0036
⇋692-5231
Located next to Parc des Gouverneurs and overlooking the river, the Château de Léry has comfortable rooms. Rooms facing the street offer a good view. This hotel is in a quiet neighbourhood in the old part of the city, just a few minutes' walk from the bustle of downtown.

### Auberge du Trésor
**$$$**
ℜ, ≡
20 Rue Sainte-Anne
☎694-1876 or 800-566-1876
Auberge du Trésor was built in 1676. Renovated many times since, it maintains an impressive appearance. The rooms are modern and comfortable.

### Château de Pierre
**$$$**
≡
17 Avenue Ste-Geneviève
☎694-0429 or 888-694-0429
⇋694-0153
The Château de Pierre is set in an old colonial-style house. The ostentatious entrance of this hotel is quite striking and some-

what flashy. The rooms are comfortable.

### Hôtel Sainte-Anne
**$$$-$$$$ bkfst incl.**
ℜ
32 Rue Ste-Anne
☎266-2165 or 877-778-8977
This establishment has the advantage of offering modern comfort in a historical setting. Its decor is somewhat minimalist. In addition, the hotel is home to the Grill Sainte-Anne, which is only open in summer and whose terrace happily spills onto Rue Sainte-Anne. Parking.

### Maison du Fort
**$$$-$$$$ bkfst incl.**
≡, K, ⊛
21 Avenue Ste-Geneviève
☎692-4375
⇋692-5257
www.hotelmaisondufort.com
This recently renovated Gregorian-style house was designed by architect Charles Baillargé in 1851. The service is quite welcoming and there are two cats on the premises.

### Hôtel Cap-Diamant
**$$$-$$$$ bkfst incl.**
≡, ℝ, ℑ
39 Avenue Ste-Geneviève
☎694-0313
⇋692-1375
www.hcapdiamant.qc.ca
Hôtel Cap-Diamant is located in an old house in Vieux-Québec. This is the kind of house where even the walls have secrets… and many stories to tell. It is the perfect place to immerse yourself in the family

life of bygone days. The long staircase, the creaking floors, and even the wallpaper contribute to its charm and quaint appearance. You can enjoy the porch or wander in the flower-filled garden and sit by the stream. Internet access is available.

## Château Bellevue
### $$$-$$$$
≡

16 Rue de la Porte
☎692-2473 or 800-463-2617
≈692-4876

The Château Bellevue offers an impressive view of the river. The rooms are pleasant and equipped with modern-style furniture.

## Hôtel Clarendon
### $$$$
≡, ℜ, ⊛, ✪, ⊘, ♿
57 Rue Sainte-Anne
☎692-2480 or 888-554-6001
≈692-4652
www.botelclarendon.com

Built in 1870, Hôtel Clarendon is one of the oldest hotels in the city (see p 69). The hotel has an unpretentious exterior while the elegant interior is decorated in Art Deco style. The entrance hall is very attractive. The rooms in this hotel have been renovated many times over the years and are spacious and comfortable, making this a very good place to stay in Vieux-Québec. Its restaurant, **Le Charles-Baillargé** (see p 203), serves elegant meals, and there is also a lively bar, **L'Emprise** (see p 228), which hosts live jazz.

## Le Clos Saint-Louis
### $$$$-$$$$$ bkfst incl.
⊛, ≡, ℑ
71 Rue St-Louis
☎694-1311 or 800-461-1311
≈694-9411
www.clossaintlouis.com

Le Clos Saint-Louis comprises two imposing Victorian houses dating from 1844 on Rue St-Louis. Located close to Vieux-Québec and its attractions, this hotel has 18 rooms with Internet access spread out on four floors. The rooms have all been arranged to make their historic aspect especially welcoming: some have four-poster beds with canopies, others old-fashioned bookcases or fireplaces. The rooms on the second floor are particularly attractive, with their stone walls and exposed wooden beams. The bathrooms are all modern and well equipped. Coffee and croissants are served in the morning. No smoking.

## Manoir Victoria
### $$$$-$$$$$
≡, ≈, ⊘, △, ℜ, ⊛
44 Côte du Palais
☎692-1030 or 800-463-6283
≈692-3822
www.manoir-victoria.com

Manoir Victoria is a 156-room hotel nestled on Côte du Palais. Decorated in true Victorian style, it succeeds in being both chic and very comfortable. The lobby, at the top of a long flight of stairs, is inviting and contains both a bar and a dining room, La Table du Manoir. Manoir Victoria offers well-equipped suites and a number of cultural and sports packages.

### Château Frontenac
**$$$$$**
ℜ, ≡, &, ⊛, ≈, ⊘
1 Rue des Carrières
☎ *692-3861 or 800-441-1414*
⇰ *692-1751*
**www.fairmont.com**

The Château Frontenac is by far the most prestigious hotel in Québec City (see p 64). Enter its elegant lobby with its wood panelling and warm colours and let yourself be transported back in time. The Château Frontenac was built in 1893 and over the years has been the setting of several historic events. The decor exudes a classic, refined richness that is truly worthy of a castle. Its restaurant also offers a taste of luxury (see **Le Champlain**, p 205). The sumptuous rooms provide the most comfortable environment possible, and although the size and benefits of the hotel's 618 rooms vary greatly, all are quite pleasant. The rooms overlooking the river have beautiful bay windows and, of course, the view is magnificent.

## Tour B: Petit-Champlain to Vieux-Port

### Hôtel Belley
**$$-$$$**
K
249 Rue St-Paul
☎ *692-1694 or 888-692-1694*
⇰ *692-1696*

The pleasant Hôtel Belley stands opposite the market in the Vieux-Port. A hotel since 1877, this handsome building will leave you with fond memories for years to come. It has eight simply decorated cozy rooms, some with exposed brick walls, others with wooden beams and skylights. The ground floor is home to the **Taverne Belley** (see p 231) bar, whose breakfasts and lunches, served in two lovely rooms, are very popular with locals. A number of extremely comfortable and attractively decorated lodgings, some with terraces, are also available in another house across the street. These may be rented by the night, the week or the month.

### Hayden's Wexford House
**$$$ bkfst incl.**
*sb/pb*, ≡
450 Rue Champlain
☎ *524-0524*
⇰ *648-8995*
**www.haydenwexfordhouse.com**

Located on a magnificent street between Cap Diamant and the river, Hayden's Wexford House has proudly displayed its facade since 1832. Its name, in fact, is inscribed in the brickwork. This house has managed to maintain all of its period charm. The four small rooms nestled on the top floor have lovely views from the dormer windows and are tastefully decorated with wood trim and floral patterns. Adding to guests' comfort, quality mattresses have been made to measure. Breakfast is served in a stone-walled dining room which is every bit as charming as the rest of the house. No smoking.

## Appartements du Cap-Blanc
### $$$
*⅃, K*
444 Rue Champlain
☎524-6137
⇥648-8995
*www.haydenwexfordhouse.com*

Do you want to spend a few days in Québec City in a well-situated *pied-à-terre* with all the necessary conveniences? Appartements du Cap-Blanc will surely please you since they are located right next door to the owner's bed and breakfast (see Hayden's Wexford House above). Each apartment occupies one floor of a renovated old house and includes a living room, a well-equipped kitchenette, a dining room, a bathroom and a closed bedroom, all attractively decorated. You'll never want to leave! There is a minimum stay of two nights and smoking is not permitted.

## ⛵ Le Priori
### $$$$ bkfst incl.
⊛, ℜ, ⅃, K, ≡, ⚘
15 Rue Sault-au-Matelot
☎522-8108 or 800-351-3992
⇥692-0883

Le Priori is located on a quiet street in the Basse-Ville. The building is very old but has been renovated in a very modern style. The decor successfully contrasts the old stone walls of the building with up-to-date furnishings. Its appearance is striking and even the elevator is distinctive. Rooms have wireless Internet access. Le Priori is highly recommended.

## Auberge Saint-Pierre
### $$$$-$$$$$ bkfst incl.
⊛, ≡
79 Rue St-Pierre
☎694-7981 or 888-268-1017
⇥694-0406
*www.auberge.qc.ca*

This lovely inn is located in a building that had housed Canada's first insurance company since the end of the 19th century. The historic charm of Auberge Saint-Pierre was retained when the building was renovated. The rooms are similar to the neighbouring apartments, with their various landings and narrow hallways. Each room has beautiful, dark hardwood floors and sumptuously coloured walls. Those on the lower floors have lovely high ceilings, while those higher up provide a wonderful view. Wireless Internet connection.

## ⛵ Hôtel Dominion 1912
### $$$$$ bkfst incl.
≡, ⚘
126 Rue St-Pierre
☎692-2224 or 888-833-5253
⇥692-4403
*www.hoteldominion.com*

Dating from 1912 as its name implies, this beautiful building on Rue Saint-Pierre has been transformed into a hotel that charms its chic clientele. The luxurious Hôtel Dominion 1912 has a modern aspect with materials such as glass and wrought iron, but still maintains its original character. Elements of interior decoration such as cream-and-sand-coloured draperies and cushions and luxuriously soft sofas and bed spreads add an extremely comfortable touch. Black-and-white photographs of the neighbourhood hang in each room, inviting you to go out and visit. The upper floors have magnificent views of the river on one side and the city on the other. Wireless Internet access.

### Auberge Saint-Antoine
*$$$$$*
⊛, ≡, *K*, ℑ, ℜ
8 Rue St-Antoine
**☎692-2211 or 888-692-2211**
⇌*692-1177*
*www.saint-antoine.com*
Auberge Sainte-Antoine is located near the Musée de la Civilisation. This lovely hotel is divided into two buildings. The old rooms are wonderfully decorated according to different themes and each has its own unique charm. The hotel features 64 new, more modern rooms and an already-famous restaurant, Panache.

## Tour C:
## Grande Allée
## and Avenue Cartier

### B&B Café Krieghoff
*$$ bkfst incl.*
ℜ, ℝ, ≡
1091 Avenue Cartier
**☎522-3711**
⇌*647-1429*
*www.cafekrieghoff.com*
B&B Café Krieghoff offers travellers a bed and breakfast combination. The novelty, however, is that breakfast is served in the café itself (see p 212), which guarantees both good

food and pleasant surroundings! The friendly staff makes sure that guests feel right at home in the family-like atmosphere. The six rooms nestled above the restaurant are modest and clean. Each one has access to a private bathroom (even if it is not connected to the room), and they all share a small sitting room and balcony with a view of lively Avenue Cartier. Internet access. No smoking.

### B&B De La Tour
*$$ bkfst incl.*
*sb*
1080 Avenue de la Tour
**☎525-8775 or 877-525-8775**
The hosts of this charming bed and breakfast offer four lovely rooms in an equally lovely home. The red room, located in the front, is the most spacious, but the other three are very charming nonetheless. In the morning, an exquisite breakfast is served with fresh, delicious fruit. Parking.

### La Maison d'Elizabeth et Emma
*$$ bkfst incl.*
10 Grande Allée Ouest
**☎647-0880**
This lovely B&B features three charming, peaceful rooms, decorated with mahogany wood and beautiful drapes. Each is fitted with a pretty and well-lit bathroom. In the morning, a hearty breakfast is served in a sun-bathed dining room. The whole package is simple and refined, as hosts Jacinthe and François take marvellous care of their guests.

Accommodations

## Auberge du Quartier
### $$$ bkfst incl.
≡

170 Grande Allée Ouest
☎ 525-9726 or 800-782-9441
⇄ 521-4891

Looking for a charming little
neighbourhood inn? Situated
opposite the imposing Église
Saint-Dominique, just 5min
from the Plaines d'Abraham and
the Musée du Québec,
Auberge du Quartier should
please you. This large house
has some 15 clean, well-lit,
attractive and modern rooms.
They are spread out on three
floors, with a suite in the attic.
There is a charming terrace on
the roof-top. Reception is very
friendly.

## Relais Charles-Alexandre
### $$$ bkfst incl.
91 Grande Allée Est
☎ 523-1220
⇄ 523-9556

Relais Charles-Alexandre offers
some 20 comfortable rooms
on three floors. Breakfast is
served in a former art gallery, a
well-lit room decorated with
several reproductions. Friendly
reception.

## Auberge Louis-Hébert
### $$$ bkfst incl.
ℜ
668 Grande Allée Est
☎ 525-7812
⇄ 525-6294
*www.louishebert.com*

Directly located on lively
Grande Allée, Auberge Louis-
Hébert is a warm and charming
17th-century home. It is also
very peaceful. Rooms here
have been tastefully decorated
and offer several amenities. The
service is quite good.

## Hôtel Château Laurier
### $$$
≡, ℜ, ⊛, ℑ
1220 Place George-V Ouest
☎ 522-8108 or 800-463-4453
⇄ 524-8768
*www.vieux-quebec.com/laurier*

For several years, Château
Laurier has been situated in an
old house with a beautiful stone
facade on the corner of Grande
Allée. The hotel recently
adopted a new image. The
small guestrooms have been
renovated, retaining their original character, while a large
modern wing with classical
decor has been added at the
back. The rooms, however, are
fairly cramped and some only
offer a view of the parking lot.
They will suit people looking for
fresh new accommodations as
well as business people, since
rooms offer Internet access. A
massotherapy service is available in guests' rooms.

## Manoir Lafayette
### $$$-$$$$ bkfst incl.
≡, ℜ
661 Grande Allée Est
☎ 522-2652 or 800-363-8203
⇄ 522-4400

Manoir Lafayette is attractive
and elegant. The hotel was
recently renovated and some
rooms are equipped with comfortable antique furniture. The
Lafayette also enjoys an excellent location.

### Château Grande Allée
**$$$-$$$$**
≡
601 Grande Allée Est
☎ *647-4433 or 800-263-1471*
⇒ *646-7553*
The Château Grande Allée is a recent addition to busy Grande Allée. The well-kept rooms are so large that they look under-furnished. Making up for this slight shortcoming are various features, including large bathrooms.

### Hôtel Loews Le Concorde
**$$$-$$$$**
♿, ≡, ≈, ⊘, △, ℜ, ⊛
1225 Cours du Général-De Montcalm
☎ *647-2222 or 800-463-5256*
⇒ *647-4710*
Just outside Vieux-Québec is the Hôtel Loews Le Concorde. It is part of the Loews hotel chain and has spacious, comfortable rooms with spectacular views of Québec City and the surrounding area. There is a revolving restaurant on top of the hotel (see **L'Astral** p 217).

### Courtyard Marriott Québec
**$$$$-$$$$$**
⊘, ⊛
850 Place D'Youville
☎ *694-4004*
⇒ *694-4007*
Formerly the Le Cambré theatre, then the Trust Building, this handsome building now houses the Courtyard Marriott Québec hotel and its restaurant, **Que Sera Sera** (voir p 220). The loveliest rooms overlook Place D'Youville.

### Palace Royal
**$$$$-$$$$$**
≈, ⊗, ⊘
775 Avenue Honoré-Mercier
☎ *694-2000*
*www.jaro.qc.ca*
The Palace Royal offers beautiful, hushed rooms dominated by a Victorian decor that is both simple and luxurious. The indoor garden, with its Mediterranean accents, features a pool and a whirlpool surrounded with trees and a large atrium. Valet service.

---

## Tour D:
## Saint-Jean-Baptiste

---

### Chez Pierre
**$$ bkfst incl.**
*pb/sb*, ≡, *K*, ℝ
636 Rue d'Aiguillon
☎ *522-2173*
*www.chezpierre.qc.ca*
Chez Pierre is a bed and breakfast with three rooms. Two of them are situated on the second floor and offer all the charm of a faubourg Saint-Jean-Baptiste apartment. The first floor presents a studio-style room that includes a kitchenette. Pierre, your host, is a painter and his large coloured canvases brighten up the house. He serves a generous breakfast in the morning. No smoking.

**Accommodations**

## Delta Québec
*$$$$*
≈, ≡, ⊙, ⎕, △, ℜ
690 Boulevard Rene-Lévesque Est
☎ 647-1717 or 888-884-7777
⇴ 647-2146
*www.deltahotels.com*
The Delta Québec is linked to the Centre des Congrès. This hotel has over 375 rooms, all nicely decorated. Standard rooms are furnished with slightly rustic but elegant pine furniture. The hotel's heated outdoor pool is open all year.

## Hilton Québec
*$$$$*
≡, ≈, ⊙, △, ℜ, ⎕
1100 Boulevard René-Lévesque Est
☎ 647-2411 or 800-447-2411
⇴ 647-6488
*www.hiltonquebec.com*
Located just outside Vieux-Québec, the Hilton Québec offers rooms with the kind of comfort one expects from an international hotel chain. The Place Québec shopping mall is located in the lobby, which is connected to the Centre des Congrès.

## Hôtel du Capitole
*$$$$-$$$$$*
ℜ, ≡, ⊛
972 Rue St-Jean
☎ 694-9930 or 800-363-4040
⇴ 647-2146
*www.lecapitol.com*
Adjoining the theatre (see p 110), the Hôtel du Capitole is not exactly luxurious, but its rooms are amusing, with a decor that resembles a stage set. At the entrance is the **Il Teatro** (see p 220) restaurant. Wireless Internet access.

---

# Tour E:
# Chemin Sainte-Foy

---

## Sainte-Foy

### Université Laval
*$*
*sb*
Université Laval, Pavillon Parent, Office 1618
☎ 656-2801
⇴ 656-4335
*www.sres.ulaval.ca*
It is possible to rent a room on the university campus from the beginning of May to mid-August. The Service des Résidences on campus is responsible for renting these rooms, which offer the basic comfort of a single bed and a desk. The bathrooms are shared by all residents on the floor. This is an inexpensive place to stay and is worth considering. A weekly rate is also available. It is better to reserve in advance. Public transportation serves this area well; it takes about 10min to get downtown.

### YWCA
*$*
*sb*, ≈, ⎕
855 Avenue Holland
☎ 683-2155
⇴ 683-5526
The YWCA residence is located on the border of Sillery and Québec City. For a modest sum you can rent, for either a long or short stay, one of the small rudimentary rooms. There is a kitchenette, laundry

room, swimming pool and parking. Bedding is included.

### Hôtel Germain-des-Prés
**$$$-$$$$**
ℜ, ≡
1200 Avenue Germain-des-Prés
☎658-1224 or 800-463-5253
⇄658-8846
*www.germaindespres.com*
Hôtel Germain-des-Prés is a classic in the Québec City region. Established a few years ago, it was the first of what is now a chain of five extremely well-reputed boutique hotels. Its rooms, decorated with utmost care, are very welcoming and offer all the amenities you need for total relaxation: bathrobes, comfy armchairs, duvets and feather pillows... not to mention those little extras that are typical of this type of establishment, which provides personalized service despite its 126 rooms. The rooms will please business travellers, with its work desks and Internet access, as well as leisure travellers. There are also meeting rooms and the restaurant **Le Bistango** (see p 220) whose reputation is already firmly established.

### Château Bonne-Entente
**$$$$**
ℜ, ≡, ⊘, ⌂, ⊛, ≈, ✿, ⌕, &
3400 Chemin Sainte-Foy
☎653-5221 or 800-463-4390
⇄653-3098
*www.chateaubonneentente.com*
This magnificent old-English-style property is spread out over 4.5ha and is covered with greenery and flowers. The rooms are decorated with taste and refinement, and the entire inn has plenty of comfort and charm. You can participate in a number of indoor and outdoor activities here, or simply enjoy watching the ducks splash about in the nearby pond. Château Bonne-Entente offers all the advantages and benefits of a country resort right in the city. Its restaurant, Monte Cristo serves gourmet Mediterranean cuisine. There are also several conference rooms.

### Hôtel Gouverneur Sainte-Foy
**$$$$**
ℜ, ≡, ⊛, ≈
3030 Boulevard Laurier
☎651-3030 or 866-651-3030
⇄651-6797
*www.gouverneursaintefoy.com*
Hôtel Gouverneur is a top-notch establishment with warm-coloured rooms that provide maximum comfort. It is judiciously located near the bridges, a few minutes away from the shopping centres and right next to the expressways that lead to the region's various sports centres. Its dining room, La Verrière, will delight your taste buds as well as your eyes. A large area in the back has been landscaped with lush greenery and a lovely swimming pool.

## Near the Airport

The area around the airport is not particularly pleasant and travellers usually spend only one night here.

### Château Repotel Duplessis
*$$ bkfst incl.*

≡, ⊛, ♿

6555 Boulevard Wilfrid-Hamel
☎*872-1111 or 800-463-5255*
⇄*872-5989*

Château Repotel Duplessis is well-equipped to make your stay pleasant. The rooms are not luxurious but they are peaceful and have large bathrooms.

### Hôtel Le Cofortel
*$$ bkfst incl*

≡, ℝ, ⊛, ♿

6500 Boulevard Wilfrid-Hamel
☎*877-4777 or 800-363-7440*
⇄*877-0013*
*www.hotellecofortelquebec.com*

As its name indicates, the Hôtel Le Cofortel puts the emphasis on comfort. Furnished in bland colours and modern furniture, the rooms seem a bit austere but they are spacious.

### Comfort Inn L'Ancienne-Lorette
*$$$*

≡, ♿

1255 Autoroute Duplessis
☎*872-5900*
⇄*872-9550*

The Comfort Inn L'Ancienne-Lorette is on the road leading to the airport. The rooms are attractive even though they are furnished with laminated furniture. Internet access is available.

### 🏨 L'Autre Jardin
*$$$-$$$$ bkfst incl.*

≡

365 Boulevard Charest Est
☎*523-1790 or 877-747-0447*
⇄*523-9735*
*www.autrejardin.com*

L'Autre Jardin is an inn unlike any other, created thanks to Carrefour Tiers-Monde, a non-governmental organization working in the field of international development. All profits from the inn are therefore reinvested towards international solidarity projects. Now there's a great way to spend your hard-earned dollars: pampering yourself in a cozy inn while simultaneously supporting projects that aim to improve social conditions both in Québec and in developing countries. The inn's decor on each of its three floors is simple yet warm, with a few original touches here and there, and the staff is friendly and welcoming.

### Hôtel Royal William
*$$$-$$$$ bkfst incl.*

ℜ, ≡, ⊛

360 Boulevard Charest Est
☎*521-4488 or 888-541-0405*
*www.royalwilliam.com*

The Saint-Roch neighbourhood recently underwent a period of restoration. The opening of the Hôtel Royal William was in keeping with this spirit of revival. This large hotel located on Boulevard Charest has helped to liven up the surrounding area. Business people are particularly pleased with the practical aspect of the 40-odd rooms. In fact, the rooms are equipped with work tables, telephone outlets and Internet access. The decor is modern and comfortable, like most hotels in this category.

# Tour J: Heading North

## Lac-Delage

### Manoir du Lac Delage
*$$$$-$$$$$*
≡, ≈, ⊘, ℜ, ⅀, △, ✪
40 Avenue du Lac
☎*848-2551 or 800-463-2841*
⇻*848-6945*
*www.lacdelage.com*
Manoir du Lac Delage offers a wide array of installations that will charm sports-lovers in both winter and summer. The centre features a skating rink and is located near cross-country ski trails and slides. In summer, the lakeshore is ideal for practising several water sports. Take note that swimming is prohibited. The rooms and their wood furnishings are comfortable.

## Lac-Beauport

### Château du Lac-Beauport
*$$$ bkfst incl.*
≈, ℜ, ⊛, K, ≡
154 Chemin Tour-du-Lac
☎*849-1811 or 800-463-2692*
⇻*849-2895*
*www.chateaulacbeauport.com*
Resembling a large ski chalet, Château du Lac-Beauport is

quite comfortable, providing several sports facilities. Facing Lac Beauport, it features a lovely beach that allows visitors to enjoy activities such as surfing, kayaking and canoeing. In winter, a skating rink is created on the frozen lake. This site is fabulous for those who love spending time outdoors.

## Sainte-Catherine-de-la-Jacques-Cartier

### Chaumière Juchereau-Duchesnay
*$$*
ℜ, ≈
5050 Route de Fossambault
☎*875-2751 or 800-501-2122*
⇻*875-2752*
Not far from Station Touristique Duchesnay, where you can take part in a variety of outdoor activities, Chaumière Juchereau-Duchesnay offers room and board. Its nine pastel-coloured rooms are all similarly decorated. They are very comfortable despite the fact that they do not have the same antique elegance as the dining room. This inn, with its trees, swimming pool and terrace, will allow you to relax in peace and quiet.

### Station Touristique Duchesnay
*$$$*
*pb/sb*, ℜ, K
143 Route Duchesnay
☎*875-2122 or 877-511-5885*
⇻*875-2868*
*www.sepaq.com/duchesnay*
Nestled in the heart of a 90km² forest, on the shores of

**Lac Saint-Joseph** (see p 143), several cottages and log cabins were renovated to welcome visitors. A number of packages are available, all providing nature and comfort. Whether you wish to rent a cabin for the entire family and enjoy the lake and footpaths, or rent a romantic room for two and take advantage of the many cross-country ski trails, you will undoubtedly be seduced by this place.

### Ice Hotel
*$$$$$ ½ b*
*sb*
143 Route Duchesnay, Pavillon L'Aigle
☎*875-4522 or 877-505-0423*
⇌*875-2833*
*www.icehotel-canada.com*
It's hard to believe that a hotel could actually be made of ice…but it really is (see p 143)! This magnificent structure is built from thousands of tonnes of ice and snow. Adventurous travellers come from all over the continent to spend the night in this chilly castle. Note, however, that because the ice provides natural insulation, the temperature always remains between -2°C and -6°C within the hotel's walls. So you can snooze quite comfortably in one of its 32 rooms, all wrapped up in a thick sleeping bag. And if you're new to winter camping, don't worry: the hotel's staff is available day and night. Furthermore, the shared bathrooms are heated, and breakfast and dinner are served in a warm chalet. On site, guests can enjoy a multitude of

outdoor activities. An unforgettable experience is guaranteed!

## Parc national de la Jacques-Cartier

### Parc national de la Jacques-Cartier
*$*
Hwy. 175 N.
☎*848-3169 during summer or 800-665-6527*
*www.sepaq.com*
In Parc national de la Jacques-Cartier you can camp in magnificent surroundings. Along the river, there are numerous campsites, some rustic, others offering some facilities. And, of course, there's no lack of things to do!

## Tour K: Côte-de-Beaupré and Île d'Orléans

### Beauport

### Journey's End
*$$$*
&, ≡, ✺
240 Boulevard Sainte-Anne
☎*666-1226 or 800-465-6116*
⇌*666-5088*
This member of the Journey's End hotel chain lives up to company standards. It offers travellers comfortable rooms where they can relax. Journey's End is better known for its low prices than for its variety of services. No smoking.

## Ramada Hôtel Ambassadeur
**$$$**
⊖, △, ℜ, ⊛
321 Boulevard Sainte-Anne
☎*666-2828 or 800-363-4619*
⇋*666-2775*
***www.hotelambassadeur.ca***
This hotel was built on the outskirts of town in an area where travellers usually only stop for the night. The rooms are large and attractive, and there is a good Chinese restaurant on the ground floor.

---

## Château-Richer

### 🏝 Auberge du Petit Pré
**$$ bkfst incl.**
7126 Avenue Royale
☎*824-3852*
⇋*824-3098*
At the Auberge du Petit Pré, situated in an 18th-century house, you will be warmly received and well treated. Their four bedrooms are cosy and tastefully decorated. There's a large picture window which is open on warm sunny days, two lounges—one with a TV and the other with a fireplace—as well as two bathrooms with clawfoot tubs. Breakfasts are generous and finely prepared. Also, if requested in advance, the owner will prepare one of his delicious dinners for you. The splendid

aroma of home-cooking fills the house and adds to its overall warmth.

### 🛶 Auberge Baker
**$$-$$$ bkfst incl.**
ℜ, K, ≡, ⊛, ℑ
8790 Avenue Royale
☎*666-5509*
⇋*824-4412*
***www.auberge-baker.qc.ca***
For over 50 years, the Auberge Baker has been established in this hundred-year-old Côte-de-Beaupré house. Its stone walls, low ceilings, wood floors and wide-frame windows never fail to enchant visitors. The five bedrooms are on the dimly-lit upper floor but there is also a kitchenette, a bathroom and an adjoining terrace on the same floor. The rooms are meticulously decorated in authentic period-fashion and furnished with antiques. The inn's restaurant serves delicious meals (see p 225). Wireless Internet access.

---

## Sainte-Anne-de-Beaupré

### Auberge La Bécassine
**$-$$**
ℜ, ≡
9341 Boulevard Sainte-Anne
☎*827-4988 or 877-727-4988*
***www.labecassine.com***
La Bécassine is located less than 10min from Mont Sainte-Anne. It is actually a motel since most of the rooms are next to the main building. The rooms are simply but quite pleasantly decorated. The main building's dining room specializes in game meat dishes.

## Beaupré
## (Mont-Sainte-Anne)

### Camping Mont Sainte-Anne
*$*
☎827-4561, 826-2323 or
800-463-1568
Camping Mont Sainte-Anne is
located in **Station Mont-Sainte-Anne** (see p 162) and offers
166 campsites in a wooded area
traversed by the Rivière Jean-Larose. Essential services are
offered, and the campground is
superbly located close to all the
park's outdoor activities.

### Hôtel Val des Neiges
*$$-$$$*
≈, ⊘, △, ℜ, ⊛, ℑ, ✿, ≡
201 Val des Neiges
☎827-5711 or 888-554-6005
≠827-5997
*www.hotelvaldesneiges.com*
Many chalets have recently
been built in the newly developed areas around the base of
Mont Sainte-Anne. Among
these is the Hôtel Val des
Neiges The decor is rustic and
the rooms are comfortable.
The complex also includes
small, well-equipped condos.
They also offer cruise packages.

### 🏆 La Camarine
*$$$*
≡, ℜ, ℑ, ⊛, ⚲
10947 Boulevard Sainte-Anne
☎827-5703 or 800-567-3939
≠827-5430
*www.camarine.com*
La Camarine faces the Saint
Lawrence River. This charming
high-quality inn has thirty-odd
rooms. The decor successfully
combines the rustic feel of the

house with the more modern
wooden furniture. This is a
delightful spot and its restaurant
has a very good reputation (see
p 225).

### Château Mont-Sainte-Anne
*$$$-$$$$$*
≈, ⊘, ✿, △, ℜ, K, ℑ, ⚲, ≡
500 Boulevard Beau-Pré
☎827-5211 or 800-463-4467
≠827-3421
*www.chateaumontsainteanne.com*
Château Mont-Sainte-Anne is
located right at the bottom of
the ski slopes; there is no way
you could be closer to the
mountain. The rooms are spacious and are equipped with
kitchenettes that can be used
for an additional 10$. The es-
tablishment also has a spa.

### Village Touristique
### Mont-Sainte-Anne
*$$$$-$$$$$*
≡, K, ⊛, △, ℑ, ≈, ⊘
1000 Boulevard Beau-Pré
☎827-2002 or 800-463-7775
≠827-6666
*www.villagetouristique.com*
Situated at the foot of the
mountain, Village Touristique
Mont-Sainte-Anne is the dream
spot for those who prefer to
stay put rather than have to
travel from one place to another. There are several apartments of varying sizes that can
accommodate from two to
eight people. Some rooms
have whirlpool baths and a
mezzanine. All accommoda-
tions are equipped with modern kitchens and functional
fireplaces and are very comfortable. Several apartments have
views overlooking the trails.

# Île d'Orléans

On Île d'Orléans there are about 50 bed and breakfasts! A list can be obtained from the tourist office. There are also a few guesthouses with solid reputations, a hostel and a campground. There are therefore plenty of options for getting the most out of your stay on this enchanting island.

## Camping Orléans
*$*
≈
357 Chemin Royal, St-François
☎829-2953 or 888-829-2953
⇄829-2563
*www.campingorleans.com*
Camping Orléans has close to 140 campsites, most of which are shaded and offer a view of the river. Many services are offered. There is access to the river bank, where you can go for a pleasant walk. Reservations are a must.

## Auberge Le P'tit Bonheur
*$-$$ bksft incl.*
*sb*
186 Côte Lafleur, St-Jean
☎829-2588
*www.leptitbonheur.qc.ca*
Auberge Le P'tit Bonheur, situated on Île d'Orléans, is named after a song by Félix Leclerc, who fell in love with this island located in the middle of the St. Lawrence River. This youth hostel offers an affordable alternative to those who wish to discover this part of the region. Both the 300-year-old house and the site offer a most friendly atmosphere. Several

outdoor activities are available in summer and winter, when guests can go for dog-sleigh rides.

## Au Toit Rouge au bord de l'eau
*$$*
43 Rue Horacio-Walker, Sainte-Pétronille
☎828-9654 or 800-430-9946
Located near the water, this former rest home for nuns offers three charming rooms providing a superb view of Château Frontenac and the Montmorency Falls.

## 🏕️ Le Vieux-Presbytère
*$$$ bkfst incl.*
*pb/sb*, ℜ
1247 Avenue Monseigneur-d'Esgly, St-Pierre
☎828-9723 or 888-282-9723
⇄828-2189
*www.presbytere.com*
Le Vieux-Presbytère is in fact located in an old presbytery just behind the village church. The structure is predominantly made out of wood and stone. Low ceilings with wide beams, wide-frame windows and antiques such as woven bed-covers and braided rugs take you back to the era of New France. The dining room and the lounge are inviting. It is a tranquil spot with rustic charm.

## La Goéliche
*$$$ bkfst incl.*
ℜ, ≈, ≡, K, ⊛
22 Chemin du Quai, Ste-Pétronille
☎828-2248 or 888-511-2248
⇄828-2745
La Goéliche has reopened in a new building, after the former inn burned to the ground in

1996. The new establishment is slightly smaller, and does not have the antique charm that made the original such a hit. Nevertheless, the modern setup still has a certain country-style appeal. The 18 rooms are comfortable and offer a lovely view of Québec City. There is a small living room with a fireplace and games. The restaurant (see p 226) is also worth the trip.

###  Le Canard Huppé
*$$$-$$$$ bkfst incl.*

ℜ, ⊛, ℑ

2198 Chemin Royal, St-Laurent

☎ *828-2292 or 800-838-2292*

⇌ *828-0966*

*www.canard-huppe.com*

Le Canard Huppé has enjoyed a very good reputation over the last few years. Their clean, comfortable, country-style rooms are situated in two old houses, each with decorative wooden ducks scattered throughout. The restaurant is also just as renowned and appealing (see p 226). The service is conscientious, and the surroundings are beautiful.

### Auberge Chaumonot
*$$$$ bkfst incl.*

≈, ℜ

425 Chemin Royal, Saint-François

☎ *829-2735 or 800-520-2735*

⇌ *829-0483*

*www.aubergechaumonot.specialistes.com*

This small inn only has eight rooms and is open exclusively in the summer. Located on the south shore of the island, Auberge Chaumonot was built near the banks of the river and is surrounded by charming countryside, far from the village and the road. The country-style rooms are comfortable.

# **Restaurants**

## Fine dining

is without question one of Québec City's biggest attractions.

Whether you wish to enjoy a gourmet meal, a light healthy snack or simply savour an espresso, your only difficulty will in be choosing among the great selection of romantic restaurants and charming cafés.

As a general rule, restaurants offer, from Monday to Friday, daily specials that include a full menu at a reasonable price. Served at lunch only, theses *menus du jour* often feature a choice of appetizers and main courses with coffee and dessert. In the evening, the *table d'hôte* (same formula at a slightly higher cost) is often quite interesting as well.

Prices in this guide apply to **dinner** for one person **excluding** taxes, tip (see p 50) and drinks. The restaurants are listed according to their corresponding tours, starting with the least expensive. The price scale is as follows:

| | |
|---|---|
| *$* | less than $15 |
| *$$* | $15 to $25 |
| *$$$* | $26 to $50 |
| *$$$$* | more than $50 |

It is always preferable to make reservations, especially for groups. This also allows you to make sure the restaurant you have chosen is open that evening. Some restaurants are closed at the beginning of the week in the winter; however, most of them are open every day in high season (summer).

If you are travelling by car to Vieux-Québec, check with the restaurant to see if they offer valet service when you make reservations. This will save you a lot of trouble. If they do not provide this service, you should try to find an indoor parking garage. They are usually easy to locate.

## Bring Your Own Wine

There are in fact many restaurants here where you can bring your own bottle of wine, a practice that often seems unusual to Europeans. This tradition stems from the fact that, in order to serve alcohol, an establishment must purchase a rather expensive liquor license. Consequently, restaurant owners who wish to offer their clientele a more economical solution prefer a license which allows customers to bring their own wine. In such cases, there is usually a sign in the window.

Here's another unusual tradition: there exists, in addition to the liquor license, a bar license. Restaurants that only display a liquor license can only sell you beer,

wine and other drinks when you order a meal. Some restaurants, however, have both permits and can sell you alcohol without your having to order a meal.

## Cafés

Many Québécois are fans of espresso, which is why cafés and small, friendly restaurants are highly popular. These types of establishments have often been a part of their neighbourhoods for many years. The gleaming coffee machine is usually the most popular attraction, but you can also find lovely light dishes such as soups, salads and *croque-monsieur* (an open-faced sandwich with ham and cheese, broiled and served hot), as well as croissants and desserts, of course!

On weekends, breakfast is usually served until early afternoon. To find the list of cafés we recommend, look under "Restaurants by Type of Cuisine."

This chapter recommends the best places to eat. The selections were made with all budgets and tastes in mind. There are two indexes: the first is by type of cuisine (see below) and the second, in alphabetical order, can be found under "Restaurants" in the index at the end of this guide. We have also compiled a list of Ulysses's Favourites (see below), which are also marked with a boat symbol next to each establishment (see also p 172). These pointers should help you make a wise choice. *Bon appétit!*

# Ulysses' Favourites

**The finest establishments in Québec City and its surroundings:**
Initiale (p 210)
La Camarine (p 225)
La Closerie (p 217)
La Fenouillère (p 221)
Laurie Raphaël (p 211)
Le Champlain (p 205)
Michelangelo (p 221)

**For the romantic atmosphere:**
La Crémaillère (p 204)
Le Graffiti (p 217)
Le Saint-Amour (p 205)
Le Sainte-Victoire (p 222)
Michelangelo (p 221)
Poisson d'Avril (p 210)

**For the terrace:**
À la Bastille Chez Bahüaud (p 203)
Buffet du Passant (p 222)
Café-Resto du Musée (p 215)
Il Teatro (p 220)
Moulin de Saint-Laurent (p 225)

**For traditional Québec cuisine:**
Auberge Baker (p 225)
Aux Anciens Canadiens (p 204)

**For the view:**
Café de la Terrasse (p 205)
Café-Resto du Musée (p 215)
La Goéliche (p 226)
L'Astral (p 217)
Manoir Montmorency (p 224)

**For the elegant decor:**
Aviatic Club (p 209)
Café du Monde (p 209)
Cosmos Café (p 211)
Le Montego (p 223)
Marie Clarisse (p 210)
Voo Doo Grill (p 216)

**For originality:**
Café du Clocher Penché (p 222)
Dazibo Resto-Bistro (p 224)
Le Bonnet d'Âne (p 218)

Restaurants

## Restaurants by Type of Cuisine

Restaurants

## Tour A: Vieux-Québec

### Brûlerie Tatum
$
1084 Rue St-Jean
☎692-3900
Brûlerie Tatum is located in a lovely narrow building with a mezzanine and is decorated in reddish hues. This café roasts its own beans in its Vanier factory. They serve mouth-watering light meals such as *croque-monsieur*, sandwiches, salads and pasta, as well as a great selection of coffees and hot chocolates.

### Casse-Crêpe Breton
$
1136 Rue St-Jean
☎692-0438
Little Casse-Crêpe Breton is a popular spot that draws big crowds. Though it has been expanded, patrons still have to line up for a taste of its delicious crepes. Prepared right before your eyes, these delights are filled with your favourite ingredients by waitresses who manage to keep smiling in the midst of the hubbub. High-backed, upholstered seats help lend the place a warm atmosphere.

### Chez Temporel
$
25 Rue Couillard
☎694-1813
At Chez Temporel, the food is prepared right on the premises. Whether you opt for a rich butter croissant, a *croque-monsieur*, a salad or the special of the day, you can be sure it will be fresh and tasty. To top it all off, this establishment serves the best espresso in town! Tucked away on little Rue Couillard, the two-storey Temporel has been welcoming people of all ages and all stripes for over 20 years now. Open early in the morning to late at night.

### Le Petit Coin Latin
$
8½ Rue Sainte-Ursule
☎692-2022
Le Petit Coin Latin serves homestyle cooking in an ambiance reminiscent of a Parisian café. The decor is dominated by parlour chairs and mirrors, creating a relaxed, convivial atmosphere. The menu includes *croûtons au fromage*, quiche and salads. You can also snack on *raclette* (a swiss meal) served at your table on small burners with potatoes and cold cuts. Delicious! During summer, a lovely outdoor seating area enclosed by stone walls is open out back; to get there from the street, use the carriage entrance.

### Café de la Paix
$-$$$
44 Rue des Jardins
☎692-1430
Café de la Paix occupies a narrow space a few steps from the sidewalk on little Rue des Jardins. It has been around for years and enjoys a solid reputation among Québec City residents. The menu features traditional French cuisine such as frog's legs, beef Wellington, rabbit in mustard sauce and grilled salmon.

Restaurants

## L'Entrecôte Saint-Jean
*$$*
1011 Rue Saint-Jean
☎ *694-0234*
L'Entrecôte Saint-Jean serves steaks prepared in a variety of ways and accompanied by matchstick potatoes. Try the walnut salad and the chocolate profiteroles, which make a perfect ending to your meal. Great value for your money.

## Apsara
*$$*
71 Rue d'Auteuil
☎ *694-0232*
Apsara is located near Porte Saint-Louis and features Southeast Asian cuisine. Complete meals are served at both lunch and dinner time and prices are reasonable.

## Café Buade
*$$*
31 Rue de Buade
☎ *692-3909*
Near Rue du Trésor and Terrasse Dufferin, Café Buade has a large dining room with an attractive but modest decor. It is a pleasant establishment with a family atmosphere where you can enjoy a good meal without having to spend a fortune. The house specialty is roast beef. The dining rooms on the second floor have more charm but are sometimes closed.

## L'Omelette
*$$*
64 Rue St-Louis
☎ *694-9626*
L'Omelette is a very friendly place that serves copious breakfasts early in the morning. Later in the day, choose from a large variety of omelettes, pasta, pizza, hamburgers and submarines. Quality food at a reasonable price.

## Au Petit Coin Breton
*$$*
1029 Rue St-Jean
☎ *694-0758*
The atmosphere, decor and traditional costumes worn by the staff at Au Petit Coin Breton will surprise you. And the crepes, filled with your choice of ingredients, are quite satisfying. The dessert crepes are especially yummy.

## La Petite Italie
*$$*
49½ Rue St-Louis
☎ *694-0044*
La Petite Italie serves Italian specialties at affordable prices. The menu features pizza and pasta and the decor is pleasant. This restaurant is right in the heart of a lively tourist area.

## Le Saint-James
*$$*
1110 Rue St-Jean
☎ *692-1030*
The Saint-James bistro is part of **Manoir Victoria** (see p 178), even though it has its own entrance on Rue St-Jean. The decor is elegant and similar to that of the Manoir. An innovative formula lets you create your own meal combination from a large choice of pasta and sauces. There are also steaks, sandwiches and an interesting *table d'hôte*.

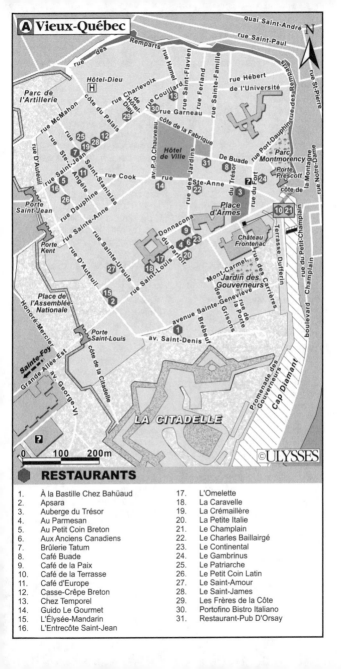

# A Vieux-Québec

## RESTAURANTS

1. À la Bastille Chez Bahüaud
2. Apsara
3. Auberge du Trésor
4. Au Parmesan
5. Au Petit Coin Breton
6. Aux Anciens Canadiens
7. Brûlerie Tatum
8. Café Buade
9. Café de la Paix
10. Café de la Terrasse
11. Café d'Europe
12. Casse-Crêpe Breton
13. Chez Temporel
14. Guido Le Gourmet
15. L'Élysée-Mandarin
16. L'Entrecôte Saint-Jean
17. L'Omelette
18. La Caravelle
19. La Crémaillère
20. La Petite Italie
21. Le Champlain
22. Le Charles Baillairgé
23. Le Continental
24. Le Gambrinus
25. Le Patriarche
26. Le Petit Coin Latin
27. Le Saint-Amour
28. Le Saint-James
29. Les Frères de la Côte
30. Portofino Bistro Italiano
31. Restaurant-Pub D'Orsay

©ULYSSES

### 🛶 Les Frères de la Côte
**$$**
1190 Rue St-Jean
☎692-5445

Les Frères de la Côte serves delicious bistro fare, including pasta, grilled meats, and thin-crust pizzas baked in a wood-burning oven and topped with delicious fresh ingredients. All-you-can-eat mussels and fries are also available on certain evenings. The atmosphere is lively yet relaxed and the place is often packed, in keeping with the bustling activity of Rue St-Jean. Guests can take in the action through the restaurant's large windows.

### Portofino Bistro Italiano
**$$-$$$**
54 Rue Couillard
☎692-8888

Portofino was designed to re-semble a typical Italian trattoria. A long bar, blue glasses, mirrors on the wall and soccer banners on the ceiling help create a warm, lively atmosphere. Don't be surprised if the owner greets you with a kiss! To top it all off, the mouth-watering Italian aro-mas will whet your appetite for the upcoming delights. The wine cellar has a good variety of Italian wines. During tourist season, the place is always packed. Formula I amateurs will enjoy the new Grand Prix-themed section. Valet parking.

### Au Parmesan
**$$-$$$**
38 Rue St-Louis
☎692-0341

Upon entering Au Parmesan, one is struck by the extensive collection of pots and bottles exhibited on the cornices along the walls. If you are looking for a quiet spot to have a private conversation, this is not the place. A *chansonnier* playing the accordion contributes to the animated atmosphere, and in the summer, it is *la dolce vita* every evening of the week! The clientele is mostly made up of tourists. The specialties are French and Italian; pasta, sea-food platters, ham and smoked salmon with melon are among the favourites.

### 🛶 L'Élysée-Mandarin
**$$-$$$**
65 Rue d'Auteuil
☎692-0909

L'Élysée-Mandarin, which also boasts prime location in Paris, serves excellent Szechuan, Cantonese and Mandarin cui-sine in a decor that features a small indoor garden and Chinese sculptures and vases. The food is always succulent and the service is extremely courteous. If you are with a group, try the sampler menu: it would be a shame not to sam-ple as many dishes as possible!

### La Caravelle
**$$-$$$**
68½ Rue St-Louis
☎694-9022

Located on Rue St-Louis, a popular street with tourists, La Caravelle is busy at all hours of the day and night. A mixed clien-tele frequents this attractive, luxuriously decorated restaurant. The stone walls and wood pan-elling give it a pleasant, inviting atmosphere. The staff here caters to your every need, attentively making every effort to serve you. Exquisite French cuisine is served here, with a few Spanish additions to the menu.

### Le Gambrinus
*$$-$$$*
15 Rue du Fort
☎*692-5144*
Le Gambrinus is a beautiful restaurant that has a good reputation with the people of Québec City. The welcoming dining room is adorned with small paned windows. The entire room is decorated with ivy, and elegant ornamental plates hang on the walls. The atmosphere could not be more enjoyable in this warm and appealing room. On certain summer evenings guests are entertained by a singer, making the ambiance even more inviting. The terrace overlooks Château Frontenac. The French and Italian cuisine features a large selection of fish and seafood.

### Le Charles-Baillargé
*$$-$$$$*
57 Rue Sainte-Anne
☎*692-2480*
The Charles-Baillargé restaurant is located on the main floor of the beautiful **Hôtel Clarendon** (see p 178). Discriminating diners come here for excellent, traditional French cuisine served in comfortable surroundings.

### Restaurant-Pub D'Orsay
*$$$*
65 Rue de Buade
☎*694-1582*
Restaurant-Pub D'Orsay is an establishment where people

congregate to eat and drink on the second floor. The lively happy hour (5pm to 7pm) on the main floor is popular with a well-to-do clientele. The menu features pasta, mussels, fish and a fabulously tender beef rib. During the summer, when the weather allows, a *chansonnier* entertains the crowd on the large back terrace. During winter, a huge fireplace warms up the ambiance.

### Le Patriarche
*$$$*
17 Rue St-Stanislas
☎*692-5488*
Le Patriarche's decor is charming and unpretentious. The dining room's beautiful stone walls create quite a relaxed, pleasant atmosphere. The reception is warm and the service is very friendly. The inviting French cuisine menu includes wild game and seafood.

### À la Bastille Chez Bahüaud
*$$$*
47 Avenue Ste-Geneviève
☎*692-2544*
À la Bastille Chez Bahüaud is located near the Plains of Abraham and is surrounded by trees. The wonderfully quiet terrace makes this the ideal spot for an intimate moonlit dinner. Inside, the decor is both elegant and comfortable. There is also a charming downstairs bar with a more intimate atmosphere. Fine French cuisine awaits you.

## Auberge du Trésor
### $$$
20 Rue Sainte-Anne
☎694-1876
Established in a house built in 1679 under the French Regime, the Auberge du Trésor's clientele is mostly made up of tourists. French cuisine is served here in an ambiance that recalls an Old French manor house. During the summer, the terrace is an ideal spot to enjoy a drink and admire the magnificent view of Château Frontenac and the various activities taking place on the Place d'Armes. Musicians perform here in the evening. Note however that a simple cup of coffee on the terrace may cost more than you expect. A second dining room, Le Relais de la Place d'Armes, also has a view of Château Frontenac and features family cuisine that includes pasta, pizza and hamburgers.

## Café d'Europe
### $$$
27 Rue Sainte-Angèle
☎692-3835
Café d'Europe has a sober, slightly outdated decor. There is a limited amount of space, and when the place is busy, the noise level gets pretty high. The service is courteous with a personal touch. Sophisticated European cuisine is presented in a traditional manner and served in generous portions. The flambéed dishes are expertly prepared, and the smooth, flavourful sauces make for an unforgettable culinary experience.

## La Crémaillère
### $$$
21 Rue St-Stanislas, at the corner of Rue St-Jean
☎692-2216
Friendly service and exquisite cooking with a European flavour await you at La Crémaillère. A great deal of attention is given here to make your meal memorable. The attractive decor adds to the charm of this inviting restaurant.

## Le Continental
### $$$-$$$$
26 Rue St-Louis
☎694-9995
Le Continental, located just steps away from Château Frontenac, is one of the oldest restaurants in Québec City. The continental cuisine includes seafood, lamb and duck, among other dishes. Service is *au guéridon* (pedestal table) in a large, comfortable dining room.

## Aux Anciens Canadiens
### $$$-$$$$
34 Rue St-Louis
☎692-1627
Located in one of the oldest houses in Québec City (see **Maison Jacquet** p 66), Aux Anciens Canadiens serves upscale versions of traditional Québécois specialties and specializes in wild game. Try the pork and beans and the blueberry or maple sugar pie.

## Guido Le Gourmet
### $$$-$$$$
73 Rue Sainte-Anne
☎692-3856
Guido Le Gourmet will transport you to the world of fine

dining. The menu, specializing in French cuisine, includes sea bass filet, wild game, rack of lamb, *foie gras* and other delicacies from both land and sea. The elegant decor and the large, lovely plates provide a good indication of the pleasures that await you.

### Le Saint-Amour
**$$$-$$$$**
48 Rue Sainte-Ursule
☎**694-0667**

Chef and co-owner Jean-Luc Boulay creates succulent, innovative cuisine that is a feast for both the eyes and the palate. The desserts concocted in the *chocolaterie* on the second floor are absolutely divine. A truly gastronomic experience! The new wine cellar is quite impressive, boasting 12,000 bottles. To top it all off, the setting is beautiful and comfortable, with a wonderful warm atmosphere. The solarium, open year-round and decorated with all sorts of flowers and plants, brightens up the decor. Valet parking.

### 🍴 Café de la Terrasse
**$$$$**
1 Rue des Carrières
☎**692-3861**

The Café de la Terrasse, in the Château Frontenac, has picture windows looking out onto Terrasse Dufferin. Attractive decor and delicious French cuisine.

### 🍴 Le Champlain
**$$$$**
1 Rue des Carrières
☎**692-3861**

Le Champlain is the Château Frontenac's main restaurant.

Needless to say, its decor is extremely luxurious, in keeping with the opulence of the rest of the hotel. The outstanding French cuisine also does justice to the Château's reputation. Chef Jean Soular, whose recipes have been published, adds a unique touch to the classic dishes. Impeccable service.

---

## Tour B: Petit-Champlain to Vieux-Port

### Buffet de l'Antiquaire
**$**
95 Rue St-Paul
☎**692-2661**

Buffet de l'Antiquaire is a pleasant snack bar that serves home-style cooking. As its name suggests, it is located in the heart of the antique dealers' quarter and is a good spot for a break from treasure-hunting. It is also one of the first restaurants to open in the morning (6am) in the area.

### Le Petit Cochon Dingue
**$**
6 Rue du Cul-de-Sac
☎**694-0303**

This small café and sandwich shop is without pretension and offers small meals and pastries, which can either be enjoyed on site or taken out.

### Casse-cou – Café-Resto
**$**
90 Rue du Petit-Champlain
The Casse-cou features two colourful floors and an uncom-

*Restaurants*

plicated menu of *croque-mon-sieur*, pizza and sandwiches.

## Café Bistro du Cap
*$$*
67 Rue Sault-au-Matelot
☎*692-1326*
Since 2002, the owners, who are passionate about sailboats, have been running this Breton *crêperie* in the heart of the Vieux-Port. Their *table d'hôte* changes regularly, and there are also Italian dishes such as bison ravioli. The dining room, decorated with plaid tablecloths, is charming.

## Le Mesclun
*$$*
93 Rue Sault-au-Matelot
☎*692-0600*
In this small room with a wrought-iron decor, you can enjoy Provencal cuisine.

## Le Brigantin
*$$*
97 Rue Sault-au-Matelot
☎*692-3737*
Monsieur Simard, the owner, welcomes you in a warm atmosphere with a smiling staff. The lovely wood-panelled bar, where hangs a large chandelier, is the focal point of this tiled-floor room. On the menu: pasta and pizza, among other dishes.

## Un Thé au Sahara
*$$*
*bring your own wine*
7 Rue Ste-Ursule
☎*692-5315*
Located in a basement on small Rue Sainte-Ursule, this cozy Moroccan restaurant is very friendly and romantic. Fra-grances of couscous, *tajines*, *merguez* and *harissa* float from the kitchen, taking patrons to another world.

## Asia
*$$*
89 Rue Sault-au-Matelot
☎*692-3799*
Asia serves excellent cuisine from Thailand and Vietnam. Vegetarians will also be delighted with the selection of dishes. Their trademark dishes are prepared on the grill or in a wok, resulting in light, healthy meals.

## Le Cochon Dingue
*$$*
46 Boulevard Champlain
☎*692-2013*
Le Cochon Dingue is a charming café-bistro located between Boulevard Champlain and Rue du Petit-Champlain. Mirrors and a checkerboard floor create a fun, attractive decor. The menu features bistro-style dishes such as *steak-frites* and *moules-frites* combos (steak and fries or mussels with fries). The desserts are heavenly!

## Pizza Mag
*$$*
363 Rue St-Paul
☎*692-1910*
For a delicious thick-crust pizza with all the works, stop at one of the Pizza Mag counters. The toppings are quite unusual, with choices like *La Biquette* (with goat cheese), *La Crème et Poireaux* (cream and leeks), *La Parmentière* (potatoes dusted with parmesan cheese), *La Louloutte Escargots* (escargots) and *La Kamouraska*, with

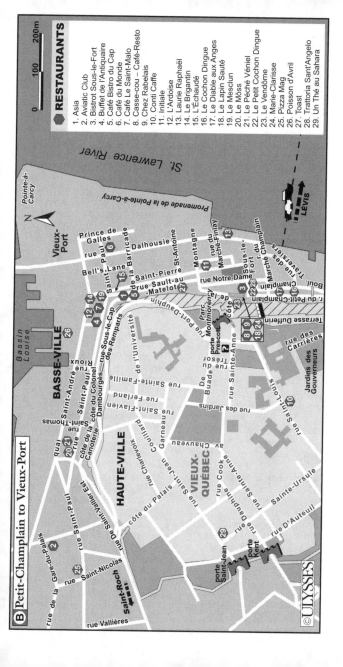

# B Petit-Champlain to Vieux-Port

## RESTAURANTS

1. Asia
2. Aviatic Club
3. Bistrot Sous-le-Fort
4. Buffet de l'Antiquaire
5. Café Bistro du Cap
6. Café du Monde
7. Café Le Saint-Malo
8. Casse-cou – Café-Resto
9. Chez Rabelais
10. Conti Caffe
11. Initiale
12. L'Ardoise
13. Laurie Raphaël
14. Le Brigantin
15. L'Échaudé
16. Le Cochon Dingue
17. Le Diable aux Anges
18. Le Lapin Sauté
19. Le Mesclun
20. Le Möss
21. Le Péché Véniel
22. Le Petit Cochon Dingue
23. Le Vendôme
24. Marie-Clarisse
25. Pizza Mag
26. Poisson d'Avril
27. Toast
28. Trattoria Sant'Angelo
29. Un Thé au Sahara

St. Lawrence River

Pointe-à-Carcy

Promenade de la Pointe-à-Carcy

LÉVIS

N

Bassin Louise

Vieux-Port

BASSE-VILLE

HAUTE-VILLE

VIEUX-QUÉBEC

Saint-Roch

© ULYSSES

0   100   200m

smoked sturgeon. Although mainly a take-out place, there are a few tables where you can sit and relax while you eat. Free delivery.

## Café Le Saint-Malo
### $$-$$$
75 Rue St-Paul
☎692-2004
Café Le Saint-Malo is a small restaurant that has been on Rue St-Paul for almost 20 years. It is decorated with many assorted objects that create a friendly atmosphere, as do the low ceilings, cozy booths and fireplace. French cuisine specialties can be enjoyed here. The *cassoulet* (bean casserole) and *boudin aux pommes* (blood sausage with apples) are particularly good.

## Le Diable aux Anges
### $$-$$$
28 Boulevard Champlain
Le Diable aux Anges, located in an old French house dating from the 18th century, features a diverse menu that is simply heavenly. The all-you-can-eat mussels and fries are served with a selection of 14 sauces.

## Bistro Sous-le-Fort
### $$-$$$
48 Rue Sous-le-Fort
☎694-0852
Bistro Sous-le-Fort has a somewhat stark decor and is mainly frequented by tourists. The restaurant serves delicious, reasonably priced Québécois cuisine that can be enjoyed, depending on the season, either on the refreshing terrace or by the warm fireplace.

## Trattoria Sant'Angelo
### $$-$$$
10 Rue du Cul-de-Sac
☎692-4862
Discover Italy at Trattoria Sant'Angelo, in the heart of the Petit-Champlain neighbourhood. The decor is a little austere but the wood fire in the centre of the restaurant provides a cheerful touch. And on a starlit summer evening, your dining experience will be enhanced if you eat out on the terrace. During high season the clientele is mostly made up of tourists, and is mixed the rest of the year. As the advertising states, "Pasta-Pizza-Amore," the menu has a great variety of pasta and pizza lovingly cooked in a wood-burning oven.

## Le Lapin Sauté
### $$-$$$
52 Rue du Petit-Champlain
☎692-5325
Located in a 200-year-old house in the Petit-Champlain neighbourhood, Le Lapin Sauté is furnished in a simple manner. The rough walls are white with a few dashes of colour. The terrace is next to the Maison de la Chanson, at the foot of Cap Diamant. You may have guessed that they serve *lapin* (rabbit), prepared in a variety of ways.

## Le Vendôme
### $$-$$$
36 Côte de la Montagne
☎692-0557
Le Vendôme is located halfway up Côte de la Montagne, and is one of the oldest restaurants in Québec City. It serves classic

French dishes like *Chateau-briand*, *coq au vin* and *duck à l'orange* in an intimate setting.

### 🍵 Café du Monde
**$$-$$$**
84 Rue Dalhousie
☎*692-4455*
Café du Monde is a large Parisian-style brasserie that serves dishes one would expect from such a place, including *magret de canard* (duck filet), *tartare* (raw minced steak with herbs), *bavette* (flank steak) and of course, *moules-frites* (mussels and french fries). The lunch menu is also interesting, with its delicious *profiteroles* (cream puffs) served for dessert. On the weekend there are great brunches as well. The bright decor is conducive to relaxation and discussion: there are black-and-white tiles on the floor, leather seats, large windows overlooking the river and a long bar adorned with an imposing copper coffee machine. There is also a bar at the entrance. The waiters, dressed in long aprons, are quite helpful.

### Toast
**$$$**
17 Rue Sault-au-Matelot
☎*692-1334*
Located in the beautiful stone building that houses the **Le Priori** hotel (see p 180), Toast distinguishes itself from the exterior thanks to its lovely red lighting. Inside, the secret to the decor is a mixture of stone walls and neon lights. The cuisine is classic but inspired by flavours from the world over. Summer terrace at the back.

### Conti Caffe
**$$$**
32 Rue St-Louis
☎*692-4191*
The Conti Caffe serves trendy Italian cuisine in an equally trendy and lively ambiance. In the middle of the dining room sits a large, crescent-shaped bar that welcomes many regulars.

### Le Péché Véniel
**$$$**
233 Rue St-Paul
☎*692-5642*
Once inside the gastronomic bistro Le Péché Véniel you will find a most enjoyable atmosphere. Whether for breakfast, lunch or dinner, the meals are always excellent. To name just a few specialties, we suggest the mussels, the various wild game offerings, the seafood and the Lac Saint-Jean *tourtière* (meat pie).

### Le Môss
**$$$**
255 Rue St-Paul
☎*692-0233*
Le Môss is a Belgian bistro that serves *moules-frites* combos, grilled meats and delicious desserts made with Belgian chocolate.

### Aviatic Club
**$$$**
450 de la Gare-du-Palais
☎*522-3555*
There are two restaurants in the magnificent Gare du Palais: a brand-new one with the evocative name of **Charbon**, which serves food from the grill, and a second, which has been there for a number of

Restaurants

years. The Aviatic Club takes you back in time with its mid-19th-century English-style decor featuring leather armchairs, beige curtains, and a Euro-Asian menu. No smoking.

### L'Échaudé
*$$$*
73 Rue Sault-au-Matelot
☎692-1299

L'Échaudé is an appealing restaurant with an Art Deco decor featuring a mirrored wall. Relaxed atmosphere. A sophisticated cuisine is prepared daily with fresh market ingredients.

### L'Ardoise
*$$$*
71 Rue St-Paul
☎694-0213

On a street lined with antique shops and art galleries, chic little bistro L'Ardoise is an ideal spot to take a break from touring the town. Although the service tends to be pretentious at times, this is a place where you will feel quite at ease. The mahogany panelling combines harmoniously with the stone walls. Among the offerings are *boudin grillé aux pommes* (grilled blood sausage with apples), *foie de veau à l'anglaise* (English-style liver), *entrecôte* (rib steak) and a selection of fish dishes. Brunch is also served on Sundays.

### Poisson d'Avril
*$$$-$$$$*
115 Rue St-André
☎692-1010

Poisson d'Avril is located in an old foundry with stone walls and wooden beams that lend a great deal of charm to the establishment. The decor is enhanced by clever lighting and the shell-patterned fabric of the chairs. The menu includes well-prepared pasta, grilled dishes and seafood. Try the mussels!

Two good restaurants are perched on the picturesque Escalier Casse-Cou, which leads to Rue du Petit-Champlain. On the top floor, **Chez Rabelais** (*$$$; 2 Rue du Petit-Champlain,* ☎694-9460) serves French fusion cuisine with an emphasis on seafood, game and local products. A little lower down is **Marie-Clarisse** (*$$$$; 12 Rue du Petit-Champlain,* ☎692-0857), where everything, except for the stone walls, is as blue as the sea—and with good reason: seafood is the house specialty. The divine dishes are served in a lovely dining room that has been very ornately decorated. When the cold weather sets in, a crackling fire warms you up.

### Initiale
*$$$$*
54 Rue St-Pierre
☎694-1818

Initiale is situated in an old bank building with a high ceiling and decorative mouldings. Formerly located in Sillery, the restaurant's devoted clientele has followed it here in appreciation of the fine food prepared by chef Yvan Lebrun. His exquisite creations feature lamb, salmon, *filet mignon*, kidneys served with *foie gras poêlé* (pan-seared *foie gras*) and, for the adventurous, pigeon! In a classical decor with a semicircular bar and light streaming in through high windows, you will be won over by these delicious dishes. The atmosphere is welcoming, although slightly stiff.

###  Laurie Raphäel
*$$$$*
17 Rue Dalhousie
☎ *692-4555*
Chef and co-owner Daniel Vézina is well known as one of the best chefs in Québec. When creating his mouth-watering dishes, Vézina draws inspiration from culinary traditions from all over the world, preparing local products with a creativity that guarantees a memorable dining experience. The menu features *foie gras*, mussels, Atlantic halibut, Ecuador tuna, venison and piglet. It goes without saying that the food at Laurie Raphaël is simply exquisite!

# Tour C:
# Grande Allée
# and Avenue Cartier

### Bügel
*$*
164 Rue Crémazie Ouest
☎ *523-7666*
Craving a bagel? You'll find all different kinds at Bügel, a bagel bakery on pretty little Rue Crémazie. In a warm atmosphere enhanced by the aroma of the wood oven, you can snack on bagels with salami, cream cheese or veggie pâté

and stock up on goodies to take back home.

### Les Finesses de Charlot
*$*
1125 Avenue Cartier
☎ *524-5636*
Les Finesses de Charlot makes excellent made-to-order submarines of all kinds. For a picnic, tuck one or two into a basket and head for the Plains of Abraham (only a 10min walk away). If it is raining you can always eat inside the restaurant. In the summer, it is also an ice cream parlour which features, among other flavours, maple and tofu ice cream.

### Cosmos Café
*$*
575 Grande Allée Est
☎ *640-0606*
Cosmos Café promises a good time in a hip atmosphere, serving burgers, sandwiches and salads with a cosmopolitan flavour. Breakfasts here are also quite good. A second Cosmos Café is located in Sainte-Foy.

### Aux 2 Violons Resto-Café
*$*
*bring your own wine*
122 Rue Crémazie Ouest
☎ *523-1111*
Nestled on Rue Crémazie, Aux 2 Violons is exactly the kind of tiny place that regulars like to keep secret and visitors love to discover. This small restaurant offers Maghrebi and Lebanese cuisine and is quite exotic, thanks to a colour scheme that recalls the contrast between the desert and the sea. Here, the

Restaurants

owners serve *fayrouz* (a malted beverage) and mint tea as diners can take their time and relax. On the Mediterranean menu, you'll find an ingenious exotic *poutine* consisting of *shish taouk*, onions and green peppers!

## Le Parlementaire
**$-$$**
*Mon-Fri*
at the corner of Avenue Honoré-Mercier and Grande Allée
☎*643-6640*
Visitors who might want to rub shoulders with members of Québec's National Assembly should have breakfast at Le Parlementaire. The menu features Québécois dishes. The restaurant is often packed,

particularly at lunch, but the food is worth the wait. Open only for breakfast and lunch.

## Café Krieghoff
**$-$$**
1089 Avenue Cartier
☎*521-3711*
Named after the Dutch-born artist whose former home is located at the end of Avenue Cartier, Café Krieghoff occupies an old house on the same street. It serves tasty light meals (quiche, salads, etc.), a fine daily menu and a more elaborate *table d'hôte*. The café is famous for its delicious espresso. Have a cup with one of their very good breakfast offerings, like the eggs benedict. The casual, convivial atmosphere is reminis-

# C Avenue Cartier

rue Crémazie

boul. René-Lévesque O.

rue Fraser

rue Aberdeen

rue Bourlamaque

rue Saunders

avenue Cartier

av. De Salaberry

Grande Allée

av. Wolfe-Montcalm

avenue Briand

avenue Galipeault

av. George-VI

National
Battlefields Park
(Plains of Abraham)

## RESTAURANTS

1. Aux 2 Violons Resto-Café
2. Bügel
3. Café Krieghoff
4. Café Resto du Musée
5. Garam Massala
6. Jaune Tomate
7. La Piazzetta
8. Le Cochon Dingue
9. Le Graffiti
10. Le Métropolitain
11. Le Momento
12. Les Finesses de Charlot
13. Mon Manège à Toi
14. Oh! Pino
15. Pizzédélic
16. Pub Java
17. Sushi Taxi

cent of a North European café. During summer, its two outdoor seating areas are often packed. No smoking.

## Pizzédélic
### $-$$
1145 Avenue Cartier
☎525-5981

This is a pizza place with a colourful setting and a welcoming staff. At Pizzédélic you can taste the latest trends in pizzas, as they prepare it in hundreds of different ways and you can choose your own combination of ingredients. The clientele here is young and lively.

## Pub Java
### $-$$$
1112 Avenue Cartier
☎522-5282

The subtle and original decor at Pub Java creates a fun atmosphere. This is an excellent place to savour a light meal when you need a bite, or to simply sit and watch the world go by.

## Mon Manège à Toi
### $$
102 Boulevard René-Lévesque Ouest
☎649-0478

Mon Manège à Toi offers a taste of Gaspésie in every meal. Its specialty, as you'll have guessed, is seafood. The menu includes mussels served with a choice of 25 different sauces, but you can also choose from many other regional dishes. The establishment's ambiance is a little theatrical, with large burgundy tablecloths, high, light-coloured ceilings and an array of paintings by Québécois artists.

## La Piazzetta
### $$
1191 Avenue Cartier
☎649-8896
(see p 218).

## Le Cochon Dingue
### $$
46 Boulevard René-Lévesque Ouest
☎523-2013

A pretty terrace in the back of this establishment's Boulevard René-Lévesque branch is heated when the temperature is cool (see also p 206).

## Garam Massala
### $$
1114 Avenue Cartier
☎522-4979

At Garam Massala you can savour curry, tandoori and other spicy Indian dishes. Though the restaurant has the disadvantage of being located in a basement, its decor is nonetheless attractive. Pleasant Indian music adds to the ambiance.

## Oh! Pino
### $$-$$$
1019 Avenue Cartier
☎525-3535

This bistro is proof that you don't have to razzle-dazzle to be unique. Despite its sober appearance, originality emanates from a thousand and one small details, starting with the place's name, which simply refers to the wine list which offers an interesting selection of Pinots. Pleasant little surprises are a-plenty, even in your plate where the chef adds his own colourful touches. On the menu you'll find such fare as tartares and seafood.

## Sushi Taxi
*$$-$$$*
813 Avenue Cartier
☎*529-0068*
*Maki, sashimi, temaki...* got a craving for raw fish? Then stop by the Sushi Taxi counter or, as its name suggests, have this delicious Japanese treat delivered to your door. You can also savour the dishes, prepared before your eyes, in the restaurant itself, a tiny room with a Zen-style decor. Sushi Taxi also has an outlet in Sainte-Foy.

## Jaune Tomate
*$$-$$$*
120 Boulevard René-Lévesque Ouest
☎*523-8777*
This pretty yellow and red restaurant on Boulevard René-Lévesque near Avenue Cartier serves good Italian cuisine in a country-style decor. Come here on Saturday and Sunday mornings to sample the delicious and inventive brunches. The eggs benedict with a hollandaise sauce flavoured with a zest of orange or teriyaki will make your weekend mornings a delight.

## Aux Vieux Canons
*$$-$$$*
650 Grande Allée Est
☎*529-9461*
The terrace at Aux Vieux Canons is very lively during the summer season. Try the delicious wine-flavoured French cooking or the succulent, expertly flambéed dishes. The atmosphere is festive thanks to

singers, dancers and musicians performing gypsy music. Quality wine list.

## Café-Restaurant du Musée
*$$-$$$*
*same hours as the museum*
1 Avenue Wolfe-Montcalm
☎*644-6780*
Inside the Musée du Québec you'll find the lovely Café-Restaurant du Musée. The restaurant's top priority is offering well-prepared food and outstanding service. Guests can gaze out on the Plains of Abraham and the river through large windows; in summer, the same view can be enjoyed from the patio.

## Le Momento
*$$-$$$*
1144 Avenue Cartier
☎*647-1313*
Le Momento is decorated in modern fashion with warm colours and a fresco taken from a Boticelli painting. As you may have guessed, they serve refined, original Italian cuisine that is sure to offer some pleasant surprises. Prepared with basil, oregano, dried tomatoes, capers and olives, the sauces are rich, but not excessively, and are quite savoury. The marinated salmon is perfectly prepared and will melt in your mouth.

## Le Rivoli
*$$-$$$*
601 Grande Allée Est
☎*529-3071*
The Rivoli is an Italian trattoria with lots of charm. Its decor features stone walls and pink

Restaurants

woodwork. You can enjoy the sun on the terrace during the summer months as you sample the pizza, which is served in countless different ways, along with veal and pasta.

## 🚢 Le Métropolitain
### $$-$$$
1188 Avenue Cartier
☎649-1096

Le Métropolitain is *the* place for sushi in Québec City. These delicious Japanese morsels are a real feast, prepared before your very eyes by expert hands behind a glass counter. Other Oriental specialties, including fish and seafood dishes, are available here as well.

## Le Bonaparte
### $$$
680 Grande Allée Est
☎647-4747

Le Bonaparte is an excellent choice when it comes to French gourmet cooking. To add to the experience, why not participate in one of the "Murder Mystery" evenings where intrigue and suspense are part of the fun? The restaurant's terrace overlooks Grande Allée and is popular with the young fashionable crowd.

## Le Louis-Hébert
### $$$
668 Grande Allée Est
☎525-7812

An elegant restaurant with a plush decor, Le Louis-Hébert serves French cuisine and delectable seafood. There is a plant-filled solarium at the back. Courteous, attentive service.

## 🚢 Voo Doo Grill
### $$$
575 Grande Allée Est
☎647-2000

This old house was once the social club of the Union Nationale, the political party of notorious Maurice Duplessis. This explains the name of the nightclub, **Maurice** (see p 231), occupying the building's two upper floors and where you can end the evening after a copious meal. Located on the second floor, the restaurant has kept some of the building's original architectural features and displays a most ingenious decor. A collection of African art work featuring masks, sculptures and dolls among other items, creates an entrancing effect. Unfortunately the music is not African, but *djumbé* players occasionally perform in the evening, adding a bit of rhythm to the already lively atmosphere. The Voo Doo Grill menu has grilled food, of course: meat, fish, fowl and wild Nunavut salmon, as well as dishes sauteed in a wok and served on spicy rice or *satay* with a choice of sauces. All are tasty, creatively prepared and beautifully presented. The kitchen is open late.

## Le Paris-Brest
### $$$
590 Grande Allée Est, at the corner of de La Chevrotière
☎529-2243

At Le Paris-Brest, French cuisine is the specialty. Prepared with care, the food here will satisfy the most demanding gourmets. In summer, the restaurant opens its small terrace which looks out onto Grande Allée.

### L'Astral
*$$$*
Hotel Loews Le Concorde, 1225 Cours du Général-De Montcalm
☎*647-2222*

A rotating restaurant located atop one of the city's largest hotels, L'Astral serves excellent French food and provides a stunning view of the river, the Plains of Abraham, the Laurentian mountains and the city. It takes about one hour for the restaurant to make a complete rotation. This is a particularly good place for Sunday brunch.

### Le Graffiti
*$$$*
1191 Avenue Cartier
☎*529-4949*

Revamped as a "Resto-Cité," Le Graffiti has managed to maintain, in addition to its lovely wood beams and brick walls, a warm ambiance. It is a bit surprising, in such as modern environment, to feel both enveloped by its beautiful interior and, thanks to a magnificent terrace, connected to the outdoors. The fine cuisine features French and Italian accents. On the menu, salmon or beef tartare is the top choice.

### La Maison du Steak
*$$$-$$$$*
624 Grande Allée Est
☎*529-3020*

La Maison du Steak is the most popular steakhouse in town. High quality food is served in a very cheerful atmosphere. In addition to the house specialty, French cuisine is also offered. Terrace.

### La Closerie
*$$$$*
1210 place George-V
☎*523-9975*

La Closerie serves fine French cuisine. The chef, who has a well-established reputation, creates meals from fresh, prime quality ingredients.

---

## Tour D: Saint-Jean-Baptiste

### Chez Victor
*$*
145 Rue St-Jean
☎*529-7702*

Located in a basement with a retro decor, Chez Victor serves salads and hamburgers—and not just any old hamburgers! The menu offers several different kinds (including four delicious veggie versions), all big, juicy and served with fresh toppings. The homemade peanut oil fries are sublime! Cordial service.

### Thang Long
*$-$$*
*bring your own wine*
869 Côte d'Abraham
☎*524-0572*

Thang Long may be tiny, but its menu will transport you to Vietnam, Thailand, China and even Japan! The decor of this neighbourhood restaurant is simple and unpretentious; the cuisine is truly up to the mark, and the service, very attentive.

Restaurants

Don't miss the *Chakis*, a Hanoï specialty that you can only find in this establishment. Try one of the meal-size soups—comfort food at bargain prices!

## Le Commensal
**$-$$**
860 Rue St-Jean
☎647-3733
The buffet style of Le Commensal has earned the public's affection over the years. Vegetarian dishes are the specialty here and are sold by weight. This open space features a modern tidy decor, making it an enjoyable setting for a meal.

## Le Bonnet d'Âne
**$$**
298 Rue St-Jean
☎647-3031
The theme here is elementary school and the menu is as varied as the subjects after which the dishes are named. Hamburgers, pizza and light meals are served on big beautiful plates that will delight both young and old. The theme extends to the decor, which includes blackboards, school desks and old toys, as well as some lovely wood trim. There is a pretty terrace in the summer.

## Le Hobbit
**$$**
700 Rue St-Jean
☎647-2677
Le Hobbit has occupied an old house in the Saint-Jean-Baptiste neighbourhood for years, and its stone walls and big windows overlooking bustling Rue St-Jean have not lost their appeal.

Here you can linger over an espresso and have a light meal or enjoy the *table d'hôte*'s delicious menu that changes daily and is never disappointing. Works by local artists are displayed here regularly.

## La Piazzetta
**$$**
707 Rue St-Jean
☎529-7489
The layout of modern-looking La Piazzetta is not really suitable for intimate dining. The restaurant is generally crowded and lively. An infinite variety of European-style pizzas is served. There are many franchises of this restaurant all over Québec; this one is the original, located in a house on Rue St-Jean.

## La Pointe des Amériques
**$$**
964 Rue St-Jean
☎694-1199
La Pointe des Amériques is located in the heart of lively Place d'Youville. This large restaurant is charming and attractively decorated, and features gourmet pizza as its specialty. Let yourself be tempted by the many exotic toppings. If you are a small party, you can choose a different kind of pizza for each person and share slices. You will certainly have a hard time deciding which is your favourite! The ambiance is delightful, and funnily enough, the wine is sold by the weight. Your bottle is weighed before and after your meal, and you only pay for the difference.

## La Campagne
*$$*
*bring your own wine*
555 Rue St-Jean
☎*525-5247*

La Campagne is located on the second floor of a house on Rue St-Jean, behind a large window filled with green plants. This establishment is well-known for its tasty, well-prepared Vietnamese dishes.

## Les Épices du Széchouan
*$$-$$$*
215 Rue St-Jean
☎*648-6440*

For exotic cuisine with succulent flavours and enticing aromas, try Les Épices du Széchouan, which occupies an old house in the Saint-Jean-Baptiste quarter. Its pretty decor is enhanced by a thousand and one Chinese trinkets. One table with a banquette is nestled beneath a corbelled wall. The house is a little ways from the street, so be careful not to miss it!

## Ciccio Café
*$$-$$$*
875 Rue Claire-Fontaine
☎*525-6161*

Ciccio Café is located on a quiet street near the Grand Théâtre de Québec. The atmosphere is relaxed and the beautiful brick walls enhance the decor. Progressive Italian cuisine, veal, fish, seafood and excellent pasta are featured on the menu.

## Carthage
*$$-$$$*
399 Rue St-Jean
☎*529-0576*

Carthage is a superb restaurant decorated in typical North African style. The ceiling is finely-crafted and adorned with gilt. Mahogany-coloured woodwork is found everywhere, as are a good number of Tunisian decorative objects. Here, a wonderful gastronomic experience awaits you. Seated on a cushion on the floor, a stool or simply at a table, you will be delighted by the Tunisian specialties. For example, the couscous served with vegetables, *merguez* (spicy sausages) or chicken, among other mouthwatering choices. Belly dancers are also occasionally on hand to liven up the celebrations.

## Le Beffroi
*$$$*
775 Avenue Honoré-Mercier
☎*694-2000*

In the Palace Royal hotel, Le Beffroi offers a menu where beef is the main staple, but which also provides a good selection of seafood dishes. The big bay window, which overlooks the entrance to the fortified town, and the lovely woodwork make this dining room a most charming spot. Edible flowers (pansies, orchids and, especially, nasturtiums) will delight your taste buds!

Restaurants

## La Grolla
### $$$
*Tue-Sun*
815 Côte d'Abraham
☎ *529-8107*

La Grolla welcomes you within its cozy Swiss chalet atmosphere. Wood beams, dried flowers and even the traditional Swiss cuckoo clock are all part of the decor. Next to a lovely wood fire, enjoy the delicious *raclette*, *grison* meats, fondue, *röstis* or crepes. The menu also features such original fare as cognac-flambéed *filet mignon* and Pernod-flambéed seafood, both prepared on a stone grill. The apple cider is light and delicious.

## Il Teatro
### $$$
972 Rue St-Jean
☎ *694-9996*

Il Teatro, located inside the magnificent Théâtre Capitole, serves excellent Italian cuisine in a lovely dining room with a long bar and big, sparkling windows all around. The courteous service is on a par with the delicious food. During summer, guests can dine in a small outdoor seating area sheltered from the hustle and bustle of Place d'Youville. Valet service.

## Que Sera Sera
### $$$-$$$$
850 Place D'Youville
☎ *694-4004*

Housed in the Courtyard Marriott Québec hotel, this restaurant serves fine market-style cuisine that is inspired by regional products. Its two floors overlook the hotel lobby.

---

# Tour E:
# Chemin Sainte-Foy

---

## Sainte-Foy

## Cosmos Café
### $
2813 Boulevard Laurier
☎ *692-2001*
See p 211.

## Mille-Feuilles
### $-$$
1394 Chemin Ste-Foy
☎ *681-4520*

Mille-Feuilles is a vegetarian restaurant. They offer dishes that are both healthy and delicious, as well as carefully prepared. Prepared meals are also available for take-out. Mille-Feuilles is located on a section of Chemin Sainte-Foy that has a few shops and restaurants.

## Le Bistango
### $$$
1200 Avenue Germain-des-Prés
☎ *658-8780*

Located in the **Hôtel Germain-des-Prés** (see p 185) complex, Le Bistango combines *savoir-faire* and casual ambiance. The good-sized dining room is decorated with taste and originality, and is very busy, both at lunch and dinner. Comfortably seated in a chair or booth, you can savour fine dishes prepared and served with care. The menu changes with the seasons and the arrival of fresh local products promises delicious surprises. This is a great spot if you find yourself in Sainte-Foy.

On certain evenings, musicians liven up the atmosphere.

### Da Cortina
**$$$**
615 80e Rue Ouest, Charlesbourg
☎ *622-3833*
Da Cortina is a big, beautiful white house whose dining room features large windows overlooking a country setting. The fine Italian cuisine includes pasta and seafood. Service is attentive.

### Le Galopin
**$$$**
3135 Chemin St-Louis
☎ *652-0991*
Le Galopin's dining room is located in a Sainte-Foy hotel, near the bridges. It is very large and comfortable, and the quality gourmet cuisine is served in a pleasant manner.

### Michelangelo
**$$$-$$$$**
3111 Chemin St-Louis
☎ *651-6262*
Michelangelo serves fine Italian cuisine that both smells and tastes wonderful. The classically decorated dining room, although busy, remains warm and intimate. The courteous and attentive service adds to the pleasure.

### La Tanière
**$$$$**
*Wen-Sun*
2115 Rang St-Ange
☎ *872-4386*
La Tanière specializes in wild game, as you might have guessed (a *tanière* is a den or lair). Although located in Sainte-

Foy, this restaurant is slightly off the tour, near the airport. Here you can experience tasty and delicious specialties from the forests of Québec.

### La Fenouillère
**$$$$**
3100 Chemin St-Louis
☎ *653-3886*
At La Fenouillère, a menu of refined and creative local cuisine promises a succulent dining experience. This restaurant also lays claim to having one of the best wine cellars in Québec. The decor is simple and comfortable.

## Tour F: Saint-Roch

### Tam Tam Café
**$**
*Mon-Fri*
421 Boulevard Langelier
☎ *523-4810*
The Tam Tam Café is an interesting spot, adjoining a youth community centre and serving as training grounds for those who wish to learn about the restaurant business. Here, you can enjoy tasty and diverse

Restaurants

dishes while supporting the staff-in-training! The decor is quaint, occasionally featuring the works of young local artists. The community centre provides various types of training to the young, as well as Internet access.

### Les Salons d'Edgar
*$$*
*Wed-Sun*
263 Rue de St-Vallier Est
☎523-7811
In the attractive Salons d'Edgar, which is also a bar (see p 233), the food is simple and hearty. European hot-dogs and beef *bourguignon*, among others, are flavourful and presented with a creative touch, such as a green salad topped with blueberries. The muffled atmosphere creates a slightly dramatic setting just right for relaxing and chatting.

### Café du Clocher Penché
*$$$*
203 Rue St-Joseph Est
☎640-0597
In an old bank building in the Saint-Roch neighbourhood, across from the church with the leaning steeple, Café du Clocher Penché serves great little dishes prepared with a touch of originality. Located on a street corner, it has several windows that make up for the austere high ceilings.

### Le Sainte-Victoire
*$$$-$$$$*
380 Boulevard Charest Est
☎525-5656
A grand piano occupies centre stage at Le Sainte-Victoire,

where a pianist plays jazz tunes on Friday and Saturday evenings. The bistro is decorated in red and gold and features banquettes, woodwork and large windows. In the kitchen is a young talented chef, Jean-François Girard. It seems he particularly enjoys concocting fish dishes, but his menu proves that he can do much more, as guinea fowl, lamb, duck, and horse create a lovely symphony of flavours.

## Tour G: Limoilou

### Le Maizerets
*$$*
2006 Chemin de la Canardière
☎661-3764
It is said that Le Maizerets serves "the best pizza west of Rome." Well, this may actually be true! For delicious pizza with a thin spicy crust, make sure to drop by here. There is also a terrace.

## Tour I: Sillery to Cap-Rouge

### Sillery

### Buffet du Passant
*$*
*Apr-Oct*
1698 Côte de l'Église
☎681-6583
In Sillery, stop in at Buffet du Passant, located halfway down steep Côte de l'Église. You may ask yourself why, since it

appears to be just another traditional snack bar serving hamburgers and french fries. But a little-known treasure lies hidden away at the back: from Rue des Voiliers, there is a superb view of the River and both its shores. A few picnic tables have been set up there so that you can eat lunch and enjoy the view. A catering service is also available.

### Brynd
*$*
1360 Rue Maguire
☎527-3844

Brynd is the place to go for smoked meat. There are also items on the menu for those who don't wish to try the house specialty (which would be a shame!). The meat is smoked and sliced right in front of your eyes, in authentic delicatessen tradition.

### Le Cochon Dingue
*$$*
1365 Avenue Maguire
☎683-8111
see p 206.

### Pizza Mag
*$$*
1465 Avenue Maguire, Sillery
☎683-1561

Like its sister establishment on Rue Saint-Paul (see p 206), this restaurant serves great pizza. Its facade is decorated with a bright, Mediterranean-inspired mural and the same artist was currently working on the interior walls when we visited the establishment.

### Le Montego
*$$$*
1460 Avenue Maguire
☎688-7991

The Montego restaurant-club promises a "sunny experience." The warmly decorated interior, large colourful plates and food presentation are indeed a pleasure. And the cooking will delight your tastebuds with sweet, hot and spicy flavours inspired by the cuisine of California and other sunny places.

### Paparazzi
*$$$*
1363 Avenue Maguire
☎683-8111

Paparazzi serves refined Italian cuisine and also features a sushi bar. The decor is modern and pleasant with pretty tables covered in ceramic tiles set up on various levels.

# Tour J: Heading North

## Wendake

### Nek8arre
*$$-$$$*
*noon-3:30pm*
575 Rue Stanislas-Kosca
☎842-4308
⇉842-3473

In the Huron-Wendat village of **Onhoüa Chetek8e** (see p 143), a pleasant restaurant whose name means "the meal is ready to be served" will introduce you to traditional Huron-Wendat cooking. Wonderful dishes such

Restaurants

as clay trout, caribou or venison brochettes with mushrooms accompanied by wild rice and corn, are some of the items on the menu. The wood tables are engraved with texts explaining the eating habits of Aboriginal cultures. Numerous objects scattered here and there will arouse your curiosity, and luckily, the waitresses also act as part-time "ethnologists" and can answer your questions. All this in a pleasant atmosphere. The entry fee to the village will be waived if you're only going to the restaurant. Wheelchair access.

### Sagamité
*$$-$$$*
10 Boulevard Maurice-Bastien
☎847-6999

At Sagamité, beautiful sculpted columns depicting hunting and war scenes remind guests that they are in the Huron-Wendat community. Among other things, it serves *potence*, a traditional grilled dish, and *sagamité*, a salty soup consisting of squash, beans, corn and ground beef.

## Sainte-Catherine-de-la-Jacques-Cartier

### Dazibo Resto-Bistro
*$-$$*
*Wen-Sun*
58 Route de Duchesnay, RR2
☎875-3301

Dazibo Resto-Bistro is quite pleasant. It is painted in warm colours and offers Irish special-

ties in a friendly family atmosphere. The most popular items on the menu are the *briks*, small crusty pastry rolls garnished to order.

## Tour K: Côte-de-Beaupré and Île d'Orléans

## Beauport

### Manoir Montmorency
*$$-$$$$*
*May to late Oct, reservations required rest of the year*
2490 Avenue Royale
☎663-3330

**Manoir Montmorency** (see p 145) benefits from a superb location above the Montmorency Falls. From May to late October, the restaurant's menu features *grillades* served on the magnificent covered and heated terrace. The rest of the year, eight luxurious rooms can hold banquets or meetings. It goes without saying that the environment is enchanting. The executive chef, Marie-Chantal Lepage, prepares a refined Québécois cuisine from the freshest local products. From the dining room surrounded by bay windows, there's an absolutely magnificent view of the falls, the river and Île d'Orléans. The entrance fee to the Parc de la Chute Montmorency (where the restaurant is located) and the parking fees are waived

A typical house in the Haute-Ville sector of Québec City. - *Patrick Escudero*

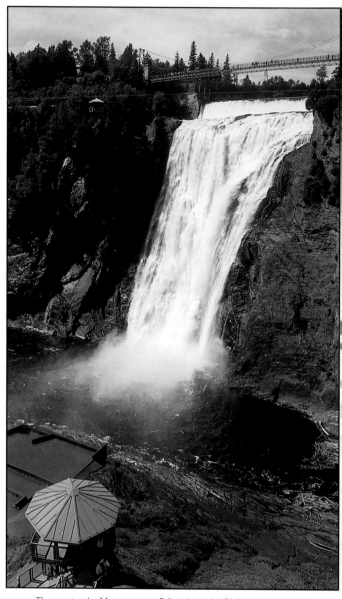

The spectacular Montmorency Falls, where the Rivière Montmorency comes to a sudden 83m drop. - *Philippe Renault*

upon presentation of your restaurant receipt or by mentioning your reservation.

## Château-Richer

### Auberge Baker
**$$$**
8790 Avenue Royale
☎824-4852 or 824-4478
**Auberge Baker** (see p 189) has two dining rooms. One features stone walls and a fireplace, while the other is set in a more sombre decor. Both serve fine traditional and gastronomic Québécois cuisine made from local products: game, meat and fowl are all well-prepared and presented with care.

## Beaupré
## (Mont Sainte-Anne)

### La Camarine
**$$$-$$$$**
10947 Boulevard Sainte-Anne
☎827-1958 or 800-567-3939
Hotel **La Camarine** (see p 190) has an excellent restaurant that serves Québec *nouvelle cuisine*. The dining room is peaceful with a simple decor. The innovative dishes are a feast for the senses. In the basement of the inn is another small restaurant, the **Bistro**, which offers the same menu and prices as upstairs, but is only open during winter. Equipped with a fireplace, it is a cozy spot for *après-ski*, and is open in the evening for drinks.

## Île d'Orléans

### Crêpe Cochonne
**$$**
*May to mid-Oct*
3963 Chemin Royal, Sainte-Famille
☎829-3656
Crêpe Cochonne offers, like its name indicates, a good selection of crêpes for all the tastes, from meal to desert. The decor is simple and the staff friendly. In the summer, the terrace has a magnificent view of the river.

### Restaurant du Manoir
**$$$**
1451 Chemin Royal, St-Jean
☎829-2630
At Manoir Mauvide-Genest, someone had the great idea of sharing the place with Chef Bolduc, which allows us to savour his delicious dishes in a simple historical setting. Here, you'll be served New France-inspired cuisine with hints of Native American traditions, and regional products are highlighted.

### Le Moulin de Saint-Laurent
**$$$-$$$$**
*May to mid-Oct*
754 Chemin Royal, St-Laurent
☎829-3888 or 888-629-3888
Le Moulin de Saint-Laurent serves Québécois cuisine and is charmingly decorated with antiques. In the large dining room, which regularly receives groups, the chairs, wooden beams, stone walls and copper utensils hung here and there harmoniously complement this old building. The food is well presented and varied. On sunny days you can sit on the

**Restaurants**

terrace, which has a view of the waterfalls beside the mill.

### Le Canard Huppé
**$$$-$$$$**
2198 Chemin Royal, St-Laurent
**☎828-2292 or 800-838-2292**
The dining room of the **Le Canard Huppé** (see p 192) serves fine regional cuisine. Prepared with the fresh ingredients that are so abundant in the area, such as duck, trout and maple products, these little dishes will delight the most demanding palate. Although the room is somewhat dark (forest green being the predominant colour) the country decor is, on the whole, quite pleasant.

### La Goéliche
**$$$-$$$$**
22 Chemin du Quai, Ste-Pétronille
**☎828-2248 or 888-511-2248**
The dining room at La Goéliche has unfortunately lost its old-time splendour (see p 191), though it is still a pleasant spot offering one of the most beautiful views of Québec City. This restaurant serves fine French cuisine: calf's sweetbread, loin of venison and *filet mignon* in morel sauce.

### Le Vieux-Presbytère
**$$$$**
1247 Avenue Monseigneur-d'Esgly, St-Pierre
**☎828-9723**
The dining room in **Le Vieux-Presbytère** (see p 191) specializes in unusual meats such as ostrich, guinea fowl and, especially, caribou. The restaurant prepares these and other dishes in a most delectable manner. The attractive dining room of this historic building also offers a superb view of the river.

# Entertainment

## As well as possessing
undeniable charm, Québec City is also a highly entertaining town.

Whether you are in the mood for cultural activities, festivals or a simple night out in its bars and nightclubs, this unique place will not disappoint you.

In many Québec City shops, restaurants and bars, you will find three newspapers containing information on current cultural activities. **Québec Scope** (*522-0440)*, published every two weeks, is a small bilingual magazine that gives a brief overview of Québec City's main cultural events. The weekly **Voir** provides a few articles on current events as well as a listing of the main cultural activities. **Le Clap** is a magazine published by the movie theatre of the same name (see p 236). It features film reviews and articles on the movie industry. All three publications are free. Ask for them!

## Bars and Nightclubs

All year long, the city's bars and nightclubs are filled with people from all walks of life. Whether it be the nightclubs on the young and dynamic Grande Allée, the cooler spots on Avenue Cartier or the few "underground" bars in the Saint-Jean-Baptiste and Vieux-Québec areas, there are countless places to choose from. Why not discover them all?

There is no cover charge in most bars and nightclubs in Québec City, except when they are hosting a special event or a show. During winter, most places require customers to check their coats, which costs a dollar or two.

## Tour A: Vieux-Québec

### L'Arlequin
1070 Rue Saint-Jean
☎694-1422
*www.arlequin.qc.ca*
For the best in underground sounds, live or mixed by a DJ, visit L'Arlequin. Located upstairs in a house on Rue Saint-Jean, its fantastic decor and party atmosphere are sure to get your feet moving.

### Le Chantauteuil
1001 Rue Saint-Jean
☎692-2030
Le Chantauteuil is a quaint bistro. The pretty decor is reminiscent of Paris, with its attractive paintings hanging on stone walls. This café has lots of character, the service is friendly and communication is easily established between staff and customers. Le Chantauteuil used to be a *boîte à chanson*

where renowned Québécois artists like Félix Leclerc and Claude Gauthier performed in the 1960s.

### Chez Son Père
24 Rue Saint-Stanislas, at the corner of Rue Saint-Jean
☎692-5308
*www.barchezsonpere.qc.ca*
This bar is one of the rare spots where you can listen to traditional Québécois music. An air of nationalism prevails in this place… The decor is nothing special: a large hall with a small stage. *Chansonniers* (loosely translated as folk singers) regularly perform hit songs by famed Québécois singers like Paul Piché, Beau Dommage, Michel Rivard and Robert Charlebois. The atmosphere is often festive, with audience members showing their enthusiasm by clapping their hands and stomping their feet.

### L'Ostradamus
29 Rue Couillard
☎694-9560
For a laid-back atmosphere, go to L'Ostradamus, a gathering place for non-conformists of all sorts. It is this peculiar ambiance that makes the place interesting. The non-mainstream music guarantees a memorable night out!

### L'Emprise
57 Rue Sainte-Anne
☎692-2480
The oldest hotel in the city (see **Hôtel Clarendon** p 178) houses L'Emprise. This elegant bar is recommended to jazz fans.

There is a long *L*-shaped bar and, in the centre of the room, a magnificent black grand piano. While relaxing comfortably in an armchair, you can listen to one of the informal shows that are frequently presented here. There is no cover charge.

## Le Kashmir
1018 Rue Saint-Jean
☎694-1648
Upstairs in a Rue Saint-Jean building is Le Kashmir, a rock and roll bar which often features live entertainment. The dance floor and the shows generally draw a large crowd.

## Le Saint-Alexandre
1087 Rue Saint-Jean
☎694-0015
Le Saint-Alexandre is a typical English pub. The Scottish-green colour scheme and stone walls blend perfectly with the mahogany wood panelling and furniture. Here, great care is given to detail and authenticity. The impressive line-up of imported beers behind the bar is eye-catching and will give you a taste of the exotic. In fact, 200 varieties of beer are served, including about 20 on tap, their handles decorating the long bar. Good light meals are also served.

## Le Sainte-Angèle
26 Rue Sainte-Angèle
☎692-2171
Tucked away in the basement of a building on Rue Sainte-Angèle, the Sainte-Angèle looks like an English pub. Its decor is a bit worn, but the place is nonetheless comfortable. Though space is cramped, that does not stop local residents of all ages from packing in here. Regulars sit at the bar and chat with the bartender. Good selection of reasonably priced scotches and cocktails.

## Bar Fixion
811 Rue St-Jean
☎694-9669
Passion dominates in this bar, all decorated in red. A lovely spiral wrought-iron staircase stands right in the middle of the dance floor, where patrons can groove to their heart's content to the sounds of Latin and tropical music. Hip hop, percussion and "karibe" (Caribbean) evenings.

## Frankie's Supper Club
48-C Côte de la Fabrique
☎692-2263
*www.frankiessupperclub.com*
You're as hungry as a wolf but want to dance a little before eating? Frankie's has you in mind with an original concept that is both eclectic club and eatery. Here, you can start the evening with a lovely meal, enjoyed to the sounds of enticing house music. On the menu you'll find Japanese fusion cuisine. At the end of the meal, the ambiance is gradually transformed, as colours change and the music's volume increases. People start to move and follow the DJ's direction and the menu becomes musical: house, funky house and trip-hop. The experience offered at this trendy spot is definitely urban!

Entertainment

**Les Yeux Bleus**
1117½ Rue Saint-Jean
☎694-9118
The *chansonniers* at Les Yeux Bleus take turns performing and give the bar a festive air. This place is not chic or exceptional, but it's fun nevertheless. This is the kind of place where friends meet for a drink or two, or perhaps three... The clientele, aged 25 to 35, is very lively. There is also a terrace.

**Soñar**
1147 Avenue Cartier
☎640-7333
Climb down a hidden staircase at the corner of Cartier and Aberdeen streets and you'll end up in a concrete basement where you'll discover one of the many surprises that keep popping up in Québec City: the Soñar. You'll first notice the off-beat lighting that makes for a dizzying atmosphere; then you'll be entranced by the Latin rhythms spun by the DJ. The Spanish influence can also be found in the *tapas* and of, course, in the establishment's name... *Soñar* means "to dream"! You'll be seduced and will gladly succumb to the

frenzy. The service is a bit lazy, but life is meant to be savoured slowly here, just like a summer afternoon on the Plaza in Seville. Terrace on warm days.

## Tour B: Petit-Champlain to Vieux-Port

**L'Inox**
37 Rue Saint-André
☎692-2877
*www.inox.qc.ca*
L'Inox is a bistro-style brewery and the last bastion of the brewing tradition in Québec City. The decor is original and the stainless steel central bar is quite eye-catching. The clientele is young and varied. As well as serving beer, they also have hot-dogs to satisfy your growling stomach. Many different activities are held throughout the year, so you should inquire; for example, it might be fun to attend a session of *peinture en direct*, where artists create paintings on the spot and then auction their works, or take part in one of the CD launches that are regularly held here.

**Le Pape Georges**
8 Rue Cul-de-Sac
☎692-1320
Le Pape Georges is a charming wine bistro. Beneath the vaults of an old house in Petit Champlain, guests can sample a wide variety of wines while nibbling on snacks like cheese and *charcuteries* (cold cuts). The atmosphere is warm, especially when there are folk and blues musicians to liven things up.

**Taverne Belley**
249 Rue Saint-Paul
☎692-4595
The Taverne Belley, located in front of the Marché du Vieux-Port, has a few typical tavern features, such as a pool table and small, round, metal tables. The decor of its two rooms is both warm and fun, with colourful paintings hanging on exposed brick walls.

**Pub Thomas Dunn**
369 Rue Saint-Paul
☎692-4693
Pub Thomas Dunn is named after the Honourable Thomas Dunn, a provincial civil servant and politician for many years. At this typical English pub situated opposite the Gare du Palais, you will find one of the best selections of beer in Québec City. The neat and tidy decor of mahogany and Scottish-green complement each other perfectly. The clientele is very mixed—from university graduates to workers of all kinds. The atmosphere is friendly and relaxed. The Pub has more than 80 different single-malt Scotches.

**Pub de l'oncle Antoine**
29 Rue Saint-Paul
☎694-9176
Located near Place-Royale, Pub de l'oncle Antoine is nestled beneath a vaulted ceiling. This place is entirely made of stone, which, in addition to the long white candles placed in bottles on the wooden tables, makes you feel as if you've stepped back in time to the Middle Ages. During winter, a crackling fire helps banish the cold.

## Tour C: Grande Allée

**Le Dagobert**
600 Grande Allée Est
☎522-0393
Better known as Le Dag, Le Dagobert is one of the largest clubs in town. According to the regulars, it is the best nightclub for flirting… Taking up three floors of an old house, Le Dag is actually very chic-looking, as is its clientele. The dance floor is quite large and a horseshoe-shaped mezzanine is ideal for those who prefer to watch rather than join the dancing crowd. Hanging above the crowd, a giant screen shows the latest rock videos. In the summer, the terrace is always packed. There are also shows upstairs.

**Maurice**
575 Grande Allée Est
☎647-2000
The Maurice nightclub resembles no other in town. The decor is so original that it is difficult to describe. A predominantly red colour scheme highlights some amazing avant-garde furniture. Comfortable sofas are nestled in the various cozy corners of the establishment. The large central dance floor is lined with small bars. Here the doormen cleverly handpick the customers, who are always hip, beautiful and aged between 20 and 35. On the upper floor, you can relax

Entertainment

in the **Charlotte Lounge** or the **Société Cigare** cigar room. Some nights feature Latino music. Cover charge.

### Jules et Jim
1060 Avenue Cartier
☎ *524-9570*
Little Jules et Jim has graced Avenue Cartier for several years now. It offers a smooth atmosphere, with banquettes and low tables reminiscent of Paris in the 1920s.

### Le Turf Pub
1179 Avenue Cartier
On lively Avenue Cartier, Le Turf is the place to be for the "beautiful" crowd (30 and over). The pub serves a nice variety of imported beers and features a satisfying pub-style menu.

### Pub Sherlock Holmes
1170 Rue d'Artigny
☎ *529-8271*
Aside from its name, there is very little evidence that Pub Sherlock Holmes is an English pub. The decor is unassuming and the music is rather commercial without being dance music. The student customers take a break from their studies by playing pool and darts. The atmosphere here is quite relaxed and easygoing.

### Vogue
1170 Rue d'Artigny
☎ *529-9973*
Located above the Pub Sherlock Holmes, Vogue is very popular with the 20 to 35 crowd. Attractively decorated, this club attracts the beautiful people. Following the beat of the infectious dance music, the frenzied crowd lets loose on the small dance floor. A small terrace overlooks the Parc de la Francophonie and Grande Allée.

## Tour D:
## Saint-Jean-Baptiste

### L'Étrange
275 Rue Saint-Jean
☎ *522-6504*
L'Étrange has been located upstairs in a house in the Saint-Jean-Baptiste neighbourhood for many years. Its specials and giant screen continue to attract the young and not-so-young. Internet access is available to customers.

### Le Fou-Bar
525 Rue Saint-Jean
☎ *522-1987*
Le Fou-Bar is an appealing place with a regular clientele who come here to drink, chat with friends or check out the current works of art on display.

### Le Sacrilège
447 Rue Saint-Jean
☎ *649-1985*
Le Sacrilège is a bar in the Saint-Jean-Baptiste neighbourhood with a lovely back terrace where you can relax and get away from the hustle and bustle of the city.

### Le Temps Partiel
698 Rue d'Aiguillon
☎ *522-1001*
For over a decade, the Fourmi Atomik club in Vieux-Québec

was the haunt of a colourful, underground crowd. Forced to shut down in the summer of 2001, it more or less reopened under this new name in the Saint-Jean-Baptiste district. The co-op team that manages the bar is the same that used to run the Fourmi. The clientele has also been transplanted from the former nightclub, as has the music, which includes a wide variety of styles, from world-beat to punk rock, alternative and 1980s techno, as well as the latest tunes.

## Tour E:
## Chemin Sainte-Foy

### Sainte-Foy

**Le Cactus**
814 Rue Myrand
☎*527-9111*
A little bit of Mexico in Québec City? Yes, it's possible! Located near the university, Le Cactus welcomes students who come for a drink and the spicy special-ties. There is a terrace.

**Le Mundial**
965 Route de l'Église
☎*652-1170*
Le Mundial's formula is sure to please everyone. The ground floor has a small bar, ideal for quiet chats or for enjoying one of the jazz shows that are regu-larly presented here. The up-stairs is reserved for those who want to don their dancing shoes. There is a lively ambi-ance on the dance floor where

the latest hits can be heard. The clientele is rather young.

## Tour F: Saint-Roch

**La Barberie**
310 Rue St-Roch
☎*522-4373*
*www.labarberie.com*
Set up in a slightly deserted neighbourhood, La Barberie was initially supposed to be just a brewery. Now open to the public, it has been revamped and painted with warm colours for the occasion. The various beers offered at the counter, which are also available in various bars around the capital and its surrounding area, are, for the most part, delicious. Their ales are fermented in oak barrels.

**Les Salons d'Edgar**
*Wen-Sun evenings*
263 Rue Saint-Vallier Est
☎*523-7811*
Can't decide whether to eat, have a drink with friends or play pool? Then go to Les Salons d'Edgar (see also p 222), where you can indulge in any or all of these activities. The beautiful

Entertainment

decor, complete with folding screens and large white draperies, will give you the slight feeling of being on stage. In a long narrow room at the back you'll find high ceilings, armchairs, pool tables and, as in any self-respecting lounge, a fireplace. The music is tastefully chosen and tango nights are often featured.

### Scanner Bistro Multimédia
291 Rue Saint-Vallier Est
☎*523-1916*
*www.scannerbistro.com*
Are you overcome by a desire to surf? No need to panic, Québec City has its fair share of Internet bars and cafés. Evocatively named, the Scanner Bistro has a few computers to help you out and a bar on two floors. Aside from the computers, there are table games like pool and soccer as well as arcade games and pinball. And when the Scanner presents its musical evenings, it would be hard to imagine remaining glued to a computer screen.

## Tour G: Limoilou

### Bal du Lézard
1049 3e Avenue
☎*529-3829*
The Bal du Lézard is a small bar in the Limoilou neighbourhood that features underground music in a funky decor. In the summer, the Bal opens out onto a terrace with wooden floors overlooking the street. Shows are regularly presented here.

## Gay and Lesbian Clubs

### L'Amour Sorcier
789 Côte Sainte-Geneviève
☎*523-3395*
L'Amour Sorcier is a small bar in the Saint-Jean-Baptiste quarter. The atmosphere really heats up here sometimes. During summer, it features a pretty patio.

### Le Drague – Cabaret Club
815 Rue St-Augustin
☎*649-7212*
*www.ledrague.com*
This gay bar, which attracts a large number of regulars, is livened up by drag shows and wild karaoke evenings.

## Cultural Events

The intensity of Québec City's cultural life varies from season to season but reaches its peak during the summer. However, you can enjoy discovering the different facets of Québec's culture all year long through the many shows, concerts and exhibitions that are presented. There are films from all over the world, concerts from here and abroad, exhibitions of all kinds and festivals for the public at large. To choose from the many possibilities, consult the region's daily newspapers, the magazines mentioned at the beginning of this chapter or the **Télégraphe de Québec** Web site *(www. telegraphe.com)*.

Ticket prices vary from one place to another. Many venues also offer student discounts.

## Outdoor Activities

In the summer many shows are presented in the city's parks, whether it be the gardens of the Hôtel-de-Ville, the Parc de la Francophonie (behind the Parlement, see p 101) or Place d'Youville. They are all very lively, especially during the **Festival d'été de Québec** (Québec City Summer Festival, see p 237). The **Agora du Vieux-Port** *(84 Rue Dalhousie, ☎692-4672)* near the river and the **Kiosque Edwin-Bélanger** *(☎648-4071)*, set up in the centre of the Plains of Abraham, also add to the excitement.

## Music

The **Orchestre Symphonique de Québec**, the oldest in Canada, often performs at the Grand Théâtre de Québec *(269 Boulevard René-Lévesque Est, ☎643-8131 or 877-643-8131)*.

## Theatres

**Théâtre Périscope**
2 Rue Crémazie Est
☎529-2183
This theatre presents experimental plays.

**Théâtre de La Bordée**
315 Rue Saint-Joseph Est
☎694-9631

**Théâtre du Trident**
Grand Théâtre de Québec
269 Boulevard René-Lévesque Est
☎643-8131

**Le Petit Théâtre de Québec**
190 Rue Dorchester
☎529-9711

Entertainment

## Concert Halls

**Auditorium Joseph-Lavergne**
Bibliothèque Gabrielle-Roy
350 Rue Saint-Joseph Est
☎529-0924
All kinds of shows are presented in this intimate theatre.

**Grand Théâtre de Québec**
269 Boulevard René-Lévesque Est
☎643-8131
See p 103.

**Maison de la Chanson/
Théâtre Petit Champlain**
68-78 Rue du Petit-Champlain
☎692-4744
Excellent concerts are held in this intimate hall.

**Le Capitole de Québec**
972 Rue Saint-Jean
☎694-4444
First inaugurated in 1903, this theatre was restored in 1992. It is now one of the most beautiful venues in Québec City.

**Salle Albert-Rousseau**
Cégep de Ste-Foy
2410 Chemin Ste-Foy, Ste-Foy
☎659-6710
Various shows are featured here.

## Movie Theatres

**Le Clap**
Centre Innovation
2360 Chemin Ste-Foy, Ste-Foy
☎650-2527
*www.clap.qc.ca*

Le Clap shows first-run and repertory films. A program is available (see p 227).

**Cinéma Imax**
5401 Boulevard des Galeries, Galeries de la Capitale
☎627-7658, *ext. 2225*

**Cinéma des Galeries de la Capitale**
5401 Boulevard des Galeries
☎628-3835

**Place Charest**
500 Rue du Pont
☎529-9745

**Cinéma Cartier**
1019 Avenue Cartier
☎522-1100
For unpretentious repertoire cinema.

## Spectator Sports

Colisée Pepsi *(2205 Avenue du Colisée,* ☎*691-7211)* is home to the **Remparts** of the Major Junior League, which always attracts hockey fans.

Right next door is the **Hippodrome de Québec** *(ExpoCité, 250 Boulevard Wilfrid-Hamel,* ☎*524-5283)* where fans can watch horse races.

The **Capitales** *(www.capitalesde quebec.com)* baseball team plays their home games at the municipal stadium in Parc Victoria.

# Festivals

## February

**Carnaval de Québec** (☎626-3716 or 866-422-7628, www.carnaval.qc.ca), Québec City's winter carnival, takes place annually during the first two weeks of February. It is an opportunity for visitors and residents of Québec City to celebrate the beauty of winter. It is also a good way to add a little life to a cold winter that often seems without end. Various activities are organized. Some of the most popular include night-time parades, canoe races over the partially frozen St. Lawrence River as well as the international ice and snow sculpture contests held on the Plains of Abraham and in front of the carved ice castle at Place du Parlement. This can be a bitterly cold period of the year, so dressing very warmly is essential.

During Carnaval (see above), the city hosts a number of sporting events, including the **Tournoi International de Hockey Pee-wee de Québec** (☎524-3311).

## July and August

The **Festival d'été de Québec** (early Jul; ☎523-4540 or 888-992-5200, www.infofestival.com) is generally held over 10 days in early July when music, songs, dancing and other kinds of entertainment from all over the world liven up Québec City. The festival has everything it takes to be the city's most important cultural event. The outdoor shows are particularly popular. For most theatres' indoor shows, you must buy tickets. However, those presented outdoors are free.

In early August, Québec City celebrates the beginnings of the colonization period with the **Fêtes de la Nouvelle-France** (☎694-3311). People dress in period costumes, a marketplace is recreated on Place-Royale and many festive activities mark the occasion which lasts a few days.

On Wednesday and Saturday evenings at the end of July and the beginning of August, the Parc de la Chute-Montmorency comes to life with the **Grands Feux Loto-Québec** (☎523-3389 or 888-523-3389). The fireworks sparkle above the falls in a spectacular show, while on the river, passengers aboard a multitude of boats admire the display of colours.

At the end of June, the **Vélirium – Festival international et Coupe du Monde de Vélo de Montagne** (World Cup Mountain Bike Race) (☎827-1122, www.velirium.com) is held at Mont-Sainte-Anne. Here you can watch the top male and female professional racers compete.

Entertainment

Place du Parlement houses the **Plein Art** *(late Jul and early Aug; every day 10am to 11pm; ☎694-0260)* exhibit. All kinds of arts and crafts are displayed and sold.

People from the Québec City region have been enjoying themselves at **Expo-Québec** *(Parc ExpoCité, ☎691-7110)* every August for 50 years now. This huge fair, complete with an amuseument park, is held in front of the coliseum for about 10 days at the end of the month.

## September

For movie buffs, the start of fall (late August, early September) marks the beginning of the **Festival International du Film de Québec** *(☎523-3456)*. This festival presents the best films from here and abroad.

## October

In October, Québec City's bars and theatres host musical entertainment and evenings featuring tales and legends during the **Festival International des Art Traditionnels** *(☎647-1598)*.

Some institutions such as the Musée de la Civilisation and the Bibliothèque Gabrielle-Roy also feature traditional craft displays as part of the festival.

The **Festival de l'Oie des Neiges de Saint-Joachim** *(Cap Tourmente, ☎827-4808 or 827-3402)* is the perfect opportunity to observe an impressive congregation of thousands of snow geese. They stop in the marshes and fields of Cap Tourmente (see p 162) before setting off on their long voyage south.

# Shopping

**W**hether you are looking for local or imported goods, you will find everything your heart desires in Québec City's shops.

There are many shopping centres in the Québec City region. Here are a few: **Galeries de la Capitale** on Boulevard des Galeries; **Place Québec** on Avenue Dufferin; **Promenades Sainte-Anne** at 10909 Boulevard Sainte-Anne that includes a few factory outlets. There are also three shopping centres on Boulevard Laurier in Sainte-Foy, namely **Place Laurier**, **Place Ste-Foy** and **Place de la Cité**.

**A**venue Maguire is Sillery's most pleasant shopping street. You can make some interesting discoveries here.

**I**n Sainte-Foy, the **Faubourg Laudance** has been set up to resemble a small European town. Brick dwellings with stores on the ground floor, an urban park and a finely designed marketplace are grouped together along **Rue du Campanile**. Adorned with a clock

tower, the covered market is a long and narrow passageway with stalls on both sides.

**H**ere are a few shops where some wonderful treasures await you.

# Antiques

If you are an antique lover, you should not miss attractive **Rue Saint-Paul**. In fact, the street is known for its many antique and second-hand shops that offer great discoveries.

Then, in the Vieux-Port, there is **Machins Chouettes** *(225 Rue St-Paul, ☎525-9898)* whose wonderful name (thingama-bobs) is a perfect description. Here, you'll find original creations made from antiques.

# Art Galleries

Fittingly for a city that inspired many artists, Québec City offers numerous art galleries exhibiting works from many periods and schools. There are also half a dozen galleries scattered around Île d'Orléans and several in the village of Saint-Jean. Here are some Québec City addresses:

**Beauchamp & Beauchamp**
10 Rue Sault-au-Matelot
☎*694-2244*

**Galerie Estampe Plus**
49 Rue Saint-Pierre
☎*694-1303*

**Galerie Linda Verge**
1049 Avenue des Érables
☎*525-8393*

**Galerie Madeleine Lacerte**
1 Côte Dinan
☎*692-1566*

**Galerie d'Art Royale**
53 Rue Saint-Pierre
☎*692-2244*

**Galerie Le Chien D'Or**
8 Rue du Fort
☎*694-9949*

**Atelier Engramme**
501 Rue de Saint-Vallier Est
☎*529-0972*

**Galerie d'art Buade**
43 Rue de Buade, third floor
☎*694-4443*
Galerie d'art Buade, a co-op that brings together some 10 artists, painters and sculptors, allows you to buy directly from the artists.

# Bookstores

Québec City has many book-stores to offer, but the ones listed here sell English-language books or books on specific topics such as art. The Saint-Jean-Baptiste neighbourhood abounds in used bookshops, although the books are mainly in French. At the following addresses you will also receive good tips:

**Globe Trotter 2000**
Place de la Cité, Sainte-Foy
☎*529-5349*
Great selection of travel books
and maps.

**Librairie du Musée national
des beaux-arts du Québec**
Parc des Champs-de-Bataille
☎*643-0529*
Beautiful books on art.

**La Maison Anglaise**
Place de la Cité, Sainte-Foy
☎*654-9523*
The best selection of English
books in Québec City.

## Clothing

### Ladieswear

**Atelier La Pomme**, **Les
Vêteries**, see "Crafts Shops and
Artisans' Studios."

**La Cache**
1150 Rue Saint-Jean
☎*692-0398*
La Cache is a Canadian chain
that sells quality clothing. The
clothes are made from beautiful
richly coloured fabrics, with unusual designs inspired by the
nature and culture of India.
There are also attractive objects
for the house as well as bed
coverings made from the same
attractive fabrics.

**L'Exile**
714 Rue Saint-Jean
☎*524-4752*
L'Exile is a charming shop
selling carefully selected qual-

ity clothing by Québécois de-
signers.

**O'Clan**
52 Boulevard Champlain
☎*692-1214*
*www.oclan.net*
At O'Clan on Boulevard Champlain you will find well-made
clothes in the latest fashions.
The men's department is upstairs and can be accessed via
Rue du Petit-Champlain (see
"Men's Clothing" below). A
stop at O'Clan is a must in
Québec City.

**Simons**
20 Côte de la Fabrique
☎*692-3630*
Place Sainte-Foy, 2450 Boulevard
Laurier
Galeries de la Capitale, 5401 Boulevard des Galeries
Simons stores have existed
since 1840 and are a part of
Québec City tradition. In Québec City homes during the
holidays, the Christmas trees
are often piled high with Simons' characteristic green
boxes. All three stores provide
everything to dress men,
women and children from head
to toe and in several different
styles. Clothing accessories and
bed linens are also sold.

**Paris Cartier**
1180 Avenue Cartier
☎*529-6083*
This shop offers lovely
women's clothing.

In a small area of Boulevard
René-Lévesque, between Rue
Turnbull and Rue Salaberry, are
several **Québec designer** bou-

Shopping

tiques selling exclusive creations for women.

In the old town, along Rue Saint-Jean, you will find large popular chains selling fashionable clothing.

## Men's Clothing

**Louis Laflamme**
1192 Rue Saint-Jean
☎**692-3774**
Louis Laflamme features two floors of chic clothing for men.

**O'Clan**
67½ Rue du Petit-Champlain
☎**692-1214**
*www.oclan.net*
If you enter O'Clan by the Rue du Petit-Champlain entrance, you will find great-looking, well-made clothes for men. Women's clothes are downstairs.

**Simons**, see above.

In the old town, large popular chain stores selling fashionable clothing like America, Bedo, Gap, Le Château and Roots are located on Rue Saint-Jean.

## Furriers

**Laliberté JB**
595 Rue St-Joseph
☎**525-4841**
The Laliberté JB department store sells a variety of fur coats as well as coats for every season.

## Shoes and Hats

In the old town, large Canadian shoe-store chains such as Aldo, Pegabo and Nero Bianco are found along Rue Saint-Jean.

For all kinds of hats, visit **Bibi & Compagnie** *(42 Rue Garneau,* ☎*694-0045).*

## Jewellery

**Lazuli**, see "Crafts Shops and Artisans' Studios."

**Origines**
54 Côte de la Fabrique
☎**694-9257**
Origines' small shop mainly sells jewellery. The pieces may be simple or elaborate, but they are all very original and elegant.

For original creations by an experienced jeweller: **Louis Perrier** *(48 Rue du Petit-Champlain,* ☎*692-4633)* or **Pierre Vives** *(23½ Rue du Petit-Champlain,* ☎*692-5566).*

# Craft Shops and Artisans' Studios

**Abaca**
38 Rue Garneau
☎**694-9761**
Hidden away on little Rue Garneau, Abaca abounds with beautiful objects from Africa and Asia.

## Atelier La Pomme
47 Rue Sous-le-Fort
☎692-2875

Atelier La Pomme makes leather goods and clothes, and is one of Petit-Champlain's oldest workshops. The various different kinds and colours of leather accentuate the originality and quality of the clothing. Some of the items you will find here include coats, skirts, hats and even mittens.

## Boutique du Musée de la Civilisation
85 Rue Dalhousie
☎643-2158

This small shop within the Musée de la Civilisation sells beautiful handcrafted objects from around the world. There are some truly great finds to be made here in all price ranges.

## Boutique du Musée national des beaux-arts du Québec
Parc des Champs-de-Bataille
☎644-1036

The Musée national des beaux-arts du Québec's gift shop also features a lovely collection of objects and reproductions.

## Galerie d'Art Indien Cinq Nations
20 Rue Cul-de-Sac
**Boutique Cinq Nations**
25½ Rue du Petit-Champlain
☎692-1009

In these two Aboriginal art galleries and stores, you can admire and purchase crafts made by First Nation artists. There is also some superb jewellery.

In Saint-Pierre on Île d'Orléans, **Boutique Hang'Art** *(751 Chemin Royal,* ☎828-2519) is also an *économusée* of rugs. In Saint-Jean, in the old presbytery in front of the church facing the river, **Les Échoueries** *(2001 Chemin Royal)* displays a great many objects made by skilled craftspeople.

## Forge à Pique-Assaut
2200 Chemin Royal, Saint-Laurent
☎828-9300

On Île d'Orléans, the Forge à Pique-Assaut is a tiny econo-museum where a guided tour introduces visitors to the black-smith's art and presents various wrought iron objects such as chandeliers, furniture pieces and curios. Visitors can also buy some beautiful crafts in the store.

## Boutique Métiers d'Art
29 Rue Notre-Dame
☎694-0267

Boutique Métiers d'Art brings together a whole range of articles made by Québec crafts-people. Located in a beautiful building on Place Royale, the gallery overflows with a variety of wonderful items that include ceramics and jewellery. The store is owned by the *Conseil des Métiers d'Arts* and offers high quality, original crafts made from raw material.

## La Corriveau
24 Côte de la Fabrique
☎694-0048

La Corriveau is a large crafts shop. With three floors to pore over, you will find any

Shopping

thing and everything you might want as a souvenir of Québec City.

### Lazuli
774 Rue Saint-Jean
☎ **525-6528**
The attractive Lazuli shop sells crafts from around the world, most notably some very beautiful jewellery. Silver, wood and ceramic objects of exceptional quality are all finely made.

### Les Trois Colombes
46 Rue Saint-Louis
☎ **694-1114**
Les Trois Colombes on Rue Saint-Louis sells crafts as well as quality clothing. Among the items on offer are some beautiful handmade wool coats.

### L'Oiseau du Paradis
80 Rue du Petit-Champlain
☎ **692-2679**
A pretty Petit-Champlain shop, L'Oiseau du Paradis sells all kinds of paper goods as well as handmade paper from Québec workshops.

### Pot-en-ciel
27 Rue du Petit-Champlain
☎ **692-1743**
Behind its large windows, Pot-en-ciel exhibits all sorts of curios that come in a rainbow of colours, especially the ceramics. The store specializes in the culinary arts and offers a wide selection of attractive items that will revitalize your kitchen and dining room.

### Le Sachem
17 Rue des Jardins
☎ **692-3056**
Le Sachem is situated in the **Antoine-Vanfelson historic house** (see p 69). Its two rooms are filled with Aboriginal and Inuit art objects and crafts. They also sell traditional fur and leather clothes and attractive Aboriginal pattern-printed t-shirts. The ubiquitous moccasins are also available here.

### La Soierie Huo
91 Rue du Petit-Champlain
☎ **692-5920**
At La Soierie Huo you can purchase lovely silk scarves with designs that are as varied as they are colourful. You may also be lucky enough to see Dominique Huot as she creates them, paintbrush in hand.

### Transparence
1193 Rue St-Jean
☎ **692-3477**
Transparence is a small, aptly named store that sells glass objects, mostly made by local craftspeople. Stop by and admire these beautiful objects which reflect the coloured light of the various tints of glass.

**Verrerie La Mailloche**
Escalier Casse-Cou
☎694-0445
**Verrerie La Mailloche** (see
p 84) sells blown-glass objects
made on the spot, such as
bottles, vases and dishes in all
shapes and colours.

**Les Vêteries**
31½ Rue du Petit-Champlain
☎694-1215
At Les Vêteries you will find
hand-woven clothing from a
regional weaving studio. The
clothes are classical in their
colours and cut, but are nonetheless quite original.

**La Perle**
27 Rue Sous-le-Fort
In a lovely stone house dating
from 1688, you'll find all kinds
of pearl necklaces.

In the **Petit-Champlain** district,
several shop-owners have
created co-ops to ensure the
quality of the neighbourhood's
establishments:

**Zazou**
31 Rue du Petit-Champlain
☎694-9990
Zazou offers ready-to-wear
clothing for women in natural
hues and fabrics. Some pieces
are inspired by Native fashion.

**Sculpteur Flamand**
49 Rue du Petit-Champlain
☎692-2813
In the boutique-workshop of
Alain Flamand, you can watch
wood sculptors at work. Its two
floors are filled with traditional
and contemporary Québécois
sculptures.

**Peau sur Peau**
85 Rue du Petit-Champlain
☎694-1921
In this shop you'll find shoes,
handbags and hats made from
quality leather. There are also
leather sculptures and 3-D
paintings, as well as a famous
belt made from, among other
things, a "mysterious braid"
invented by a Native American
from the eastern United States.

In **Wendake**, you'll find a good
selection of Native American
crafts.

**Raquettes et artisanat Gros
Louis** (*30 Boulevard Maurice-
Bastien, Wendake,* ☎843-2503)
offers snowshoes for all tastes.
You can find traditional styles
and more modern ones, which,
unfortunately, are not as
charming as the authentic handmade snowshoes.

## Decorative Objects

**La Cache**, see above under
Women's Clothing.

**La Dentellière**
56 Boulevard Champlain
☎692-2807
La Dentellière sells lace, lace and
more lace! For romantics only.

**Simons**, see above listed under
"Ladieswear."

**Zone**
999 Avenue Cartier
☎522-7373
Behind its large windows,
Zone, much like its Montréal

shops, overflows with objects for the house. You will find all sorts of items like funky lemon squeezers, shower curtains or picnic baskets that will either make your life easier or simply more colourful.

## Food

**Le CRAC** and **La Carotte Joyeuse** *(680 and 690 Rue Saint-Jean, ☎647-6881)* are two adjoining shops where you will find a whole range of health food, including organically-grown fruit and vegetables, organic fair trade coffee, organic meat and prepared meals.

### Délicatesse Tonkinoise
732 Rue Saint-Jean
☎*523-6211*
Délicatesse Tonkinoise sells Asian products you can use when preparing exotic dishes, as well as delicious take-out meals. A catering service is also available.

### Épicerie Européenne
560 Rue Saint-Jean
☎*529-4847*
Épicerie Européenne sells European gourmet products, particularly from Italy, where the shop owners are from. Whether in French or Italian, they will kindly offer you judicious culinary advice. If you like blue cheese, you must taste their Stilton with port.

### Épicerie J.-A.-Moisan
699 Rue Saint-Jean
☎*522-0685*
What a pleasure it is to shop at **Épicerie J.-A.-Moisan** (see p 112). This old grocery store carries all kinds of fresh products like fruit, vegetables, seafood, spices, bread, delicious cheeses and many local products. This gourmet shop also has a few tables where you can enjoy a snack and a counter where a delicious cuisine, including sushi, is prepared before your eyes.

For fresh fruit and vegetables in the summer, go to the **Marché du Vieux-Port** (see p 94) or the **Marché de la Place** in Sainte-Foy *(Rue de la Place, near Route de l'Église and Boulevard Hochelaga)*. Every day, farmers from the region bring their flavourful fresh products here for sale. On Sundays in Sainte-Foy, the market also houses a flea market that's sure to please anyone looking for a bargain.

## Pâtes à Tout
42 Boulevard René-Lévesque Ouest
☎529-8999
and
2500 Chemin des Quatre-Bourgeois,
Ste-Foy
☎651-8284
For fresh pasta and tasty sauces, Pâtes à Tout has it made. They also sell take-out meals and homemade bread.

Take advantage of your visit to Île d'Orléans to sample its many goodies. There are market gardeners who sell their produce at road-side stands in the summer, sugar shacks in the spring, as well as small, diverse shops scattered around the island. For example: **Chocolaterie de l'Île d'Orléans** (*150 Chemin Royal, Ste-Pétronille*, ☎828-2252) makes great ice cream during the summer; **Ferme Mona** (*723 Chemin Royal, St-Pierre*) concocts delicious liqueurs and crème de cassis (blackcurrent liqueur); and **La Boulange** (*2001 Chemin Royal*, ☎829-3162), located in the Saint-Jean presbytery, prepares wonderful bread.

## Halles du Petit-Quartier
1191 Rue Cartier
Halles du Petit-Quartier offers some of the finer things in life: a charcuterie, a bakery, a fruit store, a butcher shop, a fish shop, a pastry shop and more. An ideal place to plan a great meal or a fun picnic!

## La Cuisine du Quartier
1191 Avenue Cartier, Halles du Petit-Quartier
☎524-4185
For some fine take-out, head to La Cuisine du Quartier, which offers duck, boar and rabbit prepared with international flavours.

## SAQ Signature
1 Rue des Carrières
☎692-1182
Housed in the Château Frontenac, this branch of the Société des Alcools du Québec specializes in liqueurs and spirits. Incredibly chic, it offers a great selection.

## Sweets

When the weather is warm, Québécois are very fond of ice cream, frozen yogurt and sorbet. You have only to stroll along Avenue Cartier and spot the many ice cream shops to satisfy your sweet tooth. This short thoroughfare has at least half a dozen places that sell these tempting treats.

## Arnold
1190-A Avenue Cartier
☎522-6053
On Avenue Cartier, Arnold announces its "*chocolats cochons*" (decadent chocolates) on a sign featuring a pig. Not only the chocolates, but also the ice cream (the fresh strawberry flavour is irresistible) will tempt you to eat more and more, just like a pig!

Shopping

### Paingruël
*Tue-Sat*
375-B Rue Saint-Jean
☎ *522-7246*
Paingruël, which has only been in operation for a few years, is already one of the favourite bakeries of Québec City residents, so much so that the store had to be expanded to keep up with the demand. The bakery is constantly filled with the aroma of freshly baked bread, brioches and pastries, all created with skill and originality.

### Érico
634 Rue Saint-Jean
☎ *524-2122*
Rue Saint-Jean harbours a treasure trove for chocolate enthusiasts. Érico is a small establishment that makes these delights from the finest available products, including quality cocoa, vanilla, caramel, hazelnuts and much more. In the summer, Érico also sells rich homemade ice creams and sorbets and, of course, during winter, Érico sells delicious hot chocolate. Even if you don't have a sweet tooth, take the time to stop by, because its window design is always creative and amusing: it is entirely made of chocolate!

### Au Palais d'Or
60 Rue Garneau
☎ *692-2488*
The pastry shop Au Palais d'Or sells rich pastries made with real butter and cream. Absolutely delicious.

### Le Panetier
764 Rue Saint-Jean
☎ *522-3022*
Le Panetier makes great bread, delicious cakes and real croissants baked to perfection.

### Tutto Gelato
*closed in winter*
716 Rue St-Jean
☎ *522-0896*
On Rue Saint-Jean, Tutto Gelato serves ice cream prepared from traditional Italian recipes. The results are absolutely divine! This is a definite must for ice cream lovers.

## Music

Here are two good places to buy CDs. They both sell all kinds of music and can advise you on the latest releases.

### Sillons Le Disquaire
1149 Avenue Cartier
☎ *524-8352*

### Archambault Musique et Livres
1095 Rue Saint-Jean, Vieux-Québec
☎ *694-2088*

# Newspapers and Tobacco

For all kinds of cigars, cigarettes and cigarillos, visit the store at the corner of Rue Crémazie and Avenue Cartier, **Tabac Tremblay** *(955 Avenue Cartier,* ☎529-3910), or, opposite the Cathedral, **J.E. Giguère** *(59 Rue de Buade,* ☎692-2296). Pipes and local newspapers are also sold in these shops.

For magazines and newspapers from around the world, drop by either **Maison de la Presse Internationale** *(1050 Rue Saint-Jean)* or **Au Coin du Monde** *(1150 Avenue Cartier).*

# Outdoor Clothing and Equipment

**Azimut**
1194 Avenue Cartier
☎648-9500
Azimut sells quality tents, sleeping bags, backpacks, hiking boots… everything for Québec's great outdoors, including the famous warm *Kanuk* coats.

**DLX/Deluxe**
2480 Chemin Ste-Foy, Ste-Foy
☎653-0783
and
1028 Rue St-Jean
☎694-3553
This is where you can buy or rent snowboards, skateboards and sailboards. There are also well-known brands of sports clothing and shoes. This is *the* place in Québec City for fans of extreme sports!

**Latulippe**
637 Rue Saint-Vallier Ouest
☎529-0024
Latulippe is popular with workers who want to be well-equipped, as well as outdoor enthusiasts. All sorts of articles are sold at reasonable prices.

**Tourisme Jeunesse**
94 Boulevard René-Lévesque Ouest
☎522-2552
Tourisme Jeunesse lives up to its name. It sells everything from airline tickets to backpacks to guide books for young and not-so-young adventurers who want to explore the world.

# Stationery

**Le Copiste du Faubourg**
545 Rue Saint-Jean
☎525-5377
Le Copiste du Faubourg sells refined stationery and greeting cards, and provides a photocopy and fax service.

**Les Petits Papiers**
1170 Avenue Cartier
☎524-3860
Les Petits Papiers has greeting cards, writing paper, notebooks and wrapping paper, among other items.

Shopping

## Miscellaneous

### Animalerie Boutique Tropicale
1028 Avenue Cartier
☎522-6744

If you're travelling with Buddy the dog or Fluffy the cat, you will certainly appreciate the following address: Animalerie Boutique Tropicale.

### Excalibor
1055 Rue Saint-Jean
☎692-5959

Obviously, it is rare nowadays that you would need to shop for a sword or a chain mail armor. However, if you are a Medieval history buff or just curious, you will enjoy visiting Excalibor.

### L'Attitude
71 Rue Crémazie Ouest
☎522-0106

If being on vacation is not enough to relieve your stress, drop by the boutique located in the L'Attitude Relaxation and Massotherapy Centre. Here you will find many things to help you unwind, including essential oils, candles, CDs, tapes and books. You can also take this opportunity to enjoy a relaxing therapeutic massage.

### Musée de l'Abeille
8862 Boulevard Sainte-Anne, Château-Richer
☎824-4411

Adjoining the **Musée de l'Abeille** (bee museum) (see p 147) is a small shop selling a host of objects related to bees, such as honey-based beauty products, mead and, of course, honey. There's also a pastry shop offering sweet delicacies made with honey instead of sugar.

# Glossary

## GREETINGS

| | |
|---|---|
| Hi (casual) | *Salut* |
| How are you? | *Comment ça va?* |
| I'm fine | *Ça va bien* |
| Hello (during the day) | *Bonjour* |
| Good evening/night | *Bonsoir* |
| Goodbye, See you later | *Bonjour, Au revoir, à la prochaine* |
| Yes | *Oui* |
| No | *Non* |
| Maybe | *Peut-être* |
| Please | *S'il vous plaît* |
| Thank you | *Merci* |
| You're welcome | *De rien, Bienvenue* |
| Excuse me | *Excusez-moi* |
| I am a tourist. | *Je suis touriste* |
| I am American (m/f) | *Je suis Américain(e)* |
| I am Canadian (m/f) | *Je suis Canadien(ne)* |
| I am British | *Je suis Britannique* |
| I am German (m/f) | *Je suis Allemand(e)* |
| I am Italian | *Je suis Italien(ne)* |
| I am Belgian | *Je suis Belge* |
| I am Swiss | *Je suis Suisse* |
| I am sorry, I don't speak French | *Je suis désolé(e), je ne parle pas français* |
| Do you speak English? | *Parlez-vous anglais ?* |
| Slower, please. | *Plus lentement, s'il vous plaît.* |
| What is your name? | *Quel est votre nom?* |
| My name is... | *Je m'appelle...* |
| spouse (m/f) | *époux(se)* |
| brother, sister | *frère, soeur* |
| friend (m/f) | *ami(e)* |
| son, boy | *garçon* |
| daughter, girl | *fille* |
| father | *père* |
| mother | *mère* |
| single (m/f) | *celibataire* |
| married (m/f) | *marié(e)* |
| divorced (m/f) | *divorcé(e)* |
| widower/widow | *veuf(ve)* |

## DIRECTIONS

| | |
|---|---|
| Is there a tourism office near here? | *Est-ce qu'il y a un bureau de tourisme près d'ici?* |
| There is no... | *Il n'y a pas de...,* |
| Where is...? | *Où est le/la ... ?* |
| straight ahead | *tout droit* |
| to the right | *à droite* |
| to the left | *à gauche* |
| beside | *à côté de* |
| near | *près de* |
| here | *ici* |
| there, over there | *là, là-bas* |
| into, inside | *à l'intérieur* |
| outside | *à l'extérieur* |
| far from | *loin de* |
| between | *entre* |
| in front of | *devant* |
| behind | *derrière* |

## GETTING AROUND

| | |
|---|---|
| airport | *aéroport* |
| on time | *à l'heure* |
| late | *en retard* |
| cancelled | *annulé* |
| plane | *l'avion* |
| car | *la voiture* |
| train | *le train* |
| boat | *le bateau* |
| bicycle | *la bicyclette, le vélo* |
| bus | *l'autobus* |
| train station | *la gare* |
| bus stop | *un arrêt d'autobus* |
| The bus stop, please | *l'arrêt, s'il vous plaît* |
| street | *rue* |
| avenue | *avenue* |
| road | *route, chemin* |
| highway | *autoroute* |
| rural route | *rang* |
| path, trail | *sentier* |
| corner | *coin* |
| neighbourhood | *quartier* |
| square | *place* |
| tourist office | *bureau de tourisme* |
| bridge | *pont* |

| building | *immeuble* |
| safe | *sécuritaire* |
| fast | *rapide* |
| baggage | *bagages* |
| schedule | *horaire* |
| one way ticket | *aller simple* |
| return ticket | *aller retour* |
| arrival | *arrivée* |
| return | *retour* |
| departure | *départ* |
| north | *nord* |
| south | *sud* |
| east | *est* |
| west | *ouest* |

## CARS

| for rent | *à louer* |
| a stop | *un arrêt* |
| highway | *autoroute* |
| danger, be careful | *attention* |
| no passing | *défense de doubler* |
| no parking | *stationnement interdit* |
| no exit | *impasse* |
| stop! (an order) | *arrêtez!* |
| parking | *stationnement* |
| pedestrians | *piétons* |
| gas | *essence* |
| slow down | *ralentir* |
| traffic light | *feu de circulation* |
| service station | *station-service* |
| speed limit | *limite de vitesse* |

## MONEY

| bank | *banque* |
| credit union | *caisse populaire* |
| exchange | *change* |
| money | *argent* |
| I don't have any money | *je n'ai pas d'argent* |
| credit card | *carte de crédit* |
| traveller's cheques | *chèques de voyage* |
| The bill please | *l'addition, s'il vous plaît* |
| receipt | *reçu* |

## ACCOMMODATION

| | |
|---|---|
| inn | *auberge* |
| youth hostel | *auberge de jeunesse* |
| bed and breakfast | *gîte* |
| hot water | *eau chaude* |
| air conditioning | *climatisation* |
| accommodation | *logement, hébergement* |
| elevator | *ascenseur* |
| bathroom | *toilettes, salle de bain* |
| bed | *lit* |
| breakfast | *déjeuner* |
| manager, owner | *gérant, propriétaire* |
| bedroom | *chambre* |
| pool | *piscine* |
| floor (first, second...) | *étage* |
| main floor | *rez-de-chaussée* |
| high season | *haute saison* |
| off season | *basse saison* |
| fan | *ventilateur* |

## SHOPPING

| | |
|---|---|
| open | *ouvert(e)* |
| closed | *fermé(e)* |
| How much is this? | *C'est combien?* |
| I would like... | *Je voudrais...* |
| I need... | *J'ai besoin de...* |
| a store | *un magasin* |
| a department store | *un magasin à rayons* |
| the market | *le marché* |
| salesperson (m/f) | *vendeur(se)* |
| the customer (m/f) | *le / la client(e)* |
| to buy | *acheter* |
| to sell | *vendre* |
| t-shirt | *un t-shirt* |
| skirt | *une jupe* |
| shirt | *une chemise* |
| jeans | *un jeans* |
| pants | *des pantalons* |
| jacket | *un blouson* |
| blouse | *une blouse* |
| shoes | *des souliers* |
| sandals | *des sandales* |
| hat | *un chapeau* |
| eyeglasses | *des lunettes* |

| handbag | *un sac* |
| gifts | *cadeaux* |
| local crafts | *artisanat local* |
| sun protection products | *crèmes solaires* |
| cosmetics and perfumes | *cosmétiques et parfums* |
| camera | *appareil photo* |
| photographic film | *pellicule* |
| records, cassettes | *disques, cassettes* |
| newspapers | *journaux* |
| magazines | *revues, magazines* |
| batteries | *piles* |
| watches | *montres* |
| jewellery | *bijouterie* |
| gold | *or* |
| silver | *argent* |
| precious stones | *pierres précieuses* |
| fabric | *tissu* |
| wool | *laine* |
| cotton | *coton* |
| leather | *cuir* |

## MISCELLANEOUS

| new | *nouveau* |
| old | *vieux* |
| expensive | *cher, dispendieux* |
| inexpensive | *pas cher* |
| pretty | *joli* |
| beautiful | *beau* |
| ugly | *laid(e)* |
| big, tall (person) | *grand(e)* |
| small, short (person) | *petit(e)* |
| short (length) | *court(e)* |
| low | *bas(se)* |
| wide | *large* |
| narrow | *étroit(e)* |
| dark | *foncé* |
| light (colour) | *clair* |
| fat (person) | *gros(se)* |
| slim, skinny (person) | *mince* |
| a little | *peu* |
| a lot | *beaucoup* |
| something | *quelque chose* |
| nothing | *rien* |
| good | *bon* |
| bad | *mauvais* |

| | |
|---|---|
| more | *plus* |
| less | *moins* |
| do not touch | *ne pas toucher* |
| quickly | *vite* |
| slowly | *lentement* |
| big | *grand* |
| small | *petit* |
| hot | *chaud* |
| cold | *froid* |
| I am ill | *je suis malade* |
| pharmacy, drugstore | *pharmacie* |
| I am hungry | *j'ai faim* |
| I am thirsty | *j'ai soif* |
| What is this? | *Qu'est-ce que c'est?* |
| Where? | *Où?* |
| fixed price menu | *table d'hôte* |
| order courses separately | *à la carte* |

## WEATHER

| | |
|---|---|
| rain | *pluie* |
| clouds | *nuages* |
| sun | *soleil* |
| It is hot out | *Il fait chaud* |
| It is cold out | *Il fait froid* |

## TIME

| | |
|---|---|
| When? | *Quand?* |
| What time is it? | *Quelle heure est-il?* |
| minute | *minute* |
| hour | *heure* |
| day | *jour* |
| week | *semaine* |
| month | *mois* |
| year | *année* |
| yesterday | *hier* |
| today | *aujourd'hui* |
| tommorrow | *demain* |
| morning | *le matin* |
| afternoon | *l'après-midi* |
| evening | *le soir* |
| night | *la nuit* |
| now | *maintenant* |
| never | *jamais* |

| | |
|---|---|
| Sunday | *dimanche* |
| Monday | *lundi* |
| Tuesday | *mardi* |
| Wednesday | *mercredi* |
| Thursday | *jeudi* |
| Friday | *vendredi* |
| Saturday | *samedi* |
| January | *janvier* |
| February | *février* |
| March | *mars* |
| April | *avril* |
| May | *mai* |
| June | *juin* |
| July | *juillet* |
| August | *août* |
| September | *septembre* |
| October | *octobre* |
| November | *novembre* |
| December | *décembre* |

## COMMUNICATION

| | |
|---|---|
| post office | *bureau de poste* |
| air mail | *par avion* |
| stamps | *timbres* |
| envelope | *enveloppe* |
| telephone book | *bottin téléphonique* |
| long distance call | *appel outre-mer* |
| collect call | *appel collecte* |
| fax | *télécopieur, fax* |
| telegram | *télégramme* |
| rate | *tarif* |
| dial the regional code | *composer le code régional* |
| wait for the tone | *attendre la tonalité* |

## ACTIVITIES

| | |
|---|---|
| recreational swimming | *la baignade* |
| beach | *plage* |
| scuba diving | *la plongée sous-marine* |
| snorkelling | *la plongée-tuba* |
| fishing | *la pêche* |
| recreational sailing | *navigation de plaisance* |
| windsurfing | *la planche à voile* |
| bicycling | *faire du vélo* |

| | |
|---|---|
| mountain bike | *vélo tout-terrain (VTT)* |
| horseback riding | *équitation* |
| hiking | *la randonnée pédestre* |
| to walk around | *se promener* |
| museum or gallery | *musée* |
| cultural centre | *centre culturel* |
| cinema | *cinéma* |

## TOURING

| | |
|---|---|
| river | *fleuve, rivière* |
| waterfalls | *chutes* |
| viewpoint | *belvédère* |
| hill | *colline* |
| garden | *jardin* |
| wildlife reserve | *réserve faunique* |
| peninsula | *péninsule, presqu'île* |
| south/north shore | *côte sud/nord* |
| town or city hall | *hôtel de ville* |
| court house | *palais de justice* |
| church | *église* |
| house | *maison* |
| manor | *manoir* |
| bridge | *pont* |
| basin | *bassin* |
| workshop | *atelier* |
| historic site | *lieu historique* |
| train station | *gare* |
| stables | *écuries* |
| convent | *couvent* |
| door, archway, gate | *porte* |
| customs house | *douane* |
| market | *marché* |
| seaway | *voie maritime* |
| museum | *musée* |
| cemetery | *cimetière* |
| mill | *moulin* |
| windmill | *moulin à vent* |
| hospital | *Hôtel Dieu* |
| high school | *école secondaire* |
| lighthouse | *phare* |
| barn | *grange* |
| waterfall(s) | *chute(s)* |
| sandbank | *batture* |
| neighbourhood, region | *quartier* |

## NUMBERS

| | | | |
|---|---|---|---|
| 1 | *un* | 22 | *vingt-deux* |
| 2 | *deux* | 23 | *vingt-trois* |
| 3 | *trois* | 24 | *vingt-quatre* |
| 4 | *quatre* | 25 | *vingt-cinq* |
| 5 | *cinq* | 26 | *vingt-six* |
| 6 | *six* | 27 | *vingt-sept* |
| 7 | *sept* | 28 | *vingt-huit* |
| 8 | *huit* | 29 | *vingt-neuf* |
| 9 | *neuf* | 30 | *trente* |
| 10 | *dix* | 40 | *quarante* |
| 11 | *onze* | 50 | *cinquante* |
| 12 | *douze* | 60 | *soixante* |
| 13 | *treize* | 70 | *soixante-dix* |
| 14 | *quatorze* | 80 | *quatre-vingt* |
| 15 | *quinze* | 90 | *quatre-vingt-dix* |
| 16 | *seize* | 100 | *cent* |
| 17 | *dix-sept* | 200 | *deux cents* |
| 18 | *dix-huit* | 500 | *cinq cents* |
| 19 | *dix-neuf* | 1,000 | *mille* |
| 20 | *vingt* | 10,000 | *dix mille* |
| 21 | *vingt-et-un* | 1,000,000 | *un million* |

# Index

Index

Index

Index

*excellent*

*:: plus Vaneuce ::*

Index

# Order Form

## Ulysses Travel Guides

| | | |
|---|---|---|
| ☐ Acapulco | $14.95 CAD | $9.95 USD |
| ☐ Alberta's Best Hotels and Restaurants | $14.95 CAD | $12.95 USD |
| ☐ Arizona–Grand Canyon | $24.95 CAD | $17.95 USD |
| ☐ Atlantic Canada | $24.95 CAD | $19.95 USD |
| ☐ Beaches of Maine | $12.95 CAD | $9.95 USD |
| ☐ Bed and Breakfasts In Ontario | $17.95 CAD | $12.95 USD |
| ☐ Belize | $16.95 CAD | $12.95 USD |
| ☐ Boston | $17.95 CAD | $12.95 USD |
| ☐ British Columbia's Best Hotels | $14.95 CAD | $12.95 USD |
| ☐ Calgary | $16.95 CAD | $12.95 USD |
| ☐ California | $29.95 CAD | $21.95 USD |
| ☐ Canada | $29.95 CAD | $22.95 USD |
| ☐ Cancún & Riviera Maya | $19.95 CAD | $17.95 USD |
| ☐ Cape Cod, Nantucket and | $17.95 CAD | $12.95 USD |
| ☐ Cartagena (Colombia) | $12.95 CAD | $9.95 USD |
| ☐ Chicago | $19.95 CAD | $14.95 USD |
| ☐ Chile | $27.95 CAD | $17.95 USD |
| ☐ Colombia | $29.95 CAD | $21.95 USD |
| ☐ Costa Rica | $27.95 CAD | $19.95 USD |
| ☐ Cuba | $24.95 CAD | $17.95 USD |
| ☐ Dominican Republic | $24.95 CAD | $17.95 USD |
| ☐ Ecuador and Galápagos Islands | $24.95 CAD | $17.95 USD |
| ☐ Fabulous Québec | $29.95 CAD | $22.95 USD |
| ☐ Guadalajara | $17.95 CAD | $12.95 USD |
| ☐ Guadeloupe | $24.95 CAD | $17.95 USD |
| ☐ Guatemala | $24.95 CAD | $17.95 USD |
| ☐ Havana | $16.95 CAD | $12.95 USD |
| ☐ Hawaii | $29.95 CAD | $21.95 USD |
| ☐ Honduras | $24.95 CAD | $17.95 USD |
| ☐ Huatulco–Puerto Escondido | $17.95 CAD | $12.95 USD |
| ☐ Inns and Bed & Breakfasts in Québec | $17.95 CAD | $12.95 USD |
| ☐ Islands of the Bahamas | $24.95 CAD | $17.95 USD |
| ☐ Las Vegas | $17.95 CAD | $12.95 USD |
| ☐ Lisbon | $18.95 CAD | $13.95 USD |
| ☐ Los Angeles | $19.95 CAD | $14.95 USD |
| ☐ Los Cabos and La Paz | $14.95 CAD | $10.95 USD |
| ☐ Louisiana | $29.95 CAD | $21.95 USD |
| ☐ Martinique | $24.95 CAD | $17.95 USD |
| ☐ Miami | $17.95 CAD | $12.95 USD |
| ☐ Montréal | $19.95 CAD | $14.95 USD |
| ☐ New England | $29.95 CAD | $21.95 USD |
| ☐ New Orleans | $17.95 CAD | $12.95 USD |
| ☐ New York City | $19.95 CAD | $14.95 USD |